Books by Hugh Downs

YOURS TRULY, HUGH DOWNS
A SHOAL OF STARS

A SHOAL *of* STARS

A SHOAL *of* STARS

☆ ☆ ☆ *by Hugh Downs*

DOUBLEDAY & COMPANY, INC., GARDEN CITY, NEW YORK
1967

PHOTO CREDITS

No. 4 and 14 by the author; No. 9, 16, and 19 by Galyean; No. 24, 25, 26, 27, 28, 29, and 31 by Malau; remainder by H. R. Downs.

I had known H. R. Downs for nearly twenty years at the time I undertook this voyage. He is (not necessarily in this order) a photographer, a husband, a yachtsman, a member of the U. S. Armed Forces, an all-weather friend and a philosopher in the truest sense of that word. He continues to be my son.

This chronicle is dedicated to him.

☆ *Foreword*

~~~~~~

A SHOAL OF STARS is an account of a sea journey. It relates
how I chartered a tall and beautiful sailing ship, assembled an amiable, competent crew, and sailed her more
than 6000 miles in some three months, across the Pacific
Ocean to Tahiti.

But it is also a love story.

For many years now I have been carrying on an ardent
affair with that irresistible, unpredictable, and promiscu-
ous lady, the sea. And it's a kiss-and-tell story: lovers of
the sea are never discreet. We not only flaunt our ro-
mance, but avidly seek to enlist others to woo our goddess
along with us. So in this book, along with the details of
our adventure, I have tried to convey something of the
mystique of the ocean's eternal appeal and challenge to
man, hoping that even those who have never seen her
shores—as I had not in my early youth—may be intrigued
to heed her call.

During the trip I kept a log—a daily journal in which
I recorded fully the events that transpired and the activities of the company, as well as frequent digressive obser-
vations inspired by them. In this book I include occasional

extracts from that log when it seems to me the contemporary report is more revealing. Tradition demands that ships' logs, like other historical documents, stand verbatim. I confess, however, that I have had to do some slight editing here and there in those passages, so that they would be fully understandable out of context.

HUGH DOWNS

New York, N.Y. 1967

☆ *Contents*

~~~~~~

Illustrations follow page 144

And when the fragrant day is done,
Night—and a shoal of stars.

—from *The Road to Anywhere*
by Bert Leston Taylor

A SHOAL *of* STARS

THE LIGHTLESS SHORES of Rio Mar were off to starboard somewhere. It was our first night out of Panama. Far off to the east a thinning parade of freighters leaving or approaching the Canal Zone winked on and off as we rose to a crest and rolled off into a trough. Cape Mala by dawn, we'd hoped, and then the open Pacific and in ten days the Galapagos Islands.

But right now—trouble.

One of the extra fuel drums had broken loose from its lashing and was rolling around the deck. Had we been heeled over on either tack it would have been no problem, but we were rolling and so, like a blind bull, was 400 pounds of fuel, in the blackness of the dark night. Moreover, the drum had been leaking and the deck was treacherously slippery with diesel oil, as I found when I struggled to get the spreader lights on. Already the drum had splintered part of the cockpit coaming and, worse, had smashed over Jerry Galyean's foot when he tried to help. Spray and occasional seas over the bow were just enough to complicate the problem, but not enough to wash the oil off the deck. I was sick with the thought of the further damage that drum could do, and with the despairing feeling that this we definitely did not need.

We *did* need that extra fuel—against doldrum days in this strange corner of the world—and we couldn't let the drum go overboard. On the other hand we couldn't risk the further damage. I didn't know how much fuel was already lost, spilled on deck. I didn't and couldn't stop to check how badly Jerry was hurt. Nor did I know where H.R. had got to. My son, generally known as "H.R." (for Hugh Raymond), was a member of the crew; I was sure I had seen him come on deck while I was trying to get the spreader lights on, but where was he now? I didn't know how we were ever going to work off Rio Mar and back closer to the shipping lanes without either a change of wind or time-consuming tacking, or using up more precious auxiliary fuel at this early stage of the trip. And I didn't know what lay ahead of us: the mysterious field of lights three hours before dawn that same night. Finally, I didn't know what I'd gotten myself into in this trip, or how it would ever come out. But I did know why I was here.

"Why are you going to do it?" people had asked frequently in the days before June 30. After mid-October that year the question was: "Why *did* you do it?" Now I am most likely to hear: "If you do it again, count me in."

Commander Scott Carpenter said that very phrase to me during a November, 1965, broadcast of the "Today" show. I had to smile because I knew he meant it. Here is a man who orbited the earth three times at over 17,000 miles per hour and has lived for days at thirty-four fathoms beneath the sea. And he wants to cross an ocean at six miles per hour. The funny thing is I understand why.

Why did I do it? I was close to asking myself that very

question early on the day we left Panama, three weeks into the voyage.

My log entry said: "Saturday, July 24—*Thane*. Aimed at 1000 departure (in order to get away by noon). Got away 1515. That's life in the tropical latitudes. I felt no pressure to leave because of the long time I'd be away from Ruth. Jerry photographed some of the departure. . . ."

My wife Ruth had been with us in Panama. We'd had a better time, and more time together than I'd have supposed possible in the face of the hundred little incidents and delays that nibbled at our stay there. Underway, I could see her long after I could no longer distinguish others on the dock. She was wearing yellow slacks and a yellow Pucci shirt that day. Through the binoculars I saw her wave one last time and turn and walk up the ramp from the floating pier to her car. I wondered if she were thinking of the immense arc of the earth that would turn under me before we were together again, mid-September at the earliest. I knew it bothered her that H.R. and I would spend most of these weeks with two inches of teak planking and some miles of salt water between us and the earth's crust. Ruth feared the water, and was not at all impressed with our array of safety devices and procedures. A pang flickered through me when I thought of her quiet resignation to the whole trip. At first she had allied herself with the host of advisers who eloquently pointed out dozens of reasons why I shouldn't go through with it, but when she knew my mind was made up she stayed out of the way or helped when she could. All this came to me while I watched the distant speck of yellow move slowly up the ramp at Balboa.

We had about a mile to go between the Balboa Yacht Club and the Pacific end of the Canal. By law we were required to use a pilot on this last leg of the Canal, but it

was unnecessary from a safety standpoint and would
have meant further delay and cost. It seemed to us that
there was enough water on each side of the marker buoys
to do it legally without a pilot by staying outside the
channel itself. But then I noticed flats on one side, and I
decided we'd better continue in the channel. If we got
stopped we could say the pilot hitched a ride back with a
passing line-handler's launch. No one saw us, however,
and we slipped out into the Gulf of Panama under a line
of heavy, sharp-edged clouds. The wind came up.

The island of Taboga slid past. Night came on as the
wind backed and dropped. By now some sea had built
up, and we had to run a little closer to shore than we'd
intended. It was about this time that the oil drum broke
loose.

So here we were, trying to get the beast relashed as we
wallowed through the dark, at the same time attempting
to stay out of the way of a parade of southbound
freighters.

The spreader lights now illuminated the chaotic scene
from a swaying height. Most of the crew turned out, H.R.
among them, and under the lights became frantic shad-
ows that moved and shouted and struggled and somehow
accomplished the impossible task of recapturing the loose
drum. We could tell from the weight that there was not
much fuel lost from it, but the deck was a slippery mess
and needed to be washed down.

The lone casualty, Jerry Galyean, who was our camera-
man, had lost the nail on his right big toe. It was a nasty
wound, and as the mashed tissue conjured up thoughts
of gangrene and emergency surgery, we considered a return to Panama. But Jerry resisted strongly. He insisted
it would not incapacitate him in the least. And, as it
turned out, it didn't.

So we returned almost to normal.

"Normalcy," aboard ship, is when everything is so highly abnormal as to be on schedule, uneventful, in the precise position desired and predicted by the navigation. No voyage, of course, enjoys normalcy for more than twenty minutes at a time.

In our case, we were about on schedule, no untoward event was transpiring, and while our precise position was not known, I could at least certify that we were in deep water and a long way from Cape Mala and probably an adequate distance off the shoals to starboard. Jerry's foot was taken care of to the best of our ability; no gear was loose or broken; the pumps weren't being overtaken; we weren't afire; and we were afloat. It was hard to ask for more. Bob Dixon, Pete and Connie Jackson, and H.R. had returned to sleep, and Virgil Bowers and I were on watch. It was unpleasantly rough, but not unsafe, and the night was still so dark that the red compass light showed on our beards.

Virgil saw the lights first. They were far ahead and a little to port—and they had no business being there. At first I thought they were the parade of freighters, but that had long since vanished, most of them for coasting down South America (the few heading for the open Pacific had long since taken a different course from ours: we were seeking to shear Cape Mala).

Was there something jutting out from the shore to the west? The chart couldn't be wrong. I looked at it again, anxiously. Nothing there. They had to be ships. But they were lights that didn't seem to belong to floating craft of any kind.

We watched, puzzled, as we bore toward the still far-off lights. The wind continued to subside, but the sea ran high. We rolled. The gear slatted. I lit a cigar with the lighter Frank Blair had given me for the trip. It was a Zippo that had brought him luck in World War II when he was a Navy flier. The lighter was on a shock-cord lanyard as insurance against deep-sixing and Frank had had my name cut into it. Superstition is a funny thing. I will deny being superstitious, but I will be lying when I deny it. I don't believe for a minute that that lighter brought Blair any luck, and, if it had, it wouldn't follow that it would bring me any luck. But I used it, and somewhere deep down I was glad this night that I hadn't left it below.

Virgil Bowers, looking a little like a cross between Winston Churchill and a Trappist monk, was at the wheel. Virgil professed no knowledge of sailing, and persisted in expressing himself in nonnautical terms ("ropes" and "downstairs" and "right" and "left"), but he steered the straightest course of any of us. And I think he spent more time at the wheel than anyone else. He'd relieve a watch partner for a meal, a chore, a nap. He'd sit for hours, hardly moving the wheel, his eyes slits. At first glance you'd swear he was asleep. But he wasn't. He said he was thinking. No Buddhist ever meditated more serenely.

"Never saw you smoke on television," Virgil said now. I explained to him that for several years I never smoked except when I was outside the United States. He observed, perhaps correctly, that I was a bit around the bend. Virgil's habits are more ascetic and less complicated than mine. He never smokes or drinks at all, in or out of the U.S.

"I'd think you'd either smoke or not smoke," he was saying, "isn't it a strain to give it up when you go back to the States?"

"Nope. I've brainwashed myself. I enjoy it when I'm away and don't miss it when I'm home."

He moved the wheel, which meant he wasn't averaging his heading within a degree. He's like an autopilot.

"Who made the rule?" he asked as I dragged on my

cigar. The tip of it glowed with the same intensity and
color as the compass light.

"I did."

He shrugged.

The warm wind moved with us, matching our motion
for a moment. The sails fell slack and then filled and
whacked as we rolled from one side to the other. A whiff
of diesel oil rose from the deck.

"I think you may be too far gone to salvage," Virgil
muttered.

The lights were drawing nearer, and it was time to
wake Bob and Pete for their watch.

There was no moon and no break in the cloud cover.
No hint of the shape on which those lights were hung.
They seemed to be of varying heights or distances. These
were not banks waters. But then fishing fleets didn't have
to deploy in shallow water. There was not a running light
among the lot.

Virgil went below, and presently Bob came on deck
and looked at the lights.

"Fishing boats," he said.

"You're sure?" I asked him.

"No. But what else could they be?" He lowered himself
into the cockpit and looked at the compass. I offered
him the wheel and took a flashlight and pencil and logged
out.

Bob said, "They could be emergency lights on a mysterious island which rose just after the last Notices to Mariners went to press and which, since we get no newscasts,
we are destined to be the first to run aground on, thereby
having the distinction of appearing on subsequent charts
as a wreck. Our paltry lives are a cheap price indeed for
this glory. Does that answer the question?"

Pete came on deck blinking. We turned off the spreader
lights but left the mast light on.

Now we were beginning to close with the lights. Nothing about the water indicated that shoals were anywhere about: no return trains of wave. The seas were short but not confused or curling. I asked Pete what he thought. He didn't think there was any land nearby, and he too guessed the lights belonged to a fishing fleet. We never found out.

Now as we approached we heard a bell, and then a spotlight played on our rigging and deck. We played our large torch in this direction but couldn't make out any shapes. Once we thought we heard a voice. We moved spookily through, between lights, hoping there was no unlighted hulk in our path. Finally they faded behind us.

Ahead lay Cape Mala and the open Pacific, and far to the west the islands of Polynesia.

~~~~~~

II

I DO NOT KNOW how it was, years ago, that I heard the sea
in a patch of prairie field, or smelled salt air in a landlocked acre of stagnant lake. But on that sandless, loamy
shore I nodded my head and said to myself, "Yes! This
is how it smells, this is how it is, this is the sea!"

And I cannot say how it was that in the ribs of a wreck
on Takaroa I saw again the rotten mudstuck boards of a
rowboat, abandoned in a midwest pond before my childhood. But long ago my Ohio eyes discovered a truth
about the world and held it for a dream: the sea is not
outside—it is not chemical or concept—but rather a quality of being. I am of the sea, and not by choice. I am the
flotsam humankind, root and seed. I weep and sweat and
bleed salt.

In that long ago summertime I did not know that I
would one day sail across the world's longest open stretch
of water. I did not decide in a flash that I'd make a plan
and fulfill a sudden taut decision.

The thought today that I'll one day go to the moon
is more likely than the thought then that I'd sail across an
ocean. It was a dream that came, but so slim was its

chance of realization that hope was not at first a part of it.

Later, still very young, I rowed by myself in a working (but leaking) skiff to the middle of a moss-covered tarn and first sensed with a thrill that the magic buoyancy of water would work for me no less than for an admiral. And I felt then something of the feeling that I imagine must have been felt by sailors on a Rhodian man-of-war on the wine-dark waters off Crete, or on the prow and spirit lift of the great Polynesian canoes, or on a Norse Raider smashing through icy waves west of the known world.

If dreams follow any sort of law, perhaps this dream of mine of crossing the Pacific under my own sail could be traced to a definite beginning. But there is no particular point in doing this, because it formed so gradually that it would be chasing mists to try to pin down the points at which it was a first glimmer, then an attractive impossibility, then in turn an attractive possibility, a hope, a determination, a definite plan, and finally a scheduled project. The only thing with hard dates is the reality. We left on June 30, 1965, and returned October 4 of the same year. I can say that it became a scheduled project about five years before; it was a definite plan for six or seven years, a hope for maybe a decade, an attractive possibility for most of my adult life, an attractive impossibility somewhere prior to that.

At the point when the wish became a plan, I started a policy that paid off. At every turn I exposed the infant project to threat from any external factor that could keep it from growing up. The voyage plan was the Spartan baby: it deserved life only if it could survive the rigors of an environment in which it would have to exist. I reasoned that if any circumstance could be proved to threaten the project fatally, it should indeed die and spare me wasted motion and disappointment. A host of enemies was turned loose on it. Its life and vigor stemmed from my determination to see it through at almost all costs. Pressures to dissuade me came from many quarters. Among the arguments lined up by advisers, professional and amateur, were the following.

The risk that being away from broadcasting for months would cause the public to forget me completely. Nonsense. My reasoning in rebuttal was that if the public is going to turn its back on you, it can do so right while you're broadcasting.

The inordinate cost would be out of proportion to possible return even in personal satisfaction. This argument was meaningless since the proponents of this view were talking about *my* personal satisfaction and my money, and only I could judge that.

"You'll go nuts trying to cover that distance at six m.p.h." Any sailor knows this is not true, as I'll show later on.

"You're nuts to start with if you go through with it." Well, *possibly* true.

"What do you prove?" Nothing, of course, but that's hardly an argument.

"What is it you need to escape from?" As near as I can figure, this sophisticated bit of psychological probing points up a supposed axiom: no sane grown-up would do anything unless there was money in it and/or it conformed to the conventional, accepted behavior indicated by sensible materialism.

However, the voyage was supported by some of my acquaintances on the grounds that it was some sort of therapy and thereby as acceptable as joining A.A. or going through the Keeley Cure. It was deemed perfectly logical if it gave me better perspective or renewed strength or refreshment for my work.

The fact is that the money-making aspects of my television work over these last years were partly for the thera-peutic purpose of giving me the financial strength I needed to make the trip.

The most important test of the dream was my early exposure of it to the withering fire of reality in the form of my own fears and evaluation of its sanity. If *I* lost interest or heart there would be no need to submit it to tests from anyone or anything else.

I remember an outboard-powered boat I rented on Bang's Lake in Illinois in the late forties. I remember it because I experienced fright in it. The lake, lying east to west, allows a long fetch of wind. A stiff east wind came up while I ran down to the west end of the lake with my son, then three or four years old. The chop that built up amounted to swells as we ran with the wind. But on coming back I saw that we shipped some water each time the bow smashed into the next wave. Out in the open the condition intensified, and I wanted to turn and run again but was afraid of broaching. There were no life preservers in the boat. I could swim, but could I get a four-year-old safely to shore? The outboard was only a three-h.p. mo-tor, and for a time I doubt that we made any headway at all. Then and there I made notes about prevention and safety, and subsequently they went into what became long lists of procedures. It's natural to hope each time you extricate yourself from a trouble that the next crisis will also have an escape hatch built into it. And some-times that escape hatch is provided by resolution or tech-nique learned from a previous scrape.

Later on, as a guest on cruisers and sailboats, I learned a little about etiquette and operating rules. Yacht eti-quette is based on a mixture of safety, courtesy, and com-mon sense. Nautical rules of the road can be learned fast by anyone with a genuine interest—fast enough for him to apply safely on his own within a season or two, although one can spend a lifetime accumulating useful lore and refining techniques. It's a bit like chess: you can learn the rules in five minutes, but you can spend the rest of your days improving your game.

Before I moved away from the midwest I had begun to accumulate nautical experience of a special kind. I became part owner of a used sloop. The word "used" is perhaps too weak for describing the craft's condition at the time we bought it. She was built in Manitowoc, Wisconsin, had survived a couple of storms on the lakes and wintered outside at least once. When she came to the attention of my three friends and me, she was just off the end of a launch track on the west shore of Lake Michigan near the Wisconsin-Illinois border and she was sort of above water even though resting on the bottom. She looked as though she'd been launched by Buster Keaton. Apparently she had been put back in the water with her seams dry and open and if efforts were made to pump her out they were vain. She had inside-ballast of lead ingots (worth more as metal than we paid for her, ingots and all), she was twenty-four feet over-all, beamy and a bit tubby, but we were not buying her to race. Added to her very reasonable price was the cost of getting her off the bottom and onto a trailer and home to my back yard, where she stayed for a year before we got her in shape.

In the dead of winter, fearful we had not been able to drain all the water from the auxiliary engine, we kept an electric light burning to prevent freezing and cracking of the engine block. Checking and changing the bulb on this incubation system was undoubtedly the most unnautical boating activity I've ever been involved in, including a mechanical vacation I took in 1963 (on the latter occasion, most of my time was occupied in repairing a chartered ship's electrical, power, and plumbing systems). We christened our sloop the *Dutchess of Bilge-*

water. Berths along Chicago's North Shore are scarce and getting our sloop a place, and ourselves memberships, in the yacht club of the northern suburb I was living in was quite out of the question.

After I had moved east and sold my interest in this boat to my three partners, I learned of the further curious saga of the *Dutchess*. They had got her situated at a yacht club farther upshore, where they felt the snobbery was a trace less than in most places. We had all been a bit on the defensive, as the *Dutchess,* even fitted out after our year of work on her, could fairly be said to be a disreputable tub compared to the Bristol and Newport atmosphere of most crafts at the yacht clubs of the Great Lakes. Smarting keenly under the snubs and barbs of the less considerate members of this club they'd finally managed to get into, my erstwhile partners contrived one day to get back at them.

Getting out to the *Dutchess* required either leaving her dinghy tied to the dock or being taken out to the mooring buoy by the club's launch. This, they said, was a humiliating procedure, since even the youth hired to run the launch made plain his scorn and disdain for the *Dutchess* and her owners.

So one day, they rowed the dinghy to a point south of the club property and picked up a large bag of sand, which they put aboard the *Dutchess*. The next night they brought a pistol with them and summoned the launch. In sullen silence the three of them rode to the *Dutchess* and watched the launch go back, the pilot exuding his customary insolent blend of amusement and disapproval.

Now one of my friends quietly slipped overboard and swam ashore unseen, to where he had parked his car. He then drove home.

Just after ten P.M., when a rule of silence brings quiet to the club harbor, the remaining pair began to scuffle and shout. Then they fired the pistol and threw the sandbag overboard with as much noise as possible. Then they signaled for the launch. In the silence that followed, searchlights stabbed out from yachts moored nearby.

"What's wrong?" someone shouted anxiously.

"Nothing!" they called back cheerily from the deck of the *Dutchess,* "No problem!"

When the launch pulled alongside the young pilot was not sneering for once. His jaw was slack and his eyes flicked nervously across my friends, the *Dutchess'* deck, and the nearby waters.

The two stepped from the *Dutchess* into the launch. There was a moment's hesitation. "That all?" asked the launch jockey hollowly.

"That's all," said one of them.

Halfway back to the dock the pilot nervously tried again. "I brought three of you guys out," he said.

"Listen, you: you brought only two of us out. It is important to your well-being to keep in mind you brought *two* of us out!"

"You straight on that?" growled the other one.

The youth was straight on that.

I purposely do not identify my partners or the club in this anecdote, partly because there is a rumor the authorities have only stopped dragging the bottom of that mooring basin a couple of years ago, and would probably start up again if the mystery were given new publicity. Since there was no corpse and no one was reported missing, the affair died down after a bit. For a long time after, they tell me, the club abandoned its attitude of amused stand-offishness and replaced it with an attitude of *un*-amused stand-offishness. Any change, my friends felt, was for the better.

In the years after that summer my interest in pilotage, navigation, and chart study deepened, and out of the

resultant reading and practice the plan gestated, vague
at first, and recognized only after it had begun, as one
becomes aware of a human embryo only after it starts
its growth.

As the seasons passed, I was a guest and crew on a few
boats, and I chartered many. I explored Long Island
Sound, Martha's Vineyard, Block Island, Buzzard's Bay,
Provincetown, Plymouth, Falmouth, Gloucester, the
Annisquam River, "down" toward Maine, up the Hudson
River almost to Albany and down past Sandy Hook, N.J.,
Florida—from Fort Lauderdale through the Keys around
to Sarasota, the Bahamas, the Virgin Islands, the Wind-
ward and Leeward Islands, some of the West Coast of
California, Puget Sound and Vancouver Island, Hawaii,
Greece, and some of the Aegean Islands. I scouted ap-
proaches to Bermuda and Jamaica.

I read and studied Chapman and Mixter and Dutton
and Bowditch, Lloyds Registry and Jayne's Sailing Ships,
and adventures of such doughties as Joshua Slocum,
Howard Blackburn, Alan Villiers, Irving Johnson, Eric
Hiscock, Carlton Mitchell. I followed the exploits of An-
son, Nelson, and enjoyed fiction such as C. S. Forester's
Hornblower books.

Ancient navigation particularly fascinated me, and always will. The feats of sailing then were accomplished
with such primitive means of determining position, and
such limited maneuvering ability, that sailors were truly
called "iron men."

Columbus managed to get to the Indies twice, yet the
best navigation available could not have given him his
longitude within several hundred miles: he could not
know precise time, the essential to calculating longitude.
Granted that the first time he reached San Salvador was
an accident. But he came back.

Columbus' method was crude but effective. He could

determine his latitude. For accurate latitude determination, one doesn't have to know the time, only the date. When he first reached San Salvador he noted its latitude; when he came back, he merely got on that latitude and kept going west.

My avidness for boating experience continued. I borrowed prams and dagger boards, learned some tricks of small boat handling with outboard skiffs and cruisers in seasons on the Silver River in Florida. My charters included twenty-seven- and twenty-eight-foot single-screw inboard Pembroke sedans, a thirty-two-foot Chris-Craft twin (and I continued with twin screws from then on in my power boats) a thirty-six-foot Chris-Craft and a forty-foot Pacemaker, both with fishing cockpit, and forty-two-, forty-four- and forty-five-foot double-cabin cruisers.

I rented small sailboats and sailed them at first with instruction and then alone in such different waters as Ft. de France Harbor, Martinique; Hamilton Harbor, Bermuda; and St. Georges Bay, Beirut, Lebanon. I chartered larger sailing craft in the Caribbean, thirty-three-foot, forty-one-foot, eighty-four-foot, ninety-four-foot—all with auxiliary power, two of them ketch-rigged.

As the dream grew, I began to study ships with an eye to cost and suitability. Before I zeroed in on the size and rig most suitable to my purposes, I investigated a wide range. I learned a little about marine surveys—enough to know I would need to employ a surveyor. Less than forty feet of waterline length did not appeal to me—although many people have made the trip across the ocean in smaller vessels—and over 100 feet in length would have required more manpower than I could afford to feed. At one point I considered chartering Mike Burke's *Mandalay*, a beautiful schooner 100 feet long, requiring a crew of nine. (She was subsequently lost on a reef in the Bahamas.) But in order to make use of her I would have had to sell space to a score of people in order to break even on expenses—and then, in effect, I would have been in the tour business. This is all right if you know the tour business, but I don't and I could foresee headaches therein that had nothing to do with seafaring. But I did sail once on *Mandalay* across the Gulf Stream to Bimini, and then borrowed an airplane to photograph her.

At one time or another I had under consideration for my trip: *Te Vega,* 134 feet; Peter Van Beek's *Harbinger,* (a beautiful ketch I'd once chartered in the Caribbean. I think I'd have used her, but Van Beek finally admitted he didn't want to let me take her: he didn't want her gone that long and I honestly don't blame him. If I owned *Harbinger* I too would not charter her to anyone to cross the Pacific); Mystic Seaport's venerable *Bowdoin,* which Admiral McMillan took on several Arctic expeditions, but which would have required an OK from the museum board and a substantial sum for recommissioning; Jim Kimberly's *Gray Fox,* an eighty-one-foot Rhodes-designed ketch with twin diesels, too expensive for me; *Black Dog,* when Bill Tellier owned her; Jack Carstarphen's *Maverick,* a Virgin Islands charter; Greg Nicole's *Gulliver,* an eighty-four-foot schooner; and a Swedish training ship, a beautiful square-rigger that could easily have used a crew of twenty-four. The charter price of the latter was astonishingly reasonable, but unless I could get that crew not only to forego wages but also to stage a 100-day hunger strike, I'd be out of money before I was out of sight of land. I considered at one point chartering or purchasing a trimaran, a three-hull sailing ship. It has many virtues of speed and safety, but there were problems, such as load limits and my unfamiliarity with the unconventional character of trimarans.

When I could, I scouted ground I would cover in the trip, the idea being that if I went over some of the trickier passages with someone experienced, I'd be less likely to run into trouble on my own. I arranged to go with Greg Nicole, whose *Gulliver* draws nine feet, as I remember, from Nassau across the banks to Highburn Key in the Exuma chain, where there's a pass into Exuma sound— all extremely shallow and studded with coral heads. As it turned out on the trip, I made this passage in *Thane* with Pete Jackson aboard, who knows the waters well.

On the occasion of this "scouting" trip, I had been in Nassau with a broadcast of the Paar Show, and I stayed for a few days after the broadcast was over. Paar had been given a small power launch to use during his stay, and instead of returning it when he left, he gave it to me to use and I was to return it when I finished with it. Somehow I didn't get straight *where* it was to be returned or to whom it belonged. The hotel seemed to know nothing about it, and I asked around, but the boat seemed to be an orphan. Not only that, but on our way to a diving location "about a mile" off the east end of New Providence Island, we lost our power in a storm and were driven ashore at the estate of one Godfrey Higgs. (Thank heaven we hadn't got off the end of the island yet or we'd have been on our way to Cuba with two peanut-butter sandwiches and a small jug of rum as stores.) We left the boat there ("we" being my wife and I, two girls from the show, Frank Garisto, percussionist in the orchestra, and a fifteen-year-old native boy who was directing us to the site) and took a car back into Nassau.

Some days later aboard *Gulliver* we were under Rose Island, or between Rose and Athol, and in sight of New Providence when in the flat calm of dawn I spotted Higgs' Estate through binoculars. I told Greg I had left a boat there, probably now half sunk by the storm. We put a boat over and made our way ashore.

There was the launch, low in the water with much rain

and sea, but not damaged. We bailed her out and got her engine going. We brought her back to *Gulliver*, and we towed her in to Nassau. I still didn't know what to do with this boat. Greg observed that technically I had been guilty of an act of piracy: I had taken a boat which didn't belong to me from a private dock.

"What protection is there for boat owners against this sort of thing?" I asked him.

"Here? None. Just the white-helmeted bobbies in the streets of Nassau. You could steal a large ship and get almost to Portugal before the British Navy or something of the sort caught you."

"Is there much theft?"

"Never," he said. "It never happens—here. In France, though, it is a sickness."

We left the launch at a Nassau pier. I trust that eventually it got back to its owner.

In the early phases of planning the Big Trip I thought seriously about making it a family venture. But I abandoned the idea because it would have been a hardship on the distaff side of the family, which suffers from motion sickness. I kidded Ruth about her Phoenician ancestry and how shamed they would be with a daughter who disliked the sea, in view of their tradition of having pioneered navigation. She advanced a theory that neatly countered this idea. "My people," she said, "took to the sea as a means to an end. They navigated because they needed to get to distant places for other reasons than the challenge of navigation. If the airplane had been available, they'd have used it. That's what I'm going to do."

She had me.

In the course of reading of other people's planning for long ocean voyages, I ran across many "planning lists," of all kinds. So I began to make my own lists, based on theirs but with added ideas of my own. For years every now and then I would waken in the middle of the night with an item worth noting down which bore on safety or comfort.

Meanwhile, all the "sensible" discouragements of my friends, colleagues, and counselors lost out against the simple fact that I was going to go ahead with it. None of them had come up with a really telling argument in opposition. If any one of them had been able to prove to me that (1) I would certainly be killed trying it, (2) I would gain not only financial security but immortality by staying home, (3) my broadcast career would be ruined, (4) I would be disappointed and broke, too, it might have ended it right there. But the dream survived, not only because it was hardy, but because it made sense. I wanted to do it, I had the opportunity to do it, and there was no good reason for not doing it.

☆ III

~~~~~~

CHARTERING TURNED OUT TO BE a better procedure than purchase and later resale, and at last I found the right ship to charter. Jim Northrop of Northrop and Johnson, who says he at first did not think I was serious in looking for a boat, came up with *Thane* and arranged the details.

Thane was just about optimum length, ketch-rigged (my favorite but not exclusively so: I'd have used a schooner too) seaworthy by survey, traditional and picturesque.

To what extent is a charter vessel your own boat? It depends on how the contract is drawn. The circumstances can range from your being one of a group of paid passengers aboard a ship with a full professional crew, wherein the planning and command are out of your hands, up to but not including purchase and resale of a boat. In the latter case you are in fact temporarily the actual owner, not a charterer. For a time I considered this arrangement, since I had no desire to be a passenger on this trip.

What is called a "bare boat" charter involves taking over the vessel with no representative of the owner aboard. Most single-party charters of larger boats (thirty-five feet and over) involve a captain's being in command of the vessel, but with the itinerary and activities under the control of the charterer.

My contract with the owner of *Thane* left the vessel in my command with the stipulation that final say in matters of ship safety stayed with the owner's brother, Pete Jackson, who lived aboard and was himself a charter captain. I consulted Pete and deferred to him in more than safety matters, however. First of all, he knew the ship thoroughly: he knew the wiring, he knew the idiosyncrasies of its machinery, and he knew its reaction to various weathers. He had an uncanny ability to sight land some minutes before anyone else could see it, and he had the nerve to go aloft in a bosun's chair in the roughest possible seas. He loved the ship as I came to love her, with the special affection reserved for something on which your life depends and which does not let you down.

While ethically bound to try to return *Thane* to its owner in the same condition I took her, I was less conscientious than Pete about certain maintenance points because of the demands of my other projects on the trip and because my charter fee was understood to include "normal wear and tear." A suit of sails, for example, is not as new after crossing an ocean as before, but money to cover this depreciation is figured in the amount paid for the boat.

With the ship settled, my next concern was a crew.

Can there be too much care exercised in the selection of shipmates? Let me ask you how careful you would want to be in choosing six other people with whom to imprison yourself in a space smaller than the average small living room, with the knowledge that for weeks nobody could leave.

To assemble a company compatible enough to hold together across the Pacific is something of a triumph. To be part of one that makes it without irreparable hard feelings requires more than care in assessing character—it also requires some luck.

Many a crew of good friends, blissful and secure at the start of a Pacific voyage, has dispersed in the Galapagos, hoping never to see each other again.

Two days before our landfall in the Tuamotus, Pete Jackson was to say to me during one of our watches, "I'm going to enjoy the two bottles of champagne I'll get when we get back."

I asked him why he was getting two bottles of champagne.

"Some charter captains in the Virgin Islands were certain we wouldn't arrive in Tahiti with the same people we started with."

"And they bet you the bubbly that we'd bust up in the Galapagos?"

"In Panama."

Sometimes it happens that fast. Pete and I both felt that the groups most in danger of falling apart underway were those who gave no thought to the causes and prevention—or particularly of the possibility—of friction. I had thought about it for years and both of us had seen it and dealt with it in short period charters. I had listed some causes of difficulty in what I thought were in order of magnitude, and they are worth discussion:

(1) Innocence
(2) Sloppy regimen
(3) Scattered command
(4) Competition
(5) Women
(6) Formation of cliques

(7) Personal systemic health
(8) Liquor
(9) Boredom
(10) Insufficient compensation

(1) INNOCENCE. There's no better word for ignorance of the need to obviate friction. I believe a group of total strangers would actually have a better chance of compatibility than close friends, because the strangers, wary of each other's reactions, would tend consciously to display some consideration during the shakedown period of working together. Good friends are always in danger of behaving thoughtlessly, and this is instantly and particularly noticeable in close quarters.

(2) SLOPPY REGIMEN. There are yachtsmen whose informality is apparently motivated by a desire to get as far away from normal routine as possible. They "eat when they feel like it," and trade watches on an irregular basis. But most of them do not go many days this way. On our voyage we were highly informal, but the important schedule items which gave us a structured existence within which we could enjoy informality were a rigid and complicated watch schedule and hot meals served on time, day in and day out.

(3) SCATTERED COMMAND. A divided command of some sort is not unfeasible, even aboard ship, but to have diffuse command or none at all not only erodes morale, it endangers the ship. Someone must be in charge, and it must be clear to all when and what authority is delegated. More than anywhere on land, being captain on a ship seems to bring out whatever of the tyrant and martinet is in some men. I have seen one instance of the mildest-mannered man ashore sprouting horns and snorting fire as soon as lines are cast off, barking like a Prussian and running so tight a ship that he could never get the

same group aboard twice. Harshness is not a necessary element for command. (It is reported that when Alan Villiers skippered MGM's *Bounty* across the Pacific in preparation for the filming of *Mutiny on the Bounty* he did something that well might have set the remains of Captain Bligh spinning in his grave. He bounded on deck saying, "We've got to take in that top . . . oh, I'm sorry chaps, finish your coffee first." There was never any doubt, though, of Villier's position aboard.) I can't think of any instance where it would be necessary or advantageous for a captain to raise his voice in anger at any shipmate he has selected. With large, paid crews it is different.

(4) COMPETITION. Competitive situations are not always bad, but a threat is posed where two members of a small ship's company are too much alike in age, ability, strength, and duties—particularly if they are young males whose glands are more active than their brains. With our group there was little problem on this score since each man had at least one unique purpose aboard and the total psychological adjustment was sound.

(5) WOMEN. Women aboard ship are a potential threat. But when the detrimental aspects are eliminated it is certainly more pleasant to have one aboard than not. If the girl in question is unattached, and/or coquettish, if she is helpless and in the way, overdefensive of feminine rights, unwilling to pull her weight, or so unattractive as to be depressing, you've got trouble in direct proportion to the length of time you're stuck with her. If on the other hand she is with someone aboard who cares about her without worrying about her, if she makes a contribution to the voyage, if her personality is nonabrasive and she is pleasant to look at, there is a good chance it will prove better to have her along than another man in her place. (Such was Connie Jackson, who prepared almost

1500 meals without complaint or delay and was relieved of duties only on Sundays. And some of the conditions under which she worked would have taxed the patience and competence of any sea cook.)

(6) FORMATION OF CLIQUES. Single-handers and two-man teams will never have to deal with this problem, but with three or more aboard a single vessel, a clique can form. It is a destructive force and can be controlled best by a systematic avoidance of repeat watches with the same small teams.

(7) PERSONAL SYSTEMIC HEALTH. It is obvious that getting along will depend on staying cheerful and performing duties. Both are very difficult to do if one is not in sound shape. Constipation, seasickness, dehydration, simple headache, or indigestion can change a good worker and a pleasant personality into a liability.

(8) LIQUOR is obviously troublesome if anyone aboard has problems with drinking. Rules regarding its use should be agreed on before starting. We had all kinds of booze aboard, but agreed on the rule of not touching it while underway. We later amended the rule to permit a Sunday afternoon cocktail hour and a drink to celebrate special occasions, such as sighting land, passing midpoint between the Galapagos and the Marquesas, and once on a record-breaking 194-mile day. Theoretically this amendment could have unravelled in time to celebrations of Arbor Day, Charles De Gaulle's birthday, Guy Fawkes Day, Governor De Witt Clinton Day, etc., limited only by the supply of liquor, but nobody seemed to need or take more than he could handle.

(9) BOREDOM. This is generally absent where every member of the company is a crew member. But it happens to passengers, and it leads to seasickness and quarrels. We had none of it aboard. A bored person is a boring person.

(10) INSUFFICIENT COMPENSATION. An underpaid crew is a potentially unhappy crew, and where the ship's company is a crew working without pay, it may be assumed that some other form of compensation obtains for them (unless they were shanghaied). For some, the fun of sailing is adequate compensation. For others free passage to some port does it. I put this down as the last of seafaring difficulties, because if all the other stumbling blocks in this list are eliminated, a normally happy person who cares anything at all about the sea will find his compensation in the routine of voyaging.

IV

ON FRIDAY, JUNE 25, with Ruth and H.R. I went to Fort Lauderdale, where *Thane* was having installations completed: diesel generator, deep-freeze and refrigerator, radio antennas on both masts, and carpentry work inside for better storage.

Bob Clayton was coming down on the thirtieth to go with us as far as Nassau. I had first met Clayton on a CBS special broadcast from Fort Lauderdale. He was then free-lance broadcasting in the Miami area. Since then we've worked together for years on "Concentration" (NBC daytime daily) and on occasional other programs. The first time I met him he was on the water, broadcasting a boat parade in connection with a Mrs. America pageant, and somehow we've been connected by boating and sailing ever since. He went to Bimini with me on Burke's *Mandalay* when I was considering her as a charter. Bob, Phil Ford, and Mimi Hines were aboard the *Kathy Marion* when we went through the Keys around Florida. He has been an important part of many trips and plans. At one time he seriously considered accepting my invitation to ship on for the Tahiti trip. As it turned out he could not come, but he was of immense help in planning. He even had his Tahitian wife, Mireille, teach me how to say in flawless Paumotu: "Can you please guide me through the pass into the lagoon? My ship draws nine feet." (*Nehe nehe anei taoe e afai ian iroto ite ava? Etoru meitera hohonu nota pahi.*) I appreciated the fact that Bob had a marvelous opportunity here to teach me something embarrassing without my knowledge, as a practical joke; but even though I didn't trust him, I trusted his wife.

A small crowd of the curious gathered at dockside and each day it grew, until at departure it was enormous.

The ship was tied up on the long dock at Pier 66 just inside the drawbridge. She was back in the water after being hauled for inspection and cleaning. On the dock was such a mound of provisions and gear that I despaired of ever stowing it all. But sailing vessels are the only containers in God's world larger on the inside than they are on the outside. We finally stowed everything, and the waterline moved about four inches up the hull.

Sunday night I flew back to New York alone for three more days of broadcasts and some last minute details. I must confess that Wednesday, June 30, brought with it a "last day of school" feeling that I hadn't imagined I'd ever recapture, but I hadn't had a summer off since just before my last year in high school and the last time I was clear of duties into October was when I was four years old.

At 4:05 P.M., when the 727 touched down at the Fort Lauderdale airport it occurred to me that not for months would I again move at such speeds relative to the earth's surface. After the engines reversed thrust and brakes were applied the plane taxied the last hundred feet at less than 10 m.p.h.—about the speed at which I *would* move for the next 7000 miles. I felt I was already geared to this new and unfrantic pace.

At the pier, while the sun took its time to slope down the western sky through a breathless and almost cloudless atmosphere, I set about checking off some last-minute business. It seemed somehow leisurely even though there was much to be done and our movements back and forth from *Thane* to shore points were hampered somewhat by well-wishers, who by now numbered five or six hundred. State police had been called in by the management of Pier 66, not in alarm but because someone might have been accidentally hurt in the crush.

Everything was going according to schedule. Virgil Bowers expected the antenna for his Simpson ship-to-shore radiophone to be installed by our six P.M. deadline. I had said clearly that we would get underway at ten P.M. sharp, even if it meant snapping shore connections or leaving someone. It was not my intention to try to put the voyage on a rigid timetable. But I had an almost superstitious fear that if the initial departure were not extremely punctual the whole venture would be put in a tentative light.

Meantime, final touches were still being put on the new jet pump; the new Nautisport rubber boat had to be assembled, inflated, fitted with its outboard, tested, and then dismantled and stowed a couple of times for practice; the freezer was finally pronounced finished and functioning at eight P.M.; the carpentry work ended on the stowage areas; the oceanographic project equipment was checked out and stowed about five; the camera and recording gear was checked and stowed; a farewell ceremony at dockside was fitted in somehow; and my haircut was due at six P.M.

About 5:15, just after I'd showered, put on the clothes I intended to leave in, and stowed the clean laundry, some of the girls from the Mai Kai, a very good Polynesian restaurant and night club in Fort Lauderdale, came down to the dock in costume, struggling under mounds of flowered leis. Among them was Mireille. A truckload of musicians helped the police get the girls through the crowd, and they commenced in their informal way to wish us a musical Godspeed. Finally they piled back in the truck, and I began making my way to the barber shop.

The Last Haircut was covered photographically and journalistically on local, national, and, as it turned out, international levels. The barber, under my instructions and over my wife's apprehensive objections, clipped my locks down to the scalp. To the number of people who said, "What if it never grows back?" I countered that it was good for hair to be pruned like a hedge occasionally. Little did I know that much of my forelock would be very slow indeed coming back, and would come back much thinner than I thought it would be.

Bob Clayton had not arrived but was on his way. His plane was not due in until close to nine o'clock, and he could not make it to the shore dinner which we started at seven. Mireille was there, however, and so were Tom Jackson, *Thane's* owner, and his date; Martin Goodman, one of New York's top talent representatives; Bob Dixon's mother; Ruth Downs; and the people I'd be spending the next hundred days with in a space not so large as the room we were dining in.

In the latter group was my son H.R., age nineteen, lean, taller than I, darker of complexion (but not so dark as he would be in a few weeks), clever, able-bodied, and with some sailing experience, and good company since he was four. In addition to his duties as crew, he was supervising the floating first-aid department and was in charge of still photography. There was Bob Dixon, in his mid-twenties, reliable and energetic, a top-flight sailor, once mate on the *Mandalay,* skilled mechanic, journalist, and editor of a small Florida magazine.

And Jerry Galyean, twenty-seven, professional photographer, ascetic-looking and with a dry sense of humor. (On meeting Virgil for the first time Jerry had said with a straight face, "You're not the fellow who wrote *The Aeneid?"*)

Pete Jackson was there. Pete is in his early thirties, slight and very blond. He had set out for a diplomatic career but got hung up on sailing and had for the past few seasons been captaining *Thane* in the Virgin Islands for charter parties.

And there was Connie, Pete's wife, blonde and attractive. Connie had a cute figure, an attractive personality, an even temperament, and the ability to cook underway. She had never done this before, she explained, because in sailing from one island to another in the Virgins it was always possible to anchor or tie up in sheltered locations and prepare meals in an upright, untossed galley. But she learned quickly.

Finally, there was Virgil Bowers, heavy-set, sixty, with a jutting jaw and a grizzled crew-cut shock of gray hair. Little about his appearance gave an indication of the man's interests or character. He could have been a claims adjuster, a Bowery bum newly clothed by the Salvation Army, an overfond uncle at a *bar mitzvah,* or a burglar on vacation. Actually, he was a man who'd built a plastics molding company and retired from it early to do the things he wanted to. Virgil was an electronics wizard, and we came to say of him, that he could transmit a signal out of Hell.

H.R. was the only brunet of the bunch. Pete, Connie, Bob, and Jerry all were blond, Virgil was gray, and at the moment, I was bald.

The dinner got underway at seven P.M. in a room in the

hotel. Martin Goodman proposed a toast to our good fortune. We drank to each other's health, but not to the point of endangering our own.

Clayton had a car at the airport. In those days he was commuting from N.Y. to Florida (or Florida to N.Y.—he had homes in both places), and unless his plane was late he'd make it.

"Who's minding the ship?" Goodman asked.

"Six hundred Americans are standing guard on the pier," Jerry said.

"Wouldn't it be funny," said Bob, "if we got down to the ship and found the crowd had overwhelmed the police and was scattering with ten grand worth of equipment and groceries?"

"No, it wouldn't."

H.R. looked at my close-cropped pate once and shook his head, laughing. "I don't believe it," he said, "even looking straight at it I don't believe it."

"You don't laugh at Yul Brynner that way," I told him.

"I think you ought to eat with your hat on. Where are your manners?"

It was a jolly meal, although Bob Clayton didn't make it. He finally arrived at 9:35, when we were all back at the pier. By then the waterway was congested with a friendly flotilla of commercial and pleasure craft, and the crowd on the dock must have been close to a thousand.

Dixon's dog Satan, an immense black German Shepherd, was put below so he could not fall overboard as he had that afternoon.

At ten minutes to ten the "all ashore that's going ashore" was sounded. Five minutes later I started the engine and posted three line handlers. Now there was much shouting and popping of flashbulbs. I obliged in several requests to remove my cap, though why anyone would have wanted pictures of me as Erich von Stroheim is beyond me.

Suspecting that never again in this trip would we approach this punctuality, I gave the word to cast off at one minute before ten and backed *Thane* against a spring line to bring the bow away from the dock and then forward up channel. The stern and spring lines clattered aboard, and a cheer went up as we inched out at half a knot into the center of the channel. The escorting flotilla stood well away, but sent up a medley of whistles and bells. We were, as I had hopefully predicted, underway by 10:00 o'clock.

As we swung south, the drawbridge opened and we went through at about four knots. The log reads ". . . through the bascule bridge to the Port Everglades channel . . . accompanied by the fleet. Satan did well in the pitching and appears to be getting his sea legs (all four of them) rather rapidly . . . A fantastic flurry of salutes from boatwhistles, bells, and auto horns followed us to the end of the Port Everglades channel, and then in a warm head breeze and the dark of the moon we began to move toward the Gulf Stream. Polaris is low off the port quarter and the Pleiades just rising."

Later, H.R. and I were on watch, between three and six A.M. We could see the lights along the Florida shore stretching down toward Miami. We headed a little south of east in anticipation of the northerly set of the Gulf Stream, and our progress wasn't too brisk. About four o'clock I asked him, "How far do you think we've come?" He guessed ten miles.

"In six hours?"

"Twelve miles, maybe," he said.

"That's better."

"You're really asking if I think we've left the United States—outside the twelve-mile limit. Right?"

"Right."

"Well, I think we've moved twelve miles from Fort Lauderdale—from Port Everglades channel—but I don't think we're twelve miles offshore yet."

"You," I said, "are a wet blanket."

"You asked my opinion. I think we'd be arrested if we set up a gambling casino right here."

"All right, wise guy," I said. "I think you're close. But my calculations say we are eleven miles offshore and in less than one-half hour we'll be in international waters."

"That's an official opinion?"

"It is. You are hereby directed to accept it as unanswerable and canonical fact, and part of your deepest belief."

"Why don't you light your cigar now? I won't tell the Coast Guard."

"Why don't you keep your eye on the compass and get this barge a mile farther east. A rule is a rule."

I imagined him smirking in the dark. At four-thirty, I lit my cigar, the first smoke I'd had since coming back from Greece in May, and thought of other ships that had sailed these waters—and some that were still here.

Within a radius equal to our first and shortest run, a line from Fort Lauderdale's Port Everglades to the other side of the Gulf Stream, swung by giant dividers from north of Palm Beach down to the south end of Key Largo, nineteen large ships lie on the bottom, burned, storm-wrecked, torpedoed, stove, or scuttled—nineteen whose positions and cargoes are accurately known. Those which foundered with sulphur, coal, and ore will not interest divers. But there remain those whose cargo is delicious to contemplate and others with known cargo whose position is not a certainty. The *Santa Margarita*, for example, reportedly went down in 1595 off Palm Beach with $3,000,000 in silver and gold bullion; the *Almiranta* was lost in 1733 with $1,500,000 on board. And, most curiously, there is a ship whose position and cargo are known (25° 33.6' N.; 80° 05.7' W. and $2,000,000 in silver bullion), but whose identity is lost. She's in seventy-two feet of water, an easy dive.

How many are down there whose names and cargoes and positions are unknown? Whose rotting timbers are swept by the hems of tides and whose fittings are thick with generations of marine growth? Ships which may yet mark the hiding place under the silt or sand of chests with thousands of pieces of silver or gold? How do you know when you sail in waters of the Continental shelf that you aren't passing over one at any given instant? You don't.

I checked the plankton net I had set and found trouble already. The swivel had jammed and the line, one-half inch dacron yacht braid, was twisted badly. Worse, one of the three steel cables attached to the mouth ring of the long, sleevelike net had come untwisted to the point of parting. I had only one other net and didn't want to set it until I could find a working swivel. Even at low speeds the net exerted considerable drag, and getting it in was like pulling a sea anchor while underway. This was the first bit of a long string of bad luck with the oceanographic project which was to have been a side-line activity of the voyage.

The University of Miami had supplied specimen jars and nets, and I had purchased formalin and paraffin and had hopes of collecting plankton throughout the route.

Oceanographic organizations hesitate to tie up large research vessels for the project they had outlined for me, and so far they haven't got results from private yachts attempting it. I was beginning to find out why.

The log entry for July 1 summarized the conditions of this first day's sail:

"Thru this day weather mild, Gulf Stream somewhat choppy and wind, though light, perversely against our intended direction. Pointed rather high thru the night without engine and as a result made less than 2 knots [speed]. Gulf Stream current set us considerably north of Lat. 26° 05'. Consequently made for Grand Bahama to reach down to Berry Islands through 2nd night (July 1). Northernmost point of whole trip came in evening of July 1 when Downs made a moon sight for line of position at 1922 and we altered course to 125° with power. Finally went to 110° and lowered sail since wind had dropped to almost nothing."

The log also notes that during the Gulf Stream crossing I talked to Jean Ferrari, my secretary at NBC in New York, by commercial ship-to-shore phone through the Miami marine operator and again later by a short-wave ham phone patch. Virgil Bowers also managed to raise a Columbus, Ohio, ham operator and I talked to my surprised relatives there.

Again from the log of July 1:

"At 2305 sighted rocket take-off from Cape Kennedy. Brilliant orange trail rising rapidly from bearing astern and slightly north (what would be the direction of Kennedy) and arcing over into a probably orbital direction after burn-out of first-stage overhead and slightly south of us. Saw three stages in all and then the rapidly moving light grew fainter and vanished S.E. of the ship."

We later learned that this was a Tiros weather satellite. It gave an idea of where we were, as we had got slightly fuddled on position.

The log of this date omits mention of this embarrassment to the navigator. It was the only time on the whole voyage that we could be said to have gotten lost. "Lost" may be too strong a word, as I knew we were (a) east of the United States, (b) in the Gulf Stream, and (c) at least a day's sail from Nassau. I can honestly say that from the point of sighting the Berry Islands the following day to tying up in Tahiti months later, I knew the ship's position at any time within a few miles, but through the night of July 1 and some of the next day, I was certain only that we were somewhere inside an enormous expanse of Bahamian waters.

Daniel Boone, once questioned as to whether he'd ever got lost in the wilderness, replied, "I never was lost exactly. But once I was uncertain of my position for four days." This describes our plight. The reason for this embarrassment is a lesson in the dangers of overconfidence. Five of the seven of us had crossed the Gulf Stream at least once before. Making a landfall at Bimini or Great Isaac Light or Grand Bahama Island is no heroic feat and it usually doesn't take a sextant to find these places. The moon line I worked was merely for practice and could not have pinned down our precise position without another sight, no matter how accurate. Frequent course changes necessitated by weak and shifting winds made the sightings difficult to render into any good dead reckoning, and there was some debate about the speed of the Gulf Stream current. Suddenly I realized that the charts we had didn't show new construction known to be on Grand Bahama Island, and the loom of light dimly seen on our northern horizon could have been that island, or, if we were some miles to the south, it could have been Great Isaac Light. It is not in the least desirable to leave the Gulf Stream south of Great Isaac as there are treacherous shoals where you can run hard aground well out of sight of land. Our sighting of the rocket launching and the obvious conclusion that it came from Cape Kennedy gave us a bearing line to cross my doubtful moon line, and confirmed that we were in fact north of Great Isaac (the loom of which we later saw in the south). For the moment we moved cautiously eastward, and I made a note to keep track from then on of exactly where we were. Nothing is more nerve-racking than to be aboard a moving boat at night with the feeling that the depth may suddenly become less than the draft. You feel as though you don't want to let your full weight down.

Again, from the log:

"JULY 1 . . . During the day Clayton reflected on the Condition of the World at the time *Thane's* keel was laid (1911). The Kaiser was on the throne of Germany, Vienna was the gayest spot in the world and all classes 'were in their proper places.' The Gibson Girl looked as elegant as she was decorous and nobody had heard of bath-tub gin. Virgil said he was the only thing aboard built before *Thane* was. He opinioned further, to the amusement of the entire company, that the real name of the ship was *Sane* but we were calling her *Thane* in deference to the captain, who lisped. (It apparently takes less to amuse people out of sight of land than in port.)

"Concern over Satan who had not relieved himself in any fashion since boarding, and who had consumed 11 lbs. of table scraps from our last meal ashore, plus a can of Alpo, was at last dispelled when in the early evening our noses led us to the place on deck (*not* his training box) where he had solved his problem. At least he wasn't below at the time. Dixon indulged in a justifiable bit of profanity on cleaning the deck."

You can tell when you're out of the Gulf Stream. It's more a feeling than anything else, but there's something different and you don't have to make many crossings to recognize it. Farther north in the Atlantic, in what's called the "meander," a place where the Gulf Stream snakes over east and south and then north in a sink-trap shape not always found in the same place, yachtsmen identify the stream by temperature. In latitudes south of 30°N it's not so much a matter of temperature, though there is a differential, as it is this feeling one has. We felt it.

Again in the night hours of July 2 there was little breeze, and we had to proceed by power, east by south in Providence Channel. The copious notes in the log, in which I recorded as much detail as I could, continue:

". . . Some ships moved by to the south—freighters, probably. And the phosphorescent plankton in our wake winked in flashy imitation of the stars overhead. Without sail the ship rolled a little in a slight swell. Through the rigging Andromeda's hundred-billion-star nebula glowed 'like a candle flame seen through horn' and Cassiopeia moved up out of the North East and around, all as they had done before a sail or hull moved under them. The wheel moved in the hand like a living thing and a slight creaking and the slatting of halyards sent old messages to the listening stars.

"At dawn still no land visible. Sea became even more calm. Cloudless overhead but a few cumulus on horizon reflected whitely on the glassy water. Not a fishing boat or bird in sight. Could have been doldrums in the Pacific. At 0857 sighted land—the Berry Islands. Altered course to due East to stand off Stirrup Cay Light.

"Once clear by 3 or 4 miles, set a course of 150 to New Providence and estimated arrival at 2030."

In the afternoon, when the low profile of Stirrup Cay was slipping astern, a school of ten to a dozen bottle-nose dolphin escorted the ship for a half mile, cavorting in the clear blue-green water. For five minutes I stood on the bobstay, my feet under water, and reached out to them. Virgil was steering his usual auto-pilot-straight course. The dolphin would come quite close to me, and I decided they would probably let us join them swimming. It would be worth arriving at Nassau after dark. Jerry began to load a camera. But I was wrong. The instant we cut the engine, the dolphin took off.

We sighted Nassau before sundown. We set our ensign at the stern, ran up the club flag at the main, and readied the yellow quarantine flag and the courtesy flag. A digression here: the luck I had in obtaining and flying of flags for this trip was just about zero. I like to think that we had good luck in most matters because all the evil fortune was collected into this one pocket having to do with flags.

The firm I ordered my flags from is an old reputable New York sporting concern with a large yachting department. I ordered my flags almost three months in advance of departure date. The first mishap was that they weren't ready on time. Knowing Pete had the proper flag for the Bahamas, I asked that all the others be sent to me in Nassau. They missed that postal point, and the flags were finally forwarded to our agents in Panama.

The Ecuadorian flag we later flew for the Galapagos Islands turned out to be not the national colors, but a treasury department flag, similar but not proper. Moreover, on the approach to Wreck Bay, the port of entry of the Galapagos, we lost our yellow quarantine flag in a stiff breeze just four seconds after running it up and had to replace it with a yellow bag in which nylon storm gear was kept. We called this the quarantine ball as it inflated itself and bobbed about like a child's balloon.

Fate struck our colors for us once when the staff of the Yacht Ensign snapped off at the socket in an accident with the mizzen boom. Fortunately a spare was aboard and we were "repatriated" within minutes.

The crowning gaffe—wholly due to error on the part of my supplier—occurred after our landfall at Takaroa. To begin with, Takaroa is not a proper port of entry in

French Polynesia; I had to cable for permission from the French Governor General to enter. When the chief of the island said we were cleared, I got out the French tricolor and told H.R. and Jerry to fly it. On my return from the village, where I had gone to see if diesel fuel could be purchased, I saw a strange sight: the flag of France streaming backward from under our spreader. The colors of France cannot be flown upside down since they consist of three vertical stripes of blue, white, and red and are the same upside down as right side up. However they can be flown backward: red, white, and blue instead of blue, white, and red. I couldn't believe my eyes. How could they get it up that way? The grommets would have to be on the staff end and not the fly end. I looked back toward the French government weather station where the flag of France flew correctly with the blue toward the mast. Back aboard *Thane* I discovered that the flag had actually been made with grommets on the wrong end. It took an hour and a half for Dixon and Galyean to cut the grommet strip and resew it to the right edge.

But now we were coming to Nassau and the sun was low in the West.

The very light breeze had subsided to nothing, and the evening was utterly calm, in contrast to the busy-ness of our approach as we bustled through our arrival check list. We put on running lights and finally stood on deck in silence as the bow parted the mirror-like water and the ship glided along between the silhouetted trees of the shore on the Paradise Isle side of the channel and the lights of Nassau on the other side.

We dropped anchor about one-third of a mile from Customs House, very near where, some six years before, I'd boarded Irving Johnson's beautiful brigantine *Yankee*, now wrecked off Rarotonga. Virgil volunteered for the first watch as he wanted to stay aboard the first night anyway, so we took half of a walkie-talkie set and went ashore to customs. There the military sentry called up a customs official at home who said he would be down soon to clear us. "Soon" turned into more than two-and-a-half hours. Finally everyone but Virgil disembarked onto the streets of Nassau and scattered into the night. I called Ruth at the Nassau Beach Hotel. She was having dinner with friends, Bob and Isabel Souers, and they came down to pick me up later.

From time to time I spoke to Virgil on the walkie-talkie, and we gradually realized that most likely we were on an illegal frequency because a voice kept cutting in demanding to know who and where we were. We didn't use names and stopped referring to the ship and finally we just ran half-hourly checks all the way to the Nassau Beach. I talked for a while on the hour and half-hour, and finally the customs official arrived. Not wishing to explain the walkie-talkie, I snapped it off and jammed it in my hip pocket. This move unfortunately twisted its volume knob, not only turning it back on but turning it up to a good loud level. While I was filling out the customs forms, Virgil's voice came booming out of my behind to reverberate lustily and irreverently in the cavernous room:

"H.D. H.D. How do you copy? How do you copy? Hasn't the guy shown up yet? Over."

Through this I was fumbling behind me to shut the unit off and looking at the puzzled customs man. "Transistor," I said, "all us teenagers carry them."

He didn't smile, but he turned out to be a compassionate man, and gave us permission to bring the dog ashore (who by now had already *been* ashore long enough to catalog all the hydrants and trees) as well as waiving any search aboard.

Since we were at anchor the third and fourth, there was

good drill for the ship's boats. We transferred fuel, water, laundry, and supplies and spent a lot of time readying the next leg. Sunday we had a press lunch ashore and then invited the Souers and Julius Caruso and a couple of others aboard at six o'clock for cocktails. The party grew some when Bud Warburton's *Black Pearl*, a beautiful square-rigger, tied alongside. Along with the people there were two bitches in heat who swarmed aboard at the precise moment Satan cleared the rail onto their deck. Tom Jackson, who had seen us off at Fort Lauderdale, was also aboard the *Black Pearl*.

We celebrated that American Independence Day without setting off any of the fireworks we'd brought. I could see no way to avoid the risk of a rocket landing ashore on either side, or going straight into the furled sails of Warburton's ship, or our own. From an insurance standpoint the threat was formidable. So we lit ourselves up a little instead.

~~~~~~

V

THERE WAS AN EAST WIND Monday morning. This was the day that should see the last of our eastward direction—from here on the trip would be south and west. Our immediate goal was Highburn Key, east of New Providence in the Exuma chain. It was also the longest stretch of shoal water in the whole trip, across the Yellow Banks.

We got away by ten A.M. so we could have daylight all the way for pilotage. Numerous coral heads studded the passage, making it necessary to pick our way with care. The end of the run of July 5th was also the end of my familiarity with the waters of the Bahamas.

Highburn Key (or Cay) is a couple of miles long. It is private property today, but in the past a good deal of farming was carried on there. Probably the original inhabitants, called Lucayans, started farming it. But they are long gone, enslaved and taken to larger islands by the Spanish. There is a strong tidal current running through the Cut, and the proper approach is important to avoid the coral heads which dot the area. Just north of the pass is a dredged anchorage, landlocked and snug, which we identified by masts sticking up above the low headlands. Immediately to the south is Oyster Cay, where there must be oysters, although there are more conches than anything else along the shores.

I had been to Highburn but never through the pass into Exuma Sound. The sun was just setting when we arrived at the tricky pass. The Bahamas Guide was of great help in lining up our direction to get through. The west side of the pass is particularly touchy. At one point, when we were a shade south of where we intended to be, there was a thick nest of coral heads, and at a speed of about a half-knot the keel touched. The whole ship gave a shiver, along with a low ominous sound I hope I never hear again. But no damage was done to the ship, and she never touched ground again on the trip.

All that night we sailed under power, with one mainsail up until about 0330 when it began to luff and I had it taken in. The sea was fairly calm, and after the moon set and ragged clouds covered about half the sky the phosphorescent plankton flashed about our sides and in the foam of our wake. I was concerned that I had caught so few of these little beasts in the plankton net. The sparse samplings I got in Exuma Sound were lost south of Nevassa in a rough spell.

The log entry for July 6, a day bright with sunshine and blue water, describes a small triumph of H.R. He caught a small tuna, about twelve pounds in weight, which we subsequently made into a salad for the next day's lunch. We thought it was beautifully fought and boated by H.R., but H.R.'s observation was that judging from the unattractiveness of the fish, he thought he had caught "Charlie," the tuna in the Starkist commercials.

We made Cape Santa Maria, the north tip of Long Island, at six o'clock in the evening of that day, and then proceeded five hours east, in order to sail more southward to Great Inagua. The breeze continued to hold good. We touched 76° West Longitude, as far east as we would be on the trip. Again, I quote the log for the typical routine of these days: "JULY 7, Wed.—Extremely difficult to get motion picture footage, underway. The problem is this: If it is calm there is nothing of particular interest to shoot. If it is rough or any danger is upon us, the double problem of sparing Jerry as a hand and of protecting expensive equipment from the elements is too much. We are trying the following expedients: One Bolex is being put in the underwater housing both for storage and for quick, wide-angle accessibility. Jerry says there's some doubt about the outcome of leaving film in that camera for any length of time, but we will have to chance it.

"Waiting for a message from de Sylva regarding the plankton-towing nets with which I've not had the best luck. So far, with a couple of exceptions, the nights have been too rough or too moonlit for proper sampling. I now have a swivel on the one good net so it won't twist its steel cable apart, and I have a proper funnel for transferring specimens and a 'crucible' for melting the paraffin to seal the small bottles. Not easy work when there is pitch and roll.

"We eat well and manage to get enough sleep. I think of the often-repeated question put to me by friends before I left: 'What are you going to do to fill the time?' I wish the askers could be aboard for 48 hours to snap their harness cables on rigging or lifelines during a blow while trying to get sail in, holding a course for a watch period, making sightings, soundings, Walker-log readings, sun-sights and star-sights, readying position reports, logging course and speed changes and wind and weather in the wheel log, drying out after taking water aboard . . . working fixes and plotting courses and then waking up during brief night-naps to recheck that some error won't put you aground, cleaning a clogged bilge pump, repatching and reinflating one of the rubber boats punctured by a fishing lure or chafe in one of its compartments, loading diesel fuel after ferrying it out to an anchorage by dinghy . . . bringing in the same manner such fragile and tender items as fresh bread and good cameras, and a dozen other routines that help 'while away the long and boring hours.'

"And all this must be done before attention can be given to taping or filming the oceanographic project or meeting the radio schedule.

"This Wednesday started with an almost ominously calm wind and sea. The barometer was not low, however, and nothing stormy was predicted in any weather reports. Outside of a couple of squalls and an eventually stiff breeze and building seas, there was no bad weather. But after a while the chop began slamming us about a bit.

"We stood clear of Rum Cay light (about five miles to west of it) and continued south and east toward south spit of Long Island.

"Shortly after midnight went from engine to sail as our course was now enough off the wind. Galyean and H.R.D. logged at 0300 'slightly rough' . . . As a drill I had everyone wear life preserver and life harness over the foulweather gear for the next round of watches. It came in handy as a couple of times we were boarded by seas which drenched the wheel log and the Bahama Guide and a chart in the cockpit.

"Sighted south spit of Long Island far off starboard beam about 6 A.M.

"Acklins Island and Castle Light came up on schedule. We went through Mira Por Vos straits at about seven knots (good breeze) at 5:15 P.M.

"Started into the night on a course of 160 which should bring Great Inagua (the west end where Matthewtown is) into view by about daylight. I catch myself thinking

that God placed these islands in just the right positions
and at just the right distances for us to have deep water
runs through the nights, and land and shoal water in
the daylight hours—until I remember that my planning
over four years took these distances into account. For all
the minor annoyances, I take solid satisfaction in the fact
that the reality is so like the plan in structure.

"About the nights: When one has caught one's breath
after the first few nights of being overwhelmed by the
majesty of the spectacle of sky and water—their envelop-
ing friendly unconcern and their unchanging majesty—
one begins to hear the sounds. Some are commonplace
and instantly understandable: The hiss and smash of the
seas against the prow and hull . . . the slatting of halyards and flapping of sails, the creak of the wheel as it
is turned slightly . . . these are not only understood but
expected. But there are sounds that aren't familiar or expected, and in some cases are not even welcome. Some
of these are identified eventually, but some remain mysterious and give the scalp-crawling feeling that there are
indeed unknown creatures in the night sea, bobbing up
to mock the folly of a warm-blooded animal challenging
the vast deep in his cloth-rigged cockleshell. For three
nights I heard a distant man's voice calling 'Tom!' It was
real enough to make me scan the horizon expecting to
find a boat without lights a few yards off. Once H.R. and
I both heard it. Later we discovered that the hinge from
which the ship's bell hangs, when moved a certain way,
makes this sound."

That item of the log turned out to be an error. We believed it at the time, but some weeks later we discovered
the sound really came from an old block on the main
sheet which creaked in that remarkable way as the sheet
passed through it. Dixon named it "Chipoff." ("Chipoff,
the old block.")

On July 8, after a rough night, at about 5:30 in the morning we spotted a long row of palmettos to the southeast. At the far end, as we anticipated, we located the Matthewtown light and at twenty-five minutes after seven we dropped anchor in a sort of open roadstead that passes for Matthewtown's harbor.

Again, the log records an event that I'd prefer to have witnessed from outside rather than inside: "Preparing to go ashore, having dressed in white Western shirt with silver-mounted pearl buttons and piped pocket flaps, clean jeans, and captain's hat, and having placed in pockets a lighter, traveler's check, some Bahamian pound notes and U.S. long green, not to mention a small packet of Kingston cigars, and presenting withal a rather smartly august appearance, H.M.D. stepped jauntily over the side into what he thought was the *Seagull* dinghy, which he regards with affection as some sort of admiral's gig, but which turned out to be the Caribbean Sea. The dinghy was there but he overshot it. Those who witnessed this were kind enough later to say it made a dignified splash and he managed to keep his hat dry. The clothes and other items, except the cigars, dried out in half an hour ashore."

Great Inagua is the most thoroughly insular place I've ever visited. Being near Haiti and Cuba and not many miles from the U.S., it is not so isolated as the Galapagos Islands, nor so far from continental civilization as French Polynesia, but for sheer insular outlook of its inhabitants it is outstanding. It belongs almost wholly to the Morton Salt Company. West India Chemicals Ltd. technically operates it, and this island literally thinks salt. The motion picture house, for one example, is called the Salt Theatre. The island is fairly large, about forty miles long and twenty wide, but Matthewtown itself is not only small but hasn't the least urban flavor about it.

In the interior of the island there is a large shallow lake that provides the salt flats. Wild cattle, pigs, and horses roam the savannas there. Jerry photographed some of the many birds there on a brief inland expedition. There are cranes, roseate spoonbills, and ducks, among others.

We took lunch and dinner ashore that day. Virgil stayed aboard at lunchtime and Pete at dinnertime, and Satan got his first visit ashore since Nassau. (The capacity of a dog's interior plumbing, and his patience, can be astounding.) He caused something of a stir ashore because the locals tended to regard him as a man-eater. In fact, however, he is downright placid even with other dogs.

Island dogs have an air one never sees in continental dogs. They seem to sense their inferiority of scope. Satan was looked upon (and seemed to regard himself) as some real personage from not only a faraway, but a big and important place.

Jerry and H.R. and I sat for a while on a wooden bench shaded by the portico of the Salt Theatre (open Friday and Saturday only, and this was Thursday). We faced out to sea—any way you look is out to sea—and talked to Great Inaguans for an hour or so. They were all friendly and generous with advice. They asked about the dog and whether he bit people, and I could see that they reserved judgment. When we reassured them, they told us of a rather dramatic dog-bite incident within fifty yards of where we sat, "just outside the machine shop door." Then we found it had taken place in 1928, but it was still, along with The Riot of the same year, the talk of the island.

The riot, it seems, was occasioned by an action of the British Government, although one account has it launched by a local Helen of Troy. A sailor visiting the island had also visited this lady, and her husband took a shot at him. This resulted in the British gathering up and

removing all guns from the island. The infuriated popu-
lace rioted in protest. But the ban stood.

Later on, as we dawdled over our evening meal, an
islander in the dining room regaled us with reports of
piracy nearby, calculated to frighten us into staying on.
It was, in a way, flattering.

"Haitian gunboats come out and blow you out of the
water 'less you give in and give up your supplies or your
ship," the old timer said.

"They're not privateers then? They're real government
boats?" we asked him.

"You know what kind of government Haiti has?" he
asked. "Blow you out the water soon as look at you.
And it don't do no good to hug the Cuban shore."

"I suppose Cuban gunboats get you then?"

"No. Fidel's government won't do nothing like that.
But they do allow gangs in other boats to do what they
please."

This all led up to the advice that we make our night
run between Haiti and Cuba without lights. It seemed too
melodramatic to take seriously, but it did touch an earlier
fear of mine about getting too close to Cuba. As unlikely
as was a collision at night, it seemed even less likely
that we'd be taken by buccaneers in this age of single
side-band radio, so the plan held to move out normally at
night toward Jamaica. The log, written the evening of
the eighth, says "We will maintain radio contact with
Guantánamo if possible and hold off boarders long enough
for Virgil to transmit our position and plight if it comes
to that. Let us hope for no nonsense." I don't know
whether we thought the U. S. Marines would roar out of
Guantánamo, Cuba, to our rescue or what, but the
Walter Mitty in each of us ran through a short sequence
of distributing small arms and not giving up the ship. My

sequence had the cop-out ending that the pirates were a mirage and didn't really exist.

The last entry on the July 8 page was: "Ran through the night without incident, and while it was again rough, we were better secured and battened and things were taken in stride."

There was an odd feeling in leaving the Bahamas behind us. To begin with, our last stop was the farthest east we'd be on the voyage; from here on the directions would be west and south. Second, most of us had done some sailing in the Bahamas. We felt somewhat at home in these relatively shallow banks and coral islands strung out like bread crumbs, almost within sight of each other. The navigation was easily done by dead reckoning alone. But from here on the sextant and the correct time would be more and more important. Longer distances, deeper water, towering mountains lay ahead. The latitude was down to the teens now, the ocean seemed bluer, and the sense of slipping between Cuba and Haiti and approaching the open sea drew on strongly.

Now as they dropped away, I suddenly saw the Bahamas in a perspective that gave me the uneasy feeling of leaving home. So must have felt the peaceful Lucayans, whose tenure from time out of mind came to an abrupt end with the arrival of the Spaniards, led there by an Italian navigator in 1492; these first dwellers were almost entirely transported to forced labor in the mines and fields of Haiti. Their islands lay uninhabited for one hundred years. The Eleutheran adventurers from London tried, and failed, to colonize the Bahamas. Both the French and Spanish devastated Nassau early in the eighteenth century and left it to the pirates, who lost it to the British, who lost it in 1776 to the Americans, who held it only a few weeks, leaving it to the Spanish, who

restored it to Britain in 1783. The sunny islands must
have felt baffled by all these quick changes. Now they
are left to yachtsmen and tourists principally, and one
feels an odd pull at leaving them, whether flying back to
Florida or sailing south to Jamaica.

In a way the voyage was just beginning. We were now
entering strange waters for the first time. In the early
morning of July 9 we began to pitch a bit. The breeze had
come up; the seas were steepening, but generally moderate. During the morning we sighted Haiti. For all the
warnings on Inagua, it seemed the privateers were not
out that day. As evening came on we were sailing in a
really rough sea, built up from winds in some other area
and producing a sickening wallow.

Since the wind was light, we got little steadying influence from the sails. I must admit that at that point I
did not relish the prospect of the Pacific with its immense
reaches, if much of it was to be like this. What I didn't
know then is that the size of waves is not so important as
their nature and shape.

Of the rough sea the log noted: "It has brought morale
down a bit and made it difficult to secure gear and equipment both on deck and below, and impossible to pursue
projects other than those necessary to staying on course.
Two members suffering a touch of *mal de mer*, Connie
and Jerry. So far I've been lucky."

Rereading this part of the log later on, I detected a
hint of discouragement, which illustrates something I
didn't realize at the time. With me discouragement is the
first indication of onset of motion sickness. It seldom gets
beyond this stage, and I've had real motion sickness only
twice that I can remember. Once was before World War
II, aboard a friend's sailboat tied up at a pier in the
Detroit River. The motion was certainly not violent, but
I was cleaning the bilge under an old Buda auxiliary en-

gine. My head was lower than my feet, and there was an exquisite blend of oil and wood rot mixed with traces of garbage. I got off and stood on the dock for a moment, and the feeling went away. On another occasion I was trying to work a navigation problem aboard Van Beek's *Harbinger* in the channel between Guadeloupe and Antigua in a force 7 wind. *Harbinger* is a stiff ship and less easily tossed around, but again the nature of the motion is somehow more significant than the violence. I got the idea I had eaten something poisoned. I had to leave the problem and stand on deck for five minutes. But in each of these cases the feeling of nausea was not the first symptom. The first sign to me is a pronounced lack of zest, about anything. It's a time that habitual routine has to carry you through, and if you haven't enough experience to fall back on routine—in other words if you're new enough to have to *think* your way through each step of a task—you have a problem. The second stage is a positive sense of discouragement. During this first phase, a navigation problem, for example, seems boring. In the second phase, of discouragement, it becomes utterly futile. "There is no point completing this," a voice seems to say, "because it doesn't really matter that you find out where you are." From there it is but a step to the next phase, wherein the voice says, "we're all going to drown anyway when we go on the rocks." I've never been in deeper stages of seasickness, but they tell me the time comes when the prospect of death is a positive delight as an alternative to the active nausea it can produce.

Satan seemed to understand why he got stepped on a lot at this time. He'd look at us with his immense, puzzled eyes and silently seem to say "I know you aren't doing this to me intentionally, and I understand the ship rolls and it's hard to keep from bumping into and stepping on each other and I understand there is no known way to go to the bathroom. But what I fail to grasp is why the hell are you doing this to yourselves? Has some circumstance too tricky for dogs to understand forced you to leave your homes, where it is dry and steady and you have bathrooms and beds? *I'm* in this trap because I don't know any better and I'll go where my master goes, but *you* had a choice! And you chose this?"

We never had an answer for him.

But we knew now that Satan would have to go back. He was good company, but since he'd not been on a boat as a puppy, he never got the hang of it. We were certain that one day we'd lose him, and Bob decided to crate him up and ship him back from Jamaica.

On July tenth at 0450 in the first hint of dawn, we sighted Navassa, an island of disputed nationality off the southwest tip of Haiti. By 0730 it was closing. We stood off the island about a mile. Virgil wanted some pictures of it as Navassa has importance in ham radio circles.

At eight in the morning of the tenth, with a good breakfast of eggs and ham, juice, and coffee, we peeled off for Morant Point, Jamaica, seventy-five miles away. The mountains of Cuba and Haiti, now behind us, began to sink slowly into the horizon and finally faded into the haze. We got enough breeze for steadying and made about six knots. The seas did not build up any higher. The day passed quickly with chores and projects. I plotted my daily time tick from the radio now to calculate my watch error for any moment of the day, and decided that I had refined it sufficiently for the sextant accuracy I needed. Coming on Morant at night made it desirable to sharpen our position as we approached. The sky was ragged, and the evening shots were uncertain. Even with Sight Reduction tables and using Air Navigator's methods I didn't feel as secure as if I'd been a qualified Air Navigator, but I had no reason to doubt my last sun sights, and the dead reckoning had proved to be fairly accurate over short hauls.

The morale rose. A favoring wind and drying-out can do a lot for a ship's company.

Midnight came and no sign of Morant or the mountains of Jamaica. Nothing but water. The moonlit clouds on the southwestern horizon might be hiding great towers of earth and rock, but there was no noticeable difference in appearance between them and the clouds in any other direction.

The last entry in the July 10 log reads: "D.R. indicates we have to be in a position near Jamaica. Sighted light far off stbd. beam thought to be Morant."

But the light disappeared shortly after midnight. The cloud cover thickened, and I felt that to run west and risk the dark north shore of the east end of the island was unwise.

The July 11 wheel log reads: "0205 Morant light bore due North (!) Came about to 260 mag. Log 82." This meant that at five minutes after two in the morning we were straight *south* of the east tip of Jamaica. The Walker log read that we had traveled eighty-two miles, and Jamaica is only seventy-five miles from Navassa. So we had overshot. We went west for a bit since Kingston is west of Morant on the South Shore. We'd make for it at daybreak.

At dawn the sky cleared, and at the foot of Jamaica's truly majestic mountains we could see the smoke of Kingston's cement factory. The log account carries the details of our arrival.

"SUNDAY, JULY 11—Arrived at Plum Light and buoy marking range into Kingston Harbor about 8 in the morning. Sea running high . . . My turn to cook and I forgot. Nobody said anything about breakfast. (I went below about 0810 and hastily assembled the short orders I'd taken on deck. By the time breakfast was cleared away the city of Kingston was visible.)

"Just abeam of Port Royal, a ghostly remnant of a wild pirate town across the harbor from Kingston, which now houses police barracks and the port authority for entry to Jamaica, we sighted the launch *Lone Star* with several people, including Ruth, aboard. Dick Steedman was there with 16 mm. equipment grinding away. As we were under power (wind was dead astern and we'd have had to rig preventers and all, so we were simply motoring in) request was hollered across to raise sail, which we did. The boys got quite a workout putting all canvas up and tacking and wearing and then changing the anchor line to the heavy anchor as the wind increased.

"Steedman sent requests via radio to Virgil regarding our course for best photographic angles, some of which clashed with prudent seamanship. Once he called for us to continue a tack which would have set us square onto a shoal area east of the old harbor fort. Dixon figured what Steedman wanted to photograph was a shipwreck. He also called for the helm of the *Lone Star* to put his ship 'within six inches of *Thane* and hold her there!' This brought a laugh from both vessels. He was kidding of course.

"Funniest line of the day: Virgil Bowers, seeing a 20-foot cabin cruiser hovering and ducking about the larger photographic boat, proclaimed that it was 'the eight millimeter crew.'

"Port Royal is the port of entry for Jamaica. An official patrol boat directed us to the Port Royal customs station as soon as we entered the harbor. We told them we'd come back to Port Royal and clear for entry as soon as we finished the photography."

On the face of it our response seems arrogant, if not illegal. But we were not debarking or tying up and the photographer on the other boat had been hired by the Jamaican government to get pictures of us coming in. We felt there was nothing wrong with delaying the customs ceremonies by a few minutes. The customs officers did not feel the same way. The log continues:

"Whether this angered them or whether Jamaican customs are always so stuffy and thorough we may never know, but the reception we got from them clearly indicated they suspected us of bringing in contraband or intending to revive piracy in Jamaica or both, because we were subjected to considerable unnecessary inconvenience in a two-hour process. . . .

"They poked around our gear and stowage as though disappointed at not finding thirty pounds of uncut heroin or an atomic bomb. The declaration of firearms aboard created such a palpable wave of suspicious hostility that it wouldn't have been surprising if they had confiscated our arms to equip a firing squad to dispatch the lot of us."

In order to seal the long arms it was necessary to empty a locker of clothes. The guns were then put in and a glue-coated paper government seal slapped on the door. We would have felt better if they had boarded and broken the seal when we left; instead we were made to wait four hours for a harbor official who then merely said, "You may go." He apparently didn't care whether we had broken the seal and sold our guns or whether we had a hold full of stolen goods. It should be said, however, that the government treated us well—the tourist board and the military, among whom we have good friends. But Jamaica customs can be a law unto itself.

The topper was that poor Satan was not allowed ashore. This was not harassment but a law of the Country. Curiously, the Bahamas do not adhere to this basically British rule concerning dogs and quarantine, whereas Jamaica, now independent of British regulations, applies it strictly.

The irony is that Satan had to go ashore to be crated and flown out, but that could be done only with an escorting officer. We asked if the escorting officer could first escort him to a fireplug or tree. . . .

We had maneuvered *Thane* through a forest of small boats at the Royal Yacht Club anchorage. Actually we had horsed her around with considerable risk of fouling someone's anchor and mooring links. Pete showed his knowledge of *Thane's* steering characteristics in executing this maneuver against a brisk east wind. There is superb shelter in Kingston Harbor—second best in the world —against any very rough water, but the harbor is long from east to west and the wind has a long fetch, and when it blows hard little whitecaps froth up. *Thane* has high freeboard and, even with all sail in, requires careful handling in a wind.

The sizeable assemblage of locals at the dock were a little baffled at my greeting Ruth and Isabel Souers, who had accompanied her from Nassau, and Mary Sharpe (wife of Stuart Sharpe of the Jamaica Tourist Board just returned home from Florida), concluding that I was a sailor with *several* in every port.

When things were secured—and it was after noon—we went to the Sheraton Kingston, where I had arranged to stay ashore for the short time we would be in Jamaica. There we had a visit from an old friend, W. Stanley Moss, with whom we reminisced over a double sugar mill (rum) on "a rock."

This was to be the last time I ever saw Bill Moss. He came back next day while I was out and left a book he wanted me to have, *Vikings of the Sunrise*.

I had first met him early in 1962, the year after he arrived at Jamaica to write for the *Daily Gleaner,* a newspaper widely read in the Caribbean. It was trail's end for him, and I'm certain now he knew it. Some of his

friends thought they knew it too, but they were wrong
about the reason. They thought Bill was drinking himself
to death. He had given up eating almost entirely and
seemed to live on rum. He lost weight steadily until his
gauntness showed the hand of death.

Bill had a house partway down a slope from Stony
Hill Hotel. One evening he came up to a showing of a
movie based on his novel, *Ill Met By Moonlight*. This was
the first I'd met him though I was acquainted with his
book as it had been a bestseller. His way up the hill was
so painfully slow and he appeared so wasted I asked my
companion if he was ill.

"Yes, he's ill," he said. "We can't get him to eat."

We watched him take a few more steps toward us.
There was no shambling in his gait, but when Bill finally
got there I was expecting to meet the kind of a wreck
classically wrought by demon rum. Instead, through the
evening I was surprised to find behind his pale, drawn
mask a keen mind and generous personality. There was
no hint of fear or discouragement or self-deceit, or whin-
ing or sick hope. His twinkle at the world, his genuine
interest in people, his self-forgetfulness and his wit and
keenness of mind all belied the fact that the man was
obviously dying and knew it.

We watched the movie, which starred Dirk Bogarde.
It was a sound adventure yarn based on pursuit and cap-
ture of a German general in Crete during the war. Moss
had been there and the material was autobiographic.

He had been many places. He was born in Yokohama
and had been three times around the world before he
was six. His mother was a White Russian refugee and his
father a British multimillionaire who lost the whole bundle on Wall Street, of all places, in the 1929 crash. Bill
was graduated from Charterhouse and was planning to
enter Oxford when the war broke out. At the time he was

in Latvia and had to cross the North Sea in a yacht. (Much of our conversation was of yachts, and I learned a lot from Bill.)

He had dined in the Court of St. James as a member of the Coldstream Guards. According to Stede-Strephon St. Cyr, he has "smoked opium in a Siamese den and sweated it out in the French Foreign Legion dives of Siddi-bel-Abbes. He has eaten pemican in the Antarctic and caviar in the palaces of the mid-Orient . . . He worked as a secret service agent in Macedonia, Algeria . . . France, Germany, Holland, Belgium, and Italy." When he was married—in Cairo in 1945—to the Countess Zofia Tarnowski, Prince Peter of Greece was a witness and King Farouk attended the reception. He inaugurated a polar air rescue service which led him in 1957 to go parachuting in the Antarctic during the Fuchs-Hillary expeditions. After this he sailed back to the West Indies via Tahiti.

He inscribed the volume of *Vikings of the Sunrise,* which he gave me just before I sailed from Jamaica: "Dear Hugh—This book is considered to be the bible of the Pacific. It has already sailed from New Zealand to Nassau with me, and I hope you will find it useful when travelling in the opposite direction . . . Bon voyage, Bill Moss."

We were talking once about smoking and Bill said, "I don't think I could give up smoking if my life depended on it. I could quit drinking at any time, but smoking is another matter."

I looked at him and realized he was quite sincere. It didn't occur to me at the time that he not only believed what he said, but that it was probably the truth, even though his riding of alcohol to quiet intense pain had by then produced a condition that made digestion of solid food difficult. I discovered that Bill Moss was being slowly eaten away by something more devastating and hopeless than addiction to rum—cancer.

Moss was one of those rare men who faced death, aware that defeat is inevitable, without kidding himself, without burdening those around him and without any impairment of the freshness of his spirit. I never knew a more gallant man than Bill Moss.

It would not have surprised me to find that Dixon had sneaked Satan ashore as soon as it got dark. Next day arrangements were made for Satan to go back to the States in a crate, tranquilized and indifferent to the mountain of red tape attending the project. We said an emotional good-bye to him, put him in his crate and into a borrowed station wagon with the accompanying customs officer to escort him to Palisadoes airport. The handsome black German Shepherd gave us a last look as though to say, "Where are *your* crates? Surely you're not going to continue aboard that vessel where you can't go to the bathroom?" He was a good shipmate, even with all his problems, and I hated to part from him. But we were all glad at least that there would be no danger of his being lost at sea. As of this writing he is happy on dry land of the state of Florida.

On Monday, July 12, Bill Garrison, manager of the hotel, gave a dinner for all of us at the Sheraton. Whereupon we promptly talked him into coming with us to Panama. Pete and Connie went out with Dr. Roy Foster, who had lent me a boat some months before to scout the approaches to Kingston Harbor.

That morning we had gone to breakfast at Strawberry Hill north of Kingston and looked down upon the dispersing clouds. The view out over the harbor is one of the best in the world.

Strawberry Hill is partway up the foothills of Blue Mountain, which is more than 7000 feet high. From the yard of a pleasant inn one can see almost all of Kingston Harbor and the long spit of protective land out to Port Royal. It has been enlarged artificially at one point to make land for Palisadoes airport, but otherwise looks somewhat as it did in 1692. Prior to 11:43 A.M. on June 7 of that year, the old town of Port Royal had grown over the years to the roaring wickedness it enjoyed right up to the moment of its destruction.

The God-fearing of that day were not surprised at the disaster. There was probably never before or since in the world's history a city as rich or as wild and cruel. Gold, silver, fabrics, jewels, plunder by the ton was brought to this place by buccaneers who flaunted their loot publicly. Ordinary deck hands had enough personal wealth to be measured for shirts of solid gold mail. Rum brought high prices and children moderate ones.

From the height of Strawberry Hill I could see with binoculars the main and jib of a native dugout rounding Port Royal, coming into Kingston after a night of fishing. And forty feet under its skeg in the silt and murky water lie what's left of the buildings of old Port Royal. The brawling taverns were stilled when they sank as suddenly as a staved-in hull, bottles and jugs and clay pipes and lamps and all—along with weapons and the bones of men, now crusted thick with coral.

But now, winking distantly in the morning sun, it looked the same as it might have before the disaster, except for the missing land where the bulk of the city had been. I could see Gallows Point, where Governor Henry Morgan hanged scores of his fellow pirates after declaring amnesty and throwing a wild two-week party. And the little cemetery to the west of the present town where the remains of one Lewis Galdy still enjoy great reputation. Galdy was in Port Royal at the moment the quake struck and was "swallowed up in the Great Earthquake," and then was "by another Shock thrown into the Sea and miraculously saved by swimming."

Perhaps he lost his watch. Someone did. And it lay for 268 years under the water and muck until Edwin Link's recent expedition to explore the remains of Port Royal found it, still readable and stopped at 11:43. Brass gears, bright and uncorroded, fell out when the watch was opened and revealed it to have been made in 1686 by a Paul Blondel, in the Netherlands.

I could also see "Nelson's Quarterdeck," a platform on Fort Charles from which the British naval hero commanded the fortification a century later.

In recent years, from this point and from Stony Hill, people had also seen the arrival of Errol Flynn on his yacht. Flynn, for all his flamboyant living, or perhaps because of it, was extremely well-liked by the Jamaicans. He seems as much a part of their history now as the Port Royal pirates.

During an earlier visit here, I once borrowed an airplane at Palisadoes airport and flew an enormous, but empty, basketed rum bottle up to Boscabel, a little airstrip near Ocho Rios. The bottle was a decorative item I was delivering for a friend. It was a little windy that day, but not enough for updrafts through the mountain pass north of Stony Hill. The rule of thumb for weather is that if you can see the pass you can fly through it safely. I saw it, and had about 200 feet between it and clouds sitting down low over it. When I got to Boscabel, I came in a little high, but with full flaps down I thought I would have my wheels on the ground within the first third of the runway. An updraft from the banana grove put me still higher, and half the runway had flashed under me before the main gear touched the pavement. I had to get on the brakes immediately and hard, and still went off the end of the strip onto gravel before I got stopped, just short enough of the trees to turn the plane around. Some workmen putting up a cinder-block building halfway back the runway had put down their tools in anticipation of seeing a mishap, and as I taxied back they were still gaping. When I pulled the empty demijohn out of the luggage compartment they looked at each other knowingly and, shaking their heads, went back to work.

Almost literally a stone's throw from that airstrip at Boscabel is the late Ian Fleming's house, where he wrote a great many of his James Bond adventures. And farther along that shore toward Port Antonio is Noël Coward's place.

Jamaica bottles a clear liquid known as "Appleton White." This is a rum of around 170 proof, and you can put yourself right in the duffle by merely sniffing it. It makes an excellent rubbing alcohol and is occasionally actually purchased locally for that purpose. Jamaica is of course famous for fine rums, but this all-purpose elixir can double as paint remover in addition to providing an instant cure for any fit of sobriety that might overtake one.

On Tuesday, July 3, we prepared for departure the next day. Among other activities, we sealed a piece of Kleenex in the housing of the Bolex movie camera and took it to the bottom of the hotel pool. I sat on the bottom with the rig for a few minutes checking for bubbles. The idea was to leave it for a while and then bring it up and see if the Kleenex was as dry as when it was put in. I was about to come up when I saw a submarine! So help me. A fellow had brought in a little two-man sub which was about to go on the market for around $800. It was an open-cockpit affair for use with scuba gear, powered by waterproof batteries. I was invited to dive it, and it was sufficiently maneuverable so that I could work it in the pool. We had a lot of fun with it that afternoon and found ourselves wishing we could ship it aboard *Thane* slung on davits.

About ten o'clock, our young single sailors lit out again into the Kingston night. They were as fresh as if they'd slept all afternoon. They had in fact been doing some work on the ship during the first part of the day, and exerting themselves in the pool even more than I had until late afternoon. I reminded them of the ten A.M. departure time and that I'd take a dim view of anyone beat-up or missing or so badly hung over he couldn't function. My advice was as welcome as a hurricane, I'm sure, but I wasn't really worried about their ability to look out for themselves.

The wind died down late in the evening for a few hours, and we sat in the stillness of a tropical night on the terrace, smoking and talking. Mireille, who had arrived a couple of nights before, briefed me again on phrases to use in my first stop in French Polynesia, not in Tahitian but in Paumotu, the language of the Tuamotus. It occurred to me that when the time came I would hail the lead canoe in perfect Paumotu, only to have the answer come back: "I say, you don't happen to speak English, do you? Can't understand a word you say!"

Bill Garrison turned in so that he could pack what he needed for the trip. A full moon shone above the palm trees. I pointed out that it had come full exactly three hours ago and that it would rise over Tahiti five hours from now.

"That's very romantic," Ruth observed.

"You'll do well in Tahiti," said Mireille.

"The navigator's concern is to *get* to Tahiti," I answered. "One must be aware at all times of the positions of the heavenly bodies."

"They're all in Tahiti," Virgil said dryly.

On that curtain line, we broke up the gathering and went to bed. As we slept, the moon rose on Tahiti, five thousand miles west.

VI

WITH A HEAVY WIND and in spite of rather large seas we drove along the first day out at over eight knots—and then trouble began.

Sometime in the early morning hours of July 15 we lost our antenna on the mainmast. This not only meant radio silence, except for what we might be able to raise on the ship-to-shore, but sixteen feet of antenna mast, hanging by one twisted clamp, dangled from the height of the main spreader and threatened rigging and the wiring of the other antenna.

We were now approaching the toughest weather we were to see (not the most dangerous, which came with fog and calm), and I now believe I would rather cross the Pacific a half dozen times than repeat that reach from Jamaica to Panama. The waves are often larger in the Pacific, but the length from crest to crest of lively Caribbean waves are the very worst for a keel length like *Thane's*. Moreover, the seas were just confused enough to provide a sideward motion from time to time in which gimballing, for one thing, was of no avail. There was a smashing pitch, in which *Thane* would run down one steep wave to bury her bow in the next, shuddering up under green water like a destroyer in a storm in the North Sea. Also she would be jolted every few minutes by a sea from abeam that would break over the rail, drenching the deck full length. In the dark you couldn't see these coming, and each one was an annoying surprise. The foul weather gear had a workout.

During the next forty-eight hours our running lights shorted out; the jib sheet parted; we lost the mizzen halyard, the staysail club, a brand new block on the cable of the main port running backstay; and a freak accident took the jib sheet (which had come loose at its bitter end) and wound it around the propeller. We could not use power and half our working sails were not working.

At the moment, however, we were bowling along toward Panama, well clear of any navigational dangers, according to the charts and my calculations. The sextant work was in reasonable agreement with the dead reckoning as taken from the various watch entries in the wheel log.

"Connie is ill," the log reads, "and should stay in her bunk. Pete handles meals OK."

About ten minutes of three A.M., July 15, Dixon and I had been on watch since midnight, and I went below to wake Pete and H.R. for their watch. They came on deck ahead of me. I stayed to heat some coffee for the four of us. At about the time of watch change I came on deck without the coffee. I had a cigar in my mouth and my harness on. The clip was in my hand. It was my intention to clip it on a life line back in the cockpit, where I had enough cable range to crawl aft and read the Walker log with a flashlight. It was only two long steps from the doghouse to the mizzen mast.

They were nearly the last steps I ever took.

Between the time I let go of the hatch frame and reached for the mizzen, one of those beam seas hit and moved the whole ship down and out from under me. I tried to drop and grab for the rail but it all went by, and in the dim glow of the high spreader lights I saw gray foam and black water beneath me. Then I was in it. In going over the rail I had passed between two stanchions, and the line between them parted. I had grabbed the end of one of these pieces and managed to hold on to it. At least I was staying with the ship! Dixon was still at the wheel and instantly put up into the wind. This turned the ship toward me—I had gone over the windward side—and also caused her to lose way, making it less difficult to hang on. I remember two things vividly: one, being amazed that that life line was holding even though my body put a lot of strain on it, and wondering how far I'd get separated from the ship if it parted, and two, that this was extremely embarrassing after all the fuss I'd made about the importance of staying with the ship and the dangers of being lost overboard at night.

In what seemed like three minutes, but I'm sure was really only about twenty seconds, I came close to *Thane's* side. As she rolled toward me I tried to rise enough out of the water to grab the rail. She slid by. The second roll put her rail down far enough so that I could tread water and lunge up to get hold of the base of one of the stanchions. I used every ounce of strength I had. This time I saw two figures on deck by the stanchion. They reached down and grabbed my arm. On the roll to starboard they pulled me up over the rail and on board.

I think I said thanks, perfunctorily, and then, "That was a silly thing to do."

"You all right?" H.R.'s voice sounded odd. He and Pete had pulled me aboard.

"Yeah, I'm OK. It's wet out there. I just wanted to see if it's any wetter than on deck."

"You didn't lose your cigar," said Pete.

Then I noticed that my jaws were clamped in a death grip on the butt of the cigar I'd started a while back.

Dixon called from the wheel, "Hurt yourself?"

I felt a twinge in my back, and I told him I'd wrenched it. At the time I didn't realize how much damage had been done. (After a day or two the stiffness went away and during the rest of the sail it seemed all right, but I had apparently hurt some discs inside. In November, back home, two of the discs came apart and pieces drifted in the spinal canal. This raised some hell with nerves to my right leg. The leg finally simply quit working, but it was restored by spine surgery on December 20 of that year.)

I went back to get the coffee, and this time when I appeared on deck there was much joking about whether I'd make it to the cockpit. "For God's sake don't go overboard now—you've got our coffee!" And, "Now don't get carried away!" It was inevitable.

The exhilaration of the mishap carried me through without any fear during and right after the incident, but later in my bunk I got the shakes and began to worry about the others, particularly H.R. I reasoned that this was silly, since H.R. was far more agile than I—possibly the most athletic, being the youngest. He'd be OK. I also reasoned that if I allowed neurotic fear to propel me up on deck to hover over everyone's safety harness it would have a bad effect on all, so I stayed below. For three hours I shook and imagined losing people overboard, among them me. I conjured up the most morbid sequences— fire, sinking, funerals at sea, and other nightmarish situations. This was the only time I suffered insomnia on the whole trip, and the spell was all over by daylight—all but the embarrassment.

The next night I lost almost all my plankton samples plus my good line and one net. It was now easy to understand why yachts had never successfully carried out this project. It needed a large research vessel with scientists aboard free of deck duty. I was bitterly disappointed. These waters had had few samplings, according to Dr. Donald P. de Sylva of the University of Miami, and even some would be of value. Dr. de Sylva had been most cooperative and, like me, hopeful of some results.

The log of the night of July 15, among other things, details more of our woes: "A container of diesel fuel broke its lashings and has spread the deck with oil. It is gradually washing away with occasional seas which come aboard. (This was a 5-gal. jerry can—not the 55-gal. drum that got loose south of Panama.)

"Some leaks in the deck caulking are giving us unwelcome water below. Bob's and Virgil's bunks are sopping, and there is considerable dampness in the after cabin on the starboard side. No real saturation here though.

"The ship is pumping out somewhat more water than when in port, but this is to be expected as hull planks work a bit in rough water. Holding a course of 205 up to now. Changed to 185 so as to come on Panama to the east and not have to beat to the Canal entrance. Figure to pick up Punta Manzanilla early Sunday morning or in the night Saturday. Celestial position now well to south of dead reckoning . . . under 12° N. Lat. May sight land day after tomorrow before dark.

"Raised malfunctioning mizzen with the topping lift as a halyard. If it weren't for that steady main we'd be badly hampered as the engine can't be used for fear of pulling the shaft out."

Obviously we needed a wind to move, but if it would calm down a bit we could go over the side and remove the fouled line from the prop.

Our passenger, Bill Garrison, had never made a passage by sail. He must have got a hell of an impression of sailing with this, his first trip. But he was game. He was helpful where he could be and stayed out of the way where he couldn't.

In addition to everything else, we developed below an exquisite, sickening, and baffling odor. *Thane* was clean as a whistle, with no rodents or bugs aboard. Even the bilges were sweet. Normal diesel exhaust is tolerable and generally, with a breeze, unnoticeable. This odor came on gradually and had us looking at each other suspiciously, although no human ever smelled like this while he was alive. As it got stronger, the following things came under suspicion: a possible punctured can of food, exhaust from the generator, the formalin for preserving marine specimens, rancid laundry stashed away somewhere. All these we checked and dismissed as possibilities. Still the smell grew in power until we preferred sleeping on deck, rain and spray and all, to being below with that overpowering, palpable odor.

It wasn't till Panama that we discovered the source of the Mysterious Ghastly Stench. We had some dried shrimp for fish bait, and one box in the lazarette had broken and was invaded by the sea. The resultant decay was of such powerful proportions that nothing about the smell suggested shrimp, fresh or stale. It was a virulent, aggressive, poisonous fume. But once rid of the bait, we were rid of the smell.

During the afternoon of the sixteenth, the antenna clamp gave way finally, and we salvaged the antenna on deck. One trap was missing, but Virgil thought he could get one in Panama, and we would be back in commission.

By late afternoon the sea was a little less rough. The speed was cut down some but it was more comfortable and there was a lot less water on deck. We swabbed away the remainder of the diesel oil. Connie was feeling better by now, but understandingly weak after her bout with *mal de mer*.

With the calm we decided to try to free the propeller shaft. We also attempted to photograph the operation, which was, to say the least, weird. With the ship hove to but bobbing about a great deal, four of us went over the side, two to free the line and two to photograph. I took the underwater Bolex down, Jerry took the underwater Nikonos down to photograph me photographing H.R. and Bob. And once when I came up for air I saw Connie on deck with a camera shooting the scene, and Pete was taking *her* picture with Virgil's camera! All four of us underwater were troubled by being borne into the hull as it rose and fell in the chop. We finally hove to on the other tack and, for some reason we haven't figured out, suffered the same difficulty we had before.

At one point I took a whack at the line but couldn't hold my breath long enough to get more than two turns off the shaft. We had to try to stay deep to avoid getting hit by the prop or the hull, which was rising and falling with some violence.

The water below was a bright, soupy green when we first went over the side. It turned a deep gray-brown, almost black, in the space of a minute. I thought the sun had gone under a cloud, but when I surfaced, I saw it was still shining brightly. The angle of incidence apparently changed crucially at one moment as the sun slipped westward, and from that instant the depths were no longer illuminated. Sunlight never penetrates more than about 400 feet even at noon. Most of the ocean depth is lightless. Bob and H.R. finally managed to get the whole line off. It had been wound tight. The reason for this was that the propeller normally turned even when the engine was not on, as it was dragged through the water. When the line got loose and trailed under the stern it started winding onto the turning shaft until it bound the shaft. To have turned it with the engine would only have wound more line on, or, as observed earlier, would have pulled the shaft out of its bearings.

Late that afternoon, land showed to the south. We thought at first it might be Punta Manzanillo, but we were actually several miles east—not quite at the San Blas Islands. We were jubilant that our 500-mile journey to Panama was nearing an end. We turned west and ran along the shore. As it got dark we picked up Manzanillo Light.

We came through the breakwaters at the Atlantic end of the Panama Canal at 4:30 Sunday morning, July 18. There was an anchorage—a great expanse of sheltered water—shown on the chart just to the east inside the breakwater, which appeared to have no ships in it.

Just as we got the anchor down, Jerry Galyean called down, "Small craft approaching." It was the Canal authorities with a letter from the Information Officer and four pounds of paper to be filled out. They asked us to follow them into Colon for a better anchorage, and there we went through clearance formalities with one Mr. Hewitt, a very courteous and efficient gentleman who knew of our arrival and had been contacted by our agents, Boyd Bros. The letter informed me that the Information Office had received and was honoring my request to set Jerry Galyean off after the Gatun locks so he could photograph from shore. Further, it said that Ruth had set up an airplane to take him over Gatun Lake and to Gaillard Cut. Then Mr. Hewitt departed, after a cup of coffee, and we were next boarded by the Admeasurer, who measured everything aboard the boat except Connie.

A ship must be carefully measured if it has never been through the Canal before, and *Thane* hadn't. The Canal authorities can't take anybody's word about the length, width, draft, or tonnage, or the engine capabilities, lest something go wrong that would cause a snag in the endless traffic of one of the world's great strategic waterways.

Next came the agent, Mr. Dorfmeier, who got us ice and put the machinery into motion for everything else pertaining to our transit and needs. Then came a launch with His Excellency, J. D. Bazan, Minister of Justice of Panama, his son Caesar and his wife, and a younger son with his wife; and a friend, George Tillman, from the States, who made the transit with us. Ruth was there and was to be aboard *Thane* for the next ten hours in the only really calm part of the whole voyage—all sheltered water. The Bazans made us feel welcome, and after a short visit aboard disembarked with arrangements to see us at the other end.

Finally came our pilot, Captain John Dorsa, who directed the helm throughout our transit, and gave us some insight into the troubles between Zonians and Panamanians.

Line handlers came aboard at each set of locks. There was almost nothing for us to do but enjoy the scenery. H.R. was relief cook, so he missed some of the sights. But I think he cheated by getting his mother to help him. We ate sandwiches (that's what he cooked) and drank several gallons of iced tea and soft drinks and beer. The line handlers drank beer. For the only time on the voyage, somebody else was in command of the ship. Captain Dorsa drank iced tea.

Dorsa told about Russian ships going through, and how he piloted one recently—he and a detachment of marines deployed in the wheel house and engine room and any other point from which the ship could be controlled. Ramming of the lock gates is possible, and a tie-up of the Canal could of course have grave international consequences.

The captain of the Russian freighter had spoken critically of Soviet policies and with a wink had told Dorsa he'd deny, if necessary, having said any of the things he'd said.

To be a Canal pilot one must be a master mariner by U.S. standards, which are, I believe, the highest in the world. I watched Dorsa swing into action at the Cristobal piers. We were in the channel, and up to then he had acted like a guest on board. Limon Bay is wide and our exact position was not immediately important. I was at the wheel and aiming approximately for the first set of locks. When we were lined up and could see the base of the locks as well as the tower, Dorsa began to give orders as casually as if he'd been our captain from Fort Lauderdale. As we approached Gatun locks, which were the steps by which we'd be raised eighty-five feet, a large illuminated arrow on the center wall, activated by the distant Locks Control House, indicated which set of twin locks we would enter. I began to see why it would be very impractical, if not impossible, to attempt a passage of the Canal without a pilot, even if permitted.

Ahead of us was the freighter *World Jonquil,* slowed to a stop a thousand feet this side of the big gates. When the water level was equal within a few inches on each side, these gates began to swing back into recesses in the concrete wall. We moved very slowly. Then the linehandler's launch moved alongside, and the handlers boarded us. Once inside we no longer used our power; we were towed by lines. Men pulled us; locomotives pulled the *World Jonquil* but it was paying more than $5,000 to go through. Our fee was only two per cent of that, so we had neither the prestige nor the need of a locomotive.

Lines were thrown from both sides atop the high, damp, concrete walls. The handlers took up slack as the ship rose. Water came in fast from great culverts, and in a few minutes our deck was level with the wall tops. One had the feeling that we might be swept on over the walls like a child's sailboat from a swiftly overflowing bathtub. But it leveled off, and after the forward gates swung their seven-foot-thick steel leaves into the next set of concrete recesses, we followed the *Jonquil* to the next chamber and repeated the process.

"We're coming up in the world," smiled Dorsa. "Your boat is not floating as well now."

"What do you mean?"

"It floats higher in salt water. We're coming to Gatun Lake. You'll sink a little."

When we came out into the lake, our pilot relaxed a little. Our company took turns at the wheel. But Dorsa was always at the side of the helmsman to make sure the next buoy or channel marker was lined up right. Much of Gatun Lake is quite shallow. At this point the shores were low jungle and there were many islands.

Jerry got off when the line handlers left in a launch. We didn't see him again until Balboa, except in the open door of an airplane and again high on the mountain top at Gaillard Cut.

As we passed close to one of the islands, I was surprised to see a wildlife preserve under the jurisdiction of the Smithsonian Institution, said to be one of the world's most valuable natural laboratories.

Approaching Gamboa we passed a Japanese destroyer flying its rising-sun flag.

"What a startling sight that would have been here twenty-three years ago," Dixon observed.

"In 1942? You'd have had to conclude you were having hallucinations," Virgil laughed.

"Or that it was all over and we'd lost," said someone else.

"And now it's all over and we wave to them and they wave to us . . . When will men get the idea they don't have to kill each other—that there is challenge enough in the world without war?"

"Wait till you see Gaillard Cut," said Dorsa.

The wake of the Japanese destroyer set *Thane* wallowing for a moment. Ruth, who'd been napping on the freezer lid, sat up and announced that I'd betrayed her: it was supposed to be calm the whole trip. She threatened to be sick. I explained that the Japanese Navy had just committed its first hostile act since 1945.

One enters Gaillard Cut with the distinct feeling that even with all the manpower and time imaginable and all the earth-moving equipment of the world no one could have accomplished this job. The Continental Divide was demolished in a swath wide enough to let large ships pass each other easily. At one period rock and dirt were removed at a rate of more than 100,000 tons per day. The ghostly echoes of drilling and blasting still seemed to echo from the high terraced walls, and names like Shonts and Goethals and Stevens and Wallace came to my mind. A bronze plaque honoring Colonel David Gaillard, the U. S. Army engineer in charge of the excavations, is set in the face of Contractor's Hill.

At one point we saw a train speeding along, going the opposite way, where the tracks ran near the shore.

"Fastest train in the world," the local joke has it. "Goes from the Atlantic to the Pacific in an hour and a quarter."

One would need scuba gear to see the town of Miraflores now. It was founded as a labor camp by the French. American laborers lived there after the U.S. took over construction of the Canal. When the work was finished this "choice lake-floor property" ceased to be a real estate attraction. In the space of a few weeks the waters rose around and through it.

At Miraflores locks, a pith-helmeted type criticized our flying of the Panamanian flag at courtesy position.

"You're flying the wrong flag!" he shouted from high on the lock wall.

"Where?" I called back.

He merely pointed, in obvious irritation, to the Panamanian courtesy flag. I asked Dorsa if there was any reason a yacht shouldn't fly a courtesy flag the same as the freighters and some of the U.S. and foreign military ships I'd seen in the canal.

Dorsa explained that while there was nothing really wrong with flying the courtesy flag, it was not necessary since the Canal Zone is U.S. territory. I was mildly concerned about this. I didn't want trouble, and I was a little insecure about my knowledge of flag etiquette, and, as I have said, almost everything on this trip concerning flags seemed to involve trouble.

The lock foreman wasn't going to let it go. "You won't be welcome at the Balboa Yacht Club with that flag up!" he called down. Water was filling the lock now, and we were rising slowly. "You should be flying the American flag!"

I pointed to the Stars and Stripes flying at the stern and called back, "We are!"

We wrote him off as a troublemaker, and I must confess I fell into the trap of dismissing him as a typical Zonian. This is bigoted thinking and later, on talking with some military men at Fort Amador and with some Panamanians away from the Zone, I got a more balanced view.

In a way I wish I could chronicle that I'd had the guts to insist on flying the Panamanian flag at the Balboa Yacht Club to see if they'd have made trouble about it—I think now they wouldn't have—but I was on a voyage to the Pacific and not on a crusade against Zonians, so we took it in. This rationale is a prime example of how the world frequently works. Whichever side may be right is not the point here, since I can't argue the Panama flag controversy with my limited knowledge of this complex situation. But the fact that I compromised in order to ensure *my* personal voyage, *my* project, and went against my feelings at the time for personal convenience, is cut of the same cloth as the belief in equality for a minority group but not letting members of that group dine in your restaurant because it might be bad for business. This is the only entry in the log that I am ashamed of.

Ruth got some sun poisoning during the transit. Our salon and cabins, normally quite cool and comfortable, were stiflingly hot in the Canal. It seemed as though not a breath of air moved through them. The fans did not help. We were forced above decks, even though there was little shade with the sails furled. Moving at six knots created the illusion of a breeze. There were at this time fifteen people aboard, counting Ruth, George Tillman, and Bill Garrison as passengers, and Dorsa and the line handlers. The consumption of ice water, iced tea, lemonade, soft drinks, and beer was huge. H.R. made hot coffee, proclaiming the theory that it would cool us. I tried a cup and by George it did.

Our friend the *World Jonquil*, of Monrovian registry, and some 800 times our tonnage, was our lock partner all the way. Together we drained fifty-two million gallons of water out of the Canal and its lakes, which made me feel important but a bit guilty, as there was a water shortage. The lake levels were about three feet down at the time.

It was early evening as we turned out of the Channel to the mooring basin of the Balboa Yacht Club. We tied to a mooring buoy about a quarter-mile from the dock. We checked off our arrival routine, got things reasonably cleared, and laid plans for repair to standing and running rigging, radio gear, and some maintenance chores. We expected it to be all done in a day or so.

How wrong we were.

VII

Two DAYS at the most should have done it, if everyone
had known his part. But they never do. If the world always knew its part, the best laid plans of mice and men
would not gang a-gley so often. It's out when it should
be in. It doesn't answer its phones, and it says "no" when
you want it to say "yes."

It took half a day to buy a boat hook, for example. The
radio people didn't have the trap Virgil needed. He sent
for one. Stove alcohol was impossible to get. Discourag-
ing word was waiting regarding the poor exposure of
some footage shipped undeveloped from Jamaica to the
New York lab. A general letdown overtook the company,
and my plan to get away by the twentieth was definitely
scrapped.

They told us that a schooner at the club had been delayed a month for want of some necessary supplies. A
month! With an October contract deadline in New York
that kind of delay could wreck the whole Pacific voyage.

Jerry was discouraged about the prospect of preserving
raw film stock in the dampness, and voiced his doubts
about the value of his continuing. Virgil saw no point in
going on unless he could keep us in radio contact with

home. Bob was understandably concerned about the prospects of keeping a dry bunk and maintaining an equitable division of labor—he and Pete were the most experienced sailors aboard and Bob was the only qualified machinist and mechanic. Connie, I could tell, was wondering if the Pacific would be one big vicious Caribbean. I tried to assure everyone that there was a solution to each of the problems and that we would get away from Panama with everything we needed and with only slight delay.

At the height of these aggravations, Pete came down with what we thought was an Aralen tablet reaction, but which soon proved to be much worse. He developed a soaring temperature, with massive headaches and sweating, during which he shook uncontrollably and could not get enough blankets on him to keep warm.

I was jolted slightly to hear Jerry ask him, "What time do you think you'll die, Pete?"

I thought Jerry's humor was dubious and heartless, until I learned that it was inspired by Pete himself. He had a prognosis schedule, from which he would whimsically issue bulletins from time to time, like, "I'm scheduled to die at 11:40." As each deadline came and went he'd issue a revision. It was his way of making light of his condition and apparently was therapeutic for him.

"When you've decided you're not going to kick the bucket till next year, we'll sail," I told him.

None of us had visas for Panama, since we were listed as transiting crew. Technically I couldn't check in to the Panama Hilton where my wife was staying, so I wetbacked across the border on a phony military pretext and moved in. (I had overlooked the fact that the Hilton is not in the Canal Zone—that's planning!) Ruth Downs, an otherwise respectable woman, was now living with a man not registered in the hotel as her husband, and not in the country legally.

Monday morning I spent at Amador recording, under great time pressure from New York, a series of radio programs for the Army. Larry Walker flew down to record these on a portable tape machine and rush them back to New York. He made his plane back only by running for it, I think.

Afterward I had lunch in the officers' club with Captain Grady Sockwell and a Colonel Reilly, who heads the Information Office at the fort. We talked about our delay, the fickleness of Lady Luck, the Army (which I've been away from since World War II), and about an Air Rescue Unit headed by a Captain Gulick. I was thankful for the existence of Captain Gulick, but I hoped not to meet him from a rubber raft. We discussed Zonians, Panamanians, Vietnam, and the Solution of All World Problems. The lunch was an oasis in a desert of frustration.

On the morning of July 20, Ruth, H.R., Colonel J. D. Bazan, and I went by small plane to the San Blas Islands to visit the Indians there. The main island, Porvenir, has an airstrip—a level grassy stretch between palm trees. From there we went by boat to Malanega, an island not often visited by white people. It has less area than New York's Central Park, and there are some 150 families living on it.

There are 365 islands in the San Blas Archipelago. Each habitable island has its own stable society, part of a confederation of all the islands under a chief elected for life. His successor is chosen by vote from nominees representing rival political parties. They campaign vigorously. I supposed that the two major parties represent a liberal and a conservative viewpoint. I met the chief on Porvenir. Apparently he felt his life was drawing to a close, because they were campaigning on the islands and an election was scheduled.

The San Blas Indians are the smallest human beings I've ever seen. They are not so small as pygmies, but I've never seen pygmies. Whether it is a racial characteristic, or merely a matter of nutrition, I don't know. Would a San Blas Indian baby, taken from its mother and brought up on pablum and formula and Gerber's best strained fruits and vegetables, turn into a strapping six-footer? I am inclined to doubt it. But I think he'd be taller than his parents. And he'd have a good chance of living longer.

These people are relatively sophisticated. They can get into Panama fairly easily; they are acquainted with technology (they take airplanes and outboards in stride); they observe and absorb, and to a certain extent use, the world of other men; but as far as I could see they have no yearning to imitate. Although they are not hostile, there is a dark hint in their rule that white men must not remain overnight in their islands.

Certain of their women and girls wear a heavy solid gold ring in their noses. Apparently this custom has no special significance: It doesn't mark the married state or mothers or virgins or rank or station or, as far as I could make out, wealth. Some of them just wear rings in their noses and that's all there is to it.

In the house of a man named Kala-o, we watched a meal being prepared. In the center of the single room there was a fire on the dirt floor. Hanging above it was an iron kettle in which bubbled a mixture of yams and some kind of shellfish. The thick smoke from the fire, which had no way to get out, enveloped a wicker basket of fish that was being preserved in this way. Kala-o and his wife did not seem to mind the smoke.

Some of the younger folks staged a dance for us and

our cameras. As they danced, they played on curious sets of pipes made of bamboo tubes of different diameters cut to different lengths. It was an unearthly scale, not like any I'd ever heard, but curiously not a cacophony. It still sounds in my ears, a plaintive, halting sound like a weary breeze, panting to keep up with the lurching gait of the dancers.

The dance consisted of trotting around in a circle, several steps forward and one tentatively backward and then suddenly, on a hidden signal, reversing direction. Every step seemed the last one, like a runner who has just crossed the finish line and is no longer pushing but cannot quite stop.

Near Malanega is an island almost as large with a store on it. It sells sailcloth, rope and twine, canned goods and fabrics used by the Indian women for making their *molas,* which are multilayer cloth works of art, cut out and sewn, many of which are quite beautiful and some are based on very mundane objects. From the porch of the store we could see a very small island with a single hut on it. Colonel Bazan explained that it was a sort of hospital for the near group of islands.

"Either they have very little illness or very overcrowded facilities," I said.

"The treatment is somewhat drastic," he explained. "Once I saw an old man, who was seeking rejuvenation, stripped from the waist down and covered with ants. It was part of the treatment."

"Did it rejuvenate him?"

"I didn't stay to find out. It was getting dark."

We fell to discussing the psychological aspects of witchdoctoring. Perhaps if one is brought up to believe in the efficacy of such things, ants in the crotch would provide great therapy. I'm sure it would rejuvenate me in one sense: I would make a record sprint and dive into the ocean from wherever I was.

Back on Porvenir we purchased a framed *mola* inspired by the RCA Victor symbol—the listening dog and the horn of an acoustic gramaphone. It was stylized, and embellished with small figures, and from an artistic standpoint, an improvement on the original. The lettering, which to the artist was merely part of the design, was altered to suit his aesthetic ideas. It read: HI MASTERS VOICE— RCV VITOR.

The sun had not set but the chief walked ahead of us to our airplane as though to imply that he was not going to be responsible for detaining us after the traditional curfew.

The single engine of the Cessna 185 turned over many times before it caught. I wondered what would have happened with the chief's hospitality if we'd had to say, "Look, chief, we can't leave. We have engine trouble. Can you put us up for the night?" Whatever our fate, I'll wager it would have been dealt out with neither frown nor smile, but the same impassivity we had seen all day in the Indian faces.

Colonel Bazan said that although the people would not take cash for their hospitality, they needed lamps and would accept one after we'd gone. We sent them back a Coleman gasoline lamp.

A log entry for Wednesday, July 21, read: "Should be leaving Panama today but not ready . . . Pete still feeling poorly with a temperature and diarrhea. Virgil's traps have not materialized. Alcohol for the stove not legally purchasable in more than one-gallon quantities—we need three dozen. Maintenance work slow . . . need a boat hook for main antenna mast and none available . . . Ruth, H.R., Bob, and the Bazans, Sr. and Jr., dined at Florentina. Bob had driven to Darien in the early afternoon."

The work was now as far along as we could get it without certain missing items. That afternoon I had made an appearance on the Southern Command Network television station in the Zone. A Captain Crawford picked me up at the ship, and I had a brief busman's holiday. I also caught a glimpse of myself in a studio TV monitor and saw how incredibly different I looked. My beard was growing now, and my bald head had acquired a ratty-looking crew cut.

Broadcasting for the armed forces is only a quarter of a century old. It has grown in quality as well as hours of output. The Southern Command Network is particularly good in its TV and radio work. The operation is manned jointly by the Army, Navy, and Air Force and is transmitted from two locations simultaneously. Some of the men come from a civilian broadcast background, and some are trained on the job. All have a great opportunity to learn every phase of the work from technical to production.

My interviewer was skilled, and the technical aspects of the program were handled with professional ease. I have been interviewed in many places throughout the world, and this was one of the most satisfying interviews I've been involved in. The only thing I missed was a commercial; then I'd have felt at home.

From the log: "THURSDAY, JULY 22—Pete worse. Won't see a doctor. No alcohol (for the stove). Men failed to show for resetting main antenna. Virgil gloomy. Dinghy engine conked out on H.R., and he drifted toward the Pacific. . . ."

Although this latter mishap was not potentially disastrous, the current through there can be swift at times, and before he knew it H.R. had been swept almost past the last moored boat. He caught this last craft and repaired the outboard while tied alongside. Then he came back with it and it ran for fifteen minutes, just long enough for Dixon to get caught on its next failure. Bob washed up on an empty mooring buoy and took his turn at working on the motor for some time.

When he finally arrived back at the ship Connie called to him, "Have an accident?"

"No, thanks," he said cheerily. "I just had one!"

The log notes that ". . . about noon the tide of fortune began to change. Air tanks arrived from agent Heineken; I found a boat hook I could purchase. The senior Bazan sent the army with a fifty-gallon drum of proper alcohol and a sheaf of papers legalizing my receipt of it and as nearly as I can make out, licensing me to open a tavern in Panama. I'm tempted. Pete has postponed his scheduled death definitely. The inbound case of cigarettes for bartering arrived. The antenna men finally showed up and have dispelled Virgil's gloom."

The hatch covers arrived, and the food supplies were scheduled for delivery the next day definitely.

Within forty hours we had found and removed the source of the Great Stench—as already described—and replaced dried-out mattresses and carpeting, reduced deck clutter, got the radio gear functioning, received delivery of our two extra barrels of diesel oil, and replaced chafed line with new, including a 100-foot length of tow line I purchased for one last try at capturing plankton specimens with what net I had left.

On Friday, July 23, I wrote in the log: "All is falling into place. Definite plans to leave tomorrow."

An odd cold rain and wind came up at three that afternoon. We were on a mooring from a railroad wheel on the bottom, so we figured we were not too worried about anchorage. But it did blow for a while.

In the evening I called Ruth at the hotel and had her come down to the Yacht Club for dinner. Our clearance was due next morning. Our agents were most helpful and followed through on everything. Without them and the Bazans we might have lost so much time that I could not have started across the Pacific.

Fortune was smiling again. No more illness and the general mood of the company was rising.

The last meal ashore had a festive quality about it. As though in consideration of the ten or so dry days ahead each member of the ship's company felt obliged to take his personal quota of the distillation of his choice. Since Virgil doesn't drink anyway the rest of us drank for him each round. By the time the dinner came a rare glow was established. Navigating the dinghy out to the ship was something of a challenge, but five of us boarded safely while Bob and Jerry went into town and Virgil returned to the Tivoli to pack and check out in the morning. H.R., Pete, and Connie played records and tapes in the main salon. Ruth crawled onto my bunk and watched me working with the charts for a while and then she went to sleep. I finished plotting a route by which we could get out without a pilot for the remaining length of the channel. Many of the low-tide soundings showed shallow places on each side of the channel out to Flamenco Island. It was still possible to run outside the channel, hugging the buoys, which are set well inside the deep water. Then we would sail out past Naos and Perico and Changame and Tortola Islands and then to distant Taboga and the open water to Cape Mala.

It's all so neat on the charts: The dividers mark off a distance, one applies a reasonable average speed and plans to arrive at some point by a specified clock time. You build in margins for unforeseen delays and, if the planning is realistic, it's reasonable to expect to arrive on time. But it's never quite the same in reality as it was on paper. Sometimes it's better, and sometimes it may seem worse, at the moment, but with the mellowing of time it doesn't look so bad in retrospect.

About midnight, with everything repaired, provisioned, checked, and stowed for a departure at ten the next morning (in the hope of actually getting away by noon), I woke Ruth and we all had coffee.

Toward one A.M. Ruth and H.R. and I took the Nautisport dinghy ashore and left it for Bob and Jerry. Then we left the Zone by the Fort Amador gate, where we got a bus for town. The guard wanted to see passports or other identification (which could have betrayed my illegal status outside the Zone) and I said airily, indicating Ruth and H.R., "They're with me." As he mulled over just how this statement explained anything other than the obvious, we went on through.

In the morning at eight o'clock we cast off from our railroad wheel mooring and moved to the end of the Balboa Yacht Club pier. A floating dock forms a tee at the end of this structure with a long ramp on rollers, to accommodate tides up to twenty-two feet on the Pacific side of the canal. The sun shone and the breeze was mild—superb weather for a departure for the South Seas.

We finally got underway at 2:15 P.M., the delay being considered practically on time in this part of the world. Colonel Bazan and his son Caesar with his pretty wife were on hand. The colonel gave me the name of an Ecuadorian official, Oswaldo Endora, who could be of help if we hit a snag with officialdom in the Galapagos. He had also alerted the Ecuadorian Navy to our arrival there.

I have related the account of our first twelve hours out of Panama, at the beginning of the book. The strangeness of that night ended abruptly with the dawn. There was a drizzling rain—a fine gray mist of a rain, but the sea was much less rough, and the log of Saturday, July 24 reads: ". . . We are warm and dry below (when we can get below), and after Cape Mala there will be no land to worry about until Malpelo, which should come up Tuesday morning by my calculations. We are holding our average speed; the radio works well now; the food is good; and with a modicum of luck in the next day or so, we should get a good wind and enough break in the clouds to fire a sextant at something."

A yachtsman once described this area between Panama Bay and the Galapagos as "Nature's wastebasket, in which she puts scraps of weather that don't belong anywhere else." The only kind of weather that is almost never put there by nature is bad storms. There is much rain, frequent calms, fog, cold weather, hot weather, sunshine, occasionally brisk breezes, and abrupt changes from one of these conditions to another.

On Sunday, July 25, a steady, generous rain filtered a colorless dawn. Instead of breaking from the East it just gradually became a gray day. The rain was quite cool and the sea still warm—we hadn't reached the Humboldt Current yet. Just after dawn that day we sighted Cape Mala, around which to the southwest lay the Galapagos, with the rock called Malpelo about midway. It cleared a little. Samples of the log entries reflect the more leisurely pace we were hitting:

"Bob Dixon was this day the first Full-Ocean-Under-Way Relief Chef, and he set a Sunday Brunch of no mean quality: Grapefruit chunks à la Starboard Settee, followed by French Toast Lazarette, choice of milk or coffee, and optional Jellied Doughnuts served in the Gulf of Panama style. Clearing nicely. Tomorrow some projects we hope.

"MONDAY, JULY 26—All day ploughed SSW through a calm sea. Very light southerly breeze made it an easy diesel run toward Malpelo, our landmark rock in the middle of nowhere. I'm looking forward to seeing it. In spite of faith in the procedure, you never quite trust your celestial navigation without some landmark corroboration. To approach Malpelo is dangerous because of rocks submerged and awash, and to be marooned on it would be death as nothing but lichen grows on its craggy contours. But its attraction is that it's anchored to the earth, immovable and solid and dry—and man, being a land creature, finds it a welcome sight, inhospitable as it is, knowing it is always in the same position whatever currents move mysteriously around it. Looks now as if we'll come on it in the dark. There is no light on it, and it's the dark of the moon; but starlight is enough, and if clouds cut all visibility, I'll alter course to be sure we don't run into it.

"On this kind of day much can be done. H.R. whittled plugs for thru-hull fittings from the end of a boat hook, and transferred fuel from the leaky deck drums to the main tanks (we were burning it off in this run).

"Sent a position report to New York and talked with Ruth . . . As evening came on the sea was even calmer. Many of the company gathered in the cockpit and philosophized and told jokes in the close-knit camaraderie of people in a tiny world surrounded by water. H.R. took a number of still photos in black and white and color, including a sunset so flamboyant that to paint it faithfully would be to produce a painting that would seem overdone. Through some gathering but docile clouds, the equatorial sky began to show its stars—Polaris was too low on the horizon to be found, and late in the night the belt stars of Orion rose vertically, seeming larger than at latitude 40.

"What was it I knew about the stars when I was very young? Not scientific facts. But I glimpse my old knowledge again in flashes on this voyage. It has nothing to do with the distance to Rigel or the diameter of Betelgeuse or the Greenwich Hour Angle of Aries. Something deeper, that I knew intimately before I was born, comes to my mind when I see the sky spread over this boundless ocean in the silent nights at sea.

"The shape of this indescribable truth is sketched on other things. Relationships with other people, plans and ambitions, ideals of comfort and satisfaction, hope and resignation, all are shaken up and realigned in the light of this remembered insight. To a certain extent reading and thinking about the stars and the ocean produce the effect of pushing walls of the everyday world aside and provide a larger perspective. But that does not compare with being alone on the deck of a small ship in the night of an ancient ocean.

"Night comes on. Malpelo, I'm told, means 'evil hair.' Some say the rock looks like a crown."

Pete and I took turns that night—we had the 0300 to 0600 watch—in going forward and straining our eyes for a glimpse of Malpelo. It was moonless and cloudy enough to cut the starlight to nothing. Still in the blackest night there is a slight difference in the amount of light above and below the horizon. While the horizon didn't show as a precise line, you could see it, and a land mass of any kind should have shown as an irregular interruption of that dim boundary between sea and sky. But we saw nothing. Three o'clock came and went and then four. Finally, at eighteen minutes after four, I got the impression of something interrupting the horizon line just ahead to the east of our course. It seemed eerie, both smaller and closer than I knew it to be. Pete's visual acuity is better than mine. He came forward and watched it with me for several minutes. "I think that's it," he said.

About 4:45 the faintest glimmer of pre-dawn light came

out of the northeast. Now the interruption on the horizon began to take shape, and in a few minutes we could see it rather than just sense it. It sat like an evil blob off the port bow. As the dawn light grew stronger we got an idea of its distance and size.

Imagine a gigantic sculpture of a crushed felt hat made of granite, a mile long and 800 feet high, no trees, no life, except moss of a kind that dominated land masses at the end of the azoic age. From other angles it looked variously like a crown, the submerged head of a rhinoceros, and a decaying house with the chimney still standing.

Here is a fragment of a lost world. One imagines that the water around it would hold only the most rudimentary life, in keeping with its ancientness. To see Malpelo is to roll time back hundreds of millions of years. Long before giant reptiles, long before the first crustaceans, this rock (if it were yet thrust up from the bottom of the sea) brooded over the same water, under the same sun and moon.

We came abeam of this monstrous guidepost about 8:30 in the morning of July 27, and it seemed to be with us all day. It is visible for thirty miles.

Beating into the wind, we went eighteen miles west of Malpelo and then headed S.S.E. I can still see that rock today, fading and sinking like the crumbling ruin of an ancient giant's castle into the gray Pacific.

The log reads: "The wind came up still dead wrong in direction and plagued us with two minor mishaps: the mizzen halyard—brand new, half-inch line, chafed through and dropped the mizzen on Virgil for the second time. I must set down in the interest of accurate chronicling the fact that this event convulsed several members of the company. H.R. and I cracked up completely and rolled about on deck, reduced to helplessness."

The second mishap was another chafe—the staysail sheet rubbing against steel cable. It parted and had to be rerigged.

"Wind very perverse," says the log. "Any change will be good.

"WEDNESDAY, JULY 28—Moderate seas and beautiful for a reach or a run or even clawing close-hauled toward the Enchanted Isles, but the wind persists in coming from a quarter that forces us to use fuel and plunge into the teeth of it, or tack. After tacking all day, some running sun lines indicate we are hardly getting anywhere at all. Currents in this part of the ocean are setting us more and more toward the South American coast. It's as though Nature is bottling us up and packing us off to Guayaquil, and all ahead of us, over that cloud-flecked horizon, are the Southeast Trades and easy smooth sailing to the Galapagos and beyond. If we can just scrabble our way south across the equator without being driven too far east and running into Ecuador, we can pick up the wind we need. Now we must compute and check the fuel we need and calculate the wisdom of using it to force a change in our position to where the winds are *likely* (not certain) to be right. How much fuel do we need to work safely off the shores of the islands when we get among them? How much to run the generator and keep our batteries up? Not just for radio communication and refrigeration, but for running lights? What are the currents and exactly where? In this part of the ocean only probabilities are charted, and currents can only be determined after studying differences in dead reckoning and celestial fixes and allowing for the accuracy of an assortment of helmsmen, leeway of the ship at different speeds, other factors that qualify precision. Moreover, these currents are different in different positions and at different times. Some with winds, but at least one can tell from where the wind is blowing.

"Thursday, July 29—This morning talked with Frank Blair on the air on 'Today.' It seems so stiff and formal, with written introduction and prepared questions. It made me realize we have done too much of that kind of approach on the program. Far better for Frank to have picked up the phone and ad-libbed everything. Anyway, it was an interesting contact with civilization, considering that I was unable to give an exact position because of clouds and capricious currents.

"Just when we fixed a time to run the engine and dash south across the equator, the wind began to veer, and toward the end of the day we were able to make south without going too far east. If we run through the night on this heading we'll still be well off the coast of Ecuador. . . ."

In the early morning of July 30, we tacked again and the wind began to change. We kept looking astern in the expectation of seeing Malpelo, which had seemed to follow us for a time as we tacked and didn't seem to be getting anywhere. But now the wind kept swinging around to where we could be less close-hauled and on more of a reach and by mid-morning we were sailing smartly in the direction of the islands. We would not have to look at the Andes after all.

From the day's log: "The wheel worked loose. In taking it off and tightening it, Dixon and I discovered we could steer with a chain wrench, so we detached the wheel and he took it below, where its appearance produced startled surprise and then a laugh in the salon.

"Bowsprit pin worked loose and had to be replaced. Dixon is a resourceful mechanic. These things are not easy underway.

"Forward cabin leaks again. We've stashed waterproof

stuff out of the aft cabin there and invited Dixon and Virgil to split the bunk time of the remaining settee bunk.

"Oddly, as much as there is to do, a lot of it muscular activity, I don't feel I'm getting enough exercise of the type one gets from walking. You don't pace the quarter-deck here, by the way. You move from place to place by grasping lines and masts and barrels and rails and lurching from one handhold to the next. A stroll ashore will be a real luxury. Estimate the Galapagos now Tuesday."

VIII

"SATURDAY, JULY 31—Last day of the first month and how does it feel now? How thirsty am I still for the simple life at sea? How much do I now detest the hedonism of an oversoft and sedentary life ashore in a big city? I can't be such a hypocrite as to deny the attractiveness of a fresh-water shower (just to get the salt out of my beard), an air-conditioned living room with a high-fidelity sound system, a good dry martini, a properly prepared piece of beef and some fresh fruit and vegetables, a long walk on sidewalks or under trees in a park.

"But I've not got my fill of sailing and perhaps I never will have enough of it. The discomforts are merely ingredients of zest, and the satisfactions are many and deep. Only when nature appears to conspire against your plans with adverse winds and currents, or when a dangerous condition accrues, does the negative aspect of the adventure appear. Then something deep in you threatens to whimper; you realize how tiny and human you are.

"General Wild Bill Donovan said to an aide after a World War II mission, when the aide remarked on the danger, 'Nothing is any fun unless it is dangerous.'

"Why do we keep coming back for more? First of all,

not everyone does. Some, seared by a lick of danger, will stay away from similar situations the rest of their lives. Some will keep up a life-long running flirtation with mild dangers. And a few, with an inordinate thirst for it, will find destruction. It is not rational to challenge the universe, and it is pointless to petition deities. But it *is* human, it is beautiful, to test and challenge and pray.

"Today I talked to my daughter. An excellent phone patch. How real she is. She asked marvelous questions. If the average interviewer would go after what she got he would be above average. She wanted descriptions of how everybody looked, details on morale, ETA's for Galapagos and Takaroa, wind and weather, health, and geographic positions. She told us that at the school at Interlochen they are doing a production of *Once Upon a Mattress,* changing the title to *Once Upon a Time* because of the suggestiveness of 'mattress.' The kids are getting a huge kick out of this.

"Toward evening there was real evidence that the S.E. Trades are at hand. If we can just get south enough to pick them up without using too much fuel . . . But the wind is warmer and more from the south than before. The water is cold, though, and the temperature still calls for a sweater on deck."

It's hard to explain, but the Humboldt current (which we were definitely into now) has a profound effect on the temperature in this part of the world. A giant cold stream from Antarctic regions moves up and can make the air cold. It also makes frequent fogs. Often at night a bone-chilling fog enveloped us for brief periods, and it seemed the closer we got to the equator the colder the nights were.

"SUNDAY, AUGUST 1—A truly unusual day. We are bombing along at 7 knots . . . and recouping some time lost after Malpelo when the wind was forcing us to South

America and when we had to conserve fuel. Now we know we have enough and to spare to reach San Cristobal. It's overcast and cold, but it doesn't rain very much. Characteristic of the area around the Galapagos. Virgil cooked. He hated it and felt everyone was going hungry as a result. We played Monopoly in the afternoon and had a cocktail and smoked a pipe and generally steeped ourselves in some of the leisure we thought we'd left ashore.

"Bob Dixon brought out the second edition of the *Lazarette Gazette* on *Thane* press (his own typewriter). There are whole different worlds aboard a 65-foot sailboat. Great variety of mood, climate, duties, food, clothing, conversation, sea, sky, wind, and in location aboard. The main salon on a quiet tropical afternoon with the sun streaming in the skylight is vastly different from the cockpit during a squall at night. The forward deck in a brisk wind is a world away from the after cabin in a doldrum calm. The head is a challenge in any weather. The lazarette is, believe it or not, a cherished sleeping place during chilly nights. The sleeper crawls into the lazarette hatch at the forward end of the cockpit and stretches out on a shelf just inside with his head a foot and a half below the steering compass and his feet on the generator exhaust duct and slumbers till his watch partner drops a belaying pin on him to remind him it's his turn at the wheel. This was a partial violation of the rule that two had to be on deck during the night watches, but since the lazarette was not quite technically "below" and *was* in the cockpit, it was construed as above deck. On calm nights I have read or written in the log by the Pelorus light on the after deck between the fantail and the cockpit—just lying on the deck. Contrary to what I had imagined, the days don't drag on in drab similarity. Instead, they are so different and enjoyable they go by rather fast, and I haven't done as much reading as I had hoped to. The days are made up of getting to know each individual better during long conversations with watch partners (rotated), navigational challenges both near shore (where it is critical) and on deep distant runs, where the only means of checking on currents and helm reports as to courses steered is with the Plath and the Rolex. Then there are maintenance tasks, oceanographic activity, photographic work, log keeping, naps (essential since every night's sleep is chopped up by the watch schedule), steering, cleaning, checking time signals, radioing all over the world, noting weather, fuel and fresh water reserves, line chafe and deterioration, bilge levels and pump action, fire and safety systems, battery charge levels, Walker log for distances, wind direction, and a hundred miscellaneous things that still leave a modicum of time for practical jokes and idling. . . .

"Sunday was restful and different and contentment sealed it, seasoned with the anticipation of arrival at San Cristobal early Tuesday.

"MONDAY, AUGUST 2 . . . cleaned some of the salt off . . . binoculars and sextant, ate three very good meals, and slept a little after lunch. Can you ask for better than that? Add a calm sea, a breeze from away at sunset, and you have more than a group of bloody buccaneers like us deserves.

"Took some movies and stills. H.R. stitched a sail—the jib had blown out by the seams during the last blow . . . Forrest Nelson will meet us tomorrow at Wreck Bay."

That day, with a phone patch, I talked to Joey Bishop, who was hosting the Johnny Carson show. Joey had hurt his back and was in a brace in his suite at the Plaza in New York. I thanked him for mentioning me on the air—a fact I'd learned from Ruth. When he finally realized where I was calling him from, he said, "I knew you were interested in scuba diving, but this is ridiculous!"

"TUESDAY, AUGUST 3—Monday night brought decreasing visibility and some spooky incidents appropriate to nearing the Encantadas. The midnight watch got a little rain, the moon was obscured, and about 3 A.M., when watching for land became critical, a fine mist brought the horizon in to a couple of hundred feet. At 0330 the wind quit abruptly and the sea calmed further. With the very gentlest breeze we ghosted along at 5 knots."

Dixon and I came on watch a half hour earlier, and we checked the Walker log at intervals to see if our estimate of five knots was accurate. It didn't seem possible with so little wind. It was worrisome, and I thought of altering course a little to the north since I couldn't know what the currents might do in bringing us to land earlier than we'd calculated. We had hoped for a slower speed until dawn.

Just before four o'clock, Bob called to me in the dark. I was at the wheel, and he was sitting on the deck just outside the cockpit. "Hey, Hugh," he said in a soft and strange voice. "Look over here. Something's alongside us just under the surface."

I looked over the rail. "Right there," he said, pointing. "Sometimes it's within a dozen feet of us. Just gliding along at our speed."

We had noticed at times in the night that dolphins escorted us for periods of time. We could hear them breathing from time to time. And when we looked for them, we could see them glowing faintly with phosphorescence as they moved through the plankton.

"Where is it?" I didn't see anything at first. "Is it a dolphin?"

"No," Bob said. "It's more than half the length of the ship. And it doesn't come up for air. I've been watching it for ten minutes or more."

Then I saw it. A faint, ghostly glow outlining a body at

least thirty feet long, not more than six feet off to port.
I felt my hair rise. "What the hell is it? A big shark?"

"I don't know. I'm glad you see it too. I was going to
quit drinking."

Sometimes the thing would move away slowly until we
lost sight of it, but then it would drift back in, once coming in somewhat astern and catching up to us, to hover
off our flank. But it never came up to breathe.

"Probably isn't a small whale or it would blow," Bob
said.

We were silent a moment watching it. "Maybe it's the
world's first underwater flying saucer," I suggested.

"It's shaped like a cigar anyway."

For about a half hour it stuck with us, always to port,
and then it vanished without drifting out. It must have
sounded, for it looked as if it were growing fainter and
drawing closer at the same time. We watched for it to
reappear for several minutes on either side but that was
the end of it. To this day we don't know what it was.

The visibility was very poor, and about 4:45 I fell off
a little to the north, in order to reduce the chance of
coming on the north end of San Cristobal Island and, as
Dixon said, "discovering it with the bowsprit." If I had
known what a surprise awaited me at dawn, I'd have
turned straight north or even northeast.

The log reads: "At dawn land was sighted to the southeast! In fact, the north tip of San Cristobal was dead
astern—it was as though we had sailed through it. We
had obviously been set west and slightly north by the
current and set back to south after passing that north tip
of the island. We were probably pretty close at one point
in the night. What little there is of my hair again stood on
end for a moment. We sailed down the west coast and before breakfast was over had spotted Kicker Rock with

its towering flat-topped spire and thirty-foot-wide chasm."

Many ships sail through that high-walled corridor. Irving Johnson's *Yankee* started through once, but backed away. We didn't even start. Too much danger of damage to spreaders if the ship rolled in a swell. We took pictures from near it.

From the log: "The boys assembled the Nautisport boat. The black dinghy is still damaged, and the Johnson outboard is out of commission due to salt-water corrosion. We need a machine shop. In addition to the Nautisport, we still have an 8-man Winslow Raft, and the *Seagull* outboard is working well."

We headed for Wreck Bay, the port of entry, which is on the southern end of the island. It was on this run that the breeze freshened and snatched our yellow quarantine flag the instant we hoisted it. Nothing daunted, we stood into the bay smartly flying a small yellow nylon bag, the newest thing in quarantine signals, our "quarantine ball."

At noon the sun was coming out, and we were feeling our way into the harbor under power and by pilotage with Pete aloft. Not too tricky. The anchor down and holding, we stood on the deck in the sunshine and looked at the town of Wreck Bay. It is aptly named. Unpainted clapboard buildings, mostly one story, line up in a forlorn row along the south side of an unpaved street with the grand name of Avenida de Carlos Darwin. There is a statue of Darwin in front of a stone building housing the port authority offices and the island's only dentist. There is no doctor. There is no decent drinking water. There is no diesel fuel. There is no ice. The pier, put up by U.S. forces during the war, is rotting away and unsafe to walk on, let alone tie to. On the black lava shore to the east of town is a long shed, long disused, which was to have become a freezing plant for a lobster business conceived by an American promoter with more drive than luck.

At length, a launch containing an officer and rowed by two sailors drew alongside.

After all the dire reports of the idiocy and cruelty of the Ecuadorian Military Port Officials, let it be said that this entry and clearance was the most sensible and pleasant of the entire trip.

Commandante Arrera, short, neat, courteous, and friendly, went through our papers in about eight minutes, didn't seem disturbed by the presence of firearms or professional photographic gear, and offered to be of any help he could while we were there. There was no unnecessary red tape or suspicion and no officiousness on his part.

I had heard before I left of yachts seized in the Galapagos and the owners and their groups held incommunicado for weeks on some minor infraction. There is one tale of a cruise ship which, through a clerical error, reported that there were sixty bottles of liquor aboard, when there were actually 600. The liquor was seized and the passengers, after being detained for some days, went on their way boozeless.

In New York, H.R. had spent two full days getting a sheaf of papers stamped and signed and notarized, and a week later this government changed hands and we thought everything we had in the way of authorization was void.

Early in my planning I seriously considered sailing by the Galapagos and direct to French Polynesia to avoid the risk, but to have sailed by would have been unfortunate for many reasons. First, we would have missed the most interesting part of the world we had ever visited. Second, the reports of excesses were exaggerated. Third, it's a long haul across the Pacific even stopping at the Galapagos. We needed the shore time there.

Now we were here and officially and warmly welcomed. A small boat came out selling oranges. We traded some cigarettes for a supply.

We had lunch aboard, and while we were clearing that away, the Darwin Foundation's ship *Beagle* arrived from Academy Bay, at 1:30. At last we met Forrest Nelson, after months of hearing about him and talking with him on ham radio. Virgil pointed him out to us as the *Beagle* was setting her anchor three hundred feet away. A launch was lowered and Forrest came aboard *Thane*.

Though it had been years since they'd seen each other, the greeting between Virgil Bowers and Forrest Nelson was as casual as though their parting had been last week. Since they conversed daily over immense distances, their images of each other needed little refurbishing. Each observed that the other was a little older and heavier than he had thought, which was not surprising. Forrest Nelson is in his early fifties, of less than medium height, has regular features and a light complexion, topped by a graying crew cut. He wore sneakers and gray slacks and a T-shirt. Friendly and briskly businesslike, he had a high degree of self-sufficiency combined with the seemingly contradictory ease of one who has escaped clocks and calendars for all time. Forrest purchased by the barrel and dined by the position of the sun. But his tool shed was neat, and his approach to living in a wilderness was methodical and thorough. He had a grasp of reality that never let him underestimate his adversary. He has a good chance of success in some ambitious plans. He hopes to bring tourists to the Galapagos in large numbers. I think he'll do it, and it will be a favor to the kind of tourist who finds that Hilton hotels and airports and tourist-trap restaurants are the same everyplace in the world. The Galapagos are different. Forrest believes that with the help of the Ecuadorian government, already interested in tourism, he can provide enough comfort for every kind of tourist except those who shouldn't leave home to begin with, and offer something they can see nowhere in Europe or Asia or any of the South Pacific Islands.

We asked him if he had eaten lunch. He had. He suggested we plan to leave for Barrington Island, midway to Academy Bay, before dawn. In the meantime, we could see the town, and he'd help us make arrangements for killing some fresh meat in the islands.

We landed our shore party on the beach beside the rotting pier. Virgil stayed aboard. He said he'd been in Wreck Bay before and had no particular desire to go back.

The town is larger than I had thought: about 750 people, there being perhaps 1700 altogether on the island. The stores have a small assortment of canned goods, some excellent chocolate, rum and beer for five *sucres* (twenty-five cents) in enormous bottles, nearly a quart measure.

Two small boys came at us with a gunny sack containing one medium-size lobster, which they wanted to sell us for $6.00 American. Forrest said it was worth 35¢ and that they'd come down to 25¢ if one bargained hard enough. This range of haggling beat anything I'd seen in the Middle East.

Up the mountain road were large concrete aprons on which hemp or sisal fiber was drying. The town reservoir was farther up. It was low and murky. One street was paved with one-ton volcanic rocks so jagged they would have been a challenge to a mountain goat. A horse would have broken a leg in some of the three-foot-deep crevices. They were probably intended as a base for pouring some kind of paving material, but Virgil later told us he'd seen them in the same street years before. There was a partially completed church for which a bishop had long ago collected an enormous budget from the island people and then fled with it to Ecuador, where rumor had it he was living high.

An old man came to us while we were drinking our quarts of beer and begged for medicine for his wife, who had been badly burned. I was about to go to the dinghy to get our emergency painkiller and burn medication when Forrest explained that his wife had been burned a dozen years ago and was completely healed, but the man had been collecting medicine from incoming ships ever since. Whether he sold it, was neurotically hoarding supplies against another accident, had been rendered completely dotty by his wife's suffering and really felt she needed it, or whether they were hooked on analgesic drugs, we didn't find out.

"What do they do when they really need medical help?" I asked Forrest.

"They go to Ecuador."

"By boat?"

There was no other way. One woman suffering from appendicitis had to be packed in ice to wait many days for a ship to take her to a Guayaquil hospital. She lived.

"I suppose," I said, "a person's just careful not to run into unnecessary medical need."

"That would be a good idea," Forrest said, "but it's not always the case." He told us about a game played on San Cristobal in a clearing not far from where we were sitting. In the game a chicken is buried up to its neck in sand, and contestants, blindfolded and made dizzy by being turned round and round, are allowed a set number of swipes with a machete to try to decapitate the prize. The problem occurs with the audience. As the game gets more interesting, the throng of onlookers, pushing from the outside to get a better look, crowd those at ringside farther and farther into the action. There are supposed to be one-legged spectators at Wreck Bay.

The residents butchered an ox at the north end of the main drag that afternoon. It looked as though this honor crowned a lifetime of work during which the animal had toughened every muscle to the point where the oldest goat on Narborough would have more tender meat.

We ate aboard that evening. The sun set in the direction of Barrington Island, uninhabited as are most of the Galapagos. The twilight was short, as it always is on the equator, and the town lights went out very soon after dark. High on its steel tower, the range light at the shore shone like a large star. Water lapped against the hull, and distant bird cries interrupted the stillness. A haziness again enveloped the surroundings, not fog exactly, just low, indistinct cloudiness characteristic of the region much of the year. It's as though it always wants to rain in the Galapagos but seldom can, because of the temperature inversion caused by the cold Humboldt current. Much of the character of the islands is desert: cactus, lizards, sand, and a scarcity of fresh water. The location is squarely tropical, but the climate is not.

At three A.M. we came on deck sleepily and got the anchor up. In the blackness before dawn, it was hard to believe we were close to a town. Standing on deck and looking out to nothing but darkness in every direction, I could appreciate Forrest's story about a commercial fishing-boat captain who ran up onto the beach while trying to leave at night. He was somewhat drunk and turned around, thinking Dalrymple was the Wreck Bay light, and he went full speed ahead into the town instead of out the Bay.

By dawn we were nearing Barrington, which, as I said, is midway between San Cristobal and Santa Cruz. We anchored in a cove and spotted a colony of sea lions on the beach. We found that one could approach those who were sleeping and pet them or even climb over them. They do not waken because they normally lie all over each other as they sleep, and they think any contact is just another sea lion. They have no enemies on the island so they sleep rather soundly. Their fur is coarser than that of fur seals, but still sleek and clean and relatively fine. The bulls are a little harder to approach than the cows, being more alert and aggressive. They are also larger, running up to seven or eight hundred pounds. They will attack if cornered, and I suppose they could chew pretty hard.

One sleeping cow I petted woke up after a bit and looked at me with widened eyes. She blinked, as though not crediting what she saw, and then made an unbelievably human sound of astonishment, an expletive clearly meaning "What the hell is *this?*" She jumped back a foot, stared at me again, and then made off for the water, in that ungainly manner of sea lions on land. Their communication with each other vocally is limited. The sleepers will continue to sleep even when half the herd has set up a great alarm of barking and bellowing. These sounds are inarticulate and apparently mean as little to them as they do to us. At least I never saw a seal warn another as birds do. In recent years, Mexican fishing boats have landed and slaughtered them wantonly, and this began slowly to give the sea lion an idea of the true nature of humans. Along with all the indigenous wild life of the islands, they are now protected by the Ecuadorian government.

While we were back aboard for lunch, a mockingbird landed on Forrest's shoulder and stared at him. Forrest stared back, moving only slowly. The bird stayed with him for a few moments and then flew on to inspect our rigging. A yellow warbler perched on the main boom. We got out some bread crumbs for it, but it turned out to be visiting, not begging. It politely ate a couple and then flew on.

The salt water had been quietly working on the radio equipment since Panama. A log entry notes: "Virgil made one last radio contact with the deteriorating KWM2 (everything electronic and photographic, not to mention guns and cutlery, has suffered damage), and before he could sign off, it blew up. Our next schedule is for tomorrow, and we'll keep it with Forrest's shore station." I had also planned a broadcast to the "Today" program for the next morning.

Forrest had equipment for repairing radio gear, but Virgil feared this last damage was severe enough to require a new KWM2 transceiver. He also needed a new 516-F power pack.

In the afternoon we made for Academy Bay and Forrest's home. The island's highest mountain is 2800 feet, and can be seen from Wreck Bay on a clear day. Academy Bay is open to the east and south, guarded by a small island with a light on it a few miles out. The island, like all the others in the archipelago, has more than one name. (Some have three names.) It was named Santa Cruz at one time. An early expedition named it Chavez. The British, not caring to use Spanish names, and possibly not charting the group in the same location, renamed Santa Cruz/Chavez "Indefatigable Island."

A few white buildings showed from the mouth of the bay, and Forrest pointed out the Darwin Station, a store, houses built by the Angermeyers, and his own complex of buildings. It was evening when we got the anchor down. The port captain at Academy Bay was also very courteous. He said he would reissue our clearance papers next day.

While we checked to see if the anchor was holding, I

noticed a small outboard-powered skiff approaching. The sole occupant was a very good-looking Ecuadorian girl in her early twenties.

"What have we here?" I asked.

"That's my girl," Forrest said. "She and her sister work for me." He called something to her in Spanish. She answered him as she came alongside.

Forrest Nelson is not lonely in those lonely islands. He is busy and he has friends, neighbors, and employees, such as José Luis, an excellent mechanic and radio man, and Marlene and Clara, her well-built younger sister, both from Ecuador. And he has his radio on which he talks to more places in a week than I do by telephone in a year.

We took laundry and clean clothes and some cameras and gear ashore; got a fresh-water shower (Forrest collects rainwater all year long, storing it in big aboveground cisterns) and in fresh clothes, had a large gin on the rocks. After a meal in the big dining room, we played chess and read. Anticipating increasing tourist business, Forrest has built a large recreation and dining hall, a huge kitchen, and several cabins. He once housed and fed an expedition of sixty scientists who had come to the Darwin Station on a project. He has a considerable library of books in Spanish and English, a detailed set of charts covering the islands and the west coast of South America, engineering and drafting handbooks and tools. He constructed his buildings of concrete building blocks that he molded himself. Our diesel fuel, waiting in drums, was stored in his machine shed.

"THURSDAY, AUGUST 5 . . . Radio contact with Ruth through Forrest's HC8FN, and set machinery in motion for getting new equipment to Baltra I. Hope we can, KWM2 kaput."

Ruth was checking at the other end how best to get us a new transmitter without going through Ecuadorian customs. To get it to Panama was no trick, but it would be necessary to have it put in bond and send direct to Baltra Island, just to the north, since there is no customs in the Galapagos. A Colonel Fraile, a friend of Virgil and Forrest, member of the Junta Militario, and head of the Ecuadorian Air Force, could accomplish this. So could the U. S. Air Force, but we didn't want to ask them unless there were an emergency with life at stake. There was no possible means of transporting the equipment.

Also this day I broadcast a report on the air on the "Today" Program. It was great to hear Barbara Walters' voice. I remember she asked me, "What do you miss most?"

The question took me by surprise, and I presumed the answer was to exclude my family. I recall that I said something about missing certain aspects of civilization, but I realized as I was saying it that I couldn't be sincere. I thought I might eventually miss air conditioning and iced cocktails, and I gave a conventional answer. But the truth is at that moment I didn't miss anything. Later, during the long reach across the Pacific, I developed a longing to take a long walk on a sidewalk.

Aside from this and photographic activity, the following projects are noted in the ship's log of August 5: new mizzen halyard to be rigged, varnish work caught up with, fresh water and fuel loaded, repair work on jib, the bowsprit pin to be replaced and locked, one pair of binoculars with a prism jarred loose and moisture trapped inside, the Nautisport engine had a frozen part that had to be drifted, the black rubber dinghy had two compartments that wouldn't hold air, camera lenses to be wiped and dried, some repair work due on tape recorders (the Wollensak and Uher had had some damage; the Nagra was working OK), laundry to be done, etc. Meanwhile an intensive assault on the radio problems was mounted by Virgil and Forrest and José Luis.

We suspected at the time that the unusual amount of chafe we were getting on the mizzen halyard (brand new line would part in just a few hours, rubbed through) was due to bolts on an antenna draw band. It turned out we were wrong, but while we were at anchor in Academy, we filed down the bolts. What was really causing the chafe was a burr in the par block at the top of the mizzen mast. My 100-foot towline had long since been recruited as a halyard.

We finally decided not to try to have new radio equipment flown down: too much risk. There was no point in risking lives in an airplane to decrease slightly the risk to lives on a boat. Most boats make that trip without radio. Half my reason for having it was not safety, but the pleasure of keeping in touch with the rest of my family and for occasional broadcasts to TV audiences in the States. Word came that action had been started that might be impossible to stop, so we decided to leave via Baltra, where the airstrip was, in case new equipment was flown in anyway—it had already been sent to Panama.

On the morning of August 6, we got the black rubber dinghy patched up enough to use it as a tow barge for ferrying fuel drums, and more immediately for getting sound equipment across the bay for an interview with Gus Angermeyer.

This trek over and back was a saga itself. Surfing out from Forrest's dock through a curling surge that chops constantly at the black rocks, we pulled the black dinghy —filled with boxes and tripods and Jerry Galyean—with the newly repaired Johnson outboard on the Nautisport.

To understand why there is no real landing at Angermeyer Point, it is necessary to understand Gus Angermeyer and his brothers. This can be done, but it isn't easy.

Gus is now in his fifties. He is big, tough, direct, and self-sufficient; he is also a paradox because he is at the same time garrulous, sensitive, dramatic, and highly articulate in at least three languages. He manifests a love-hate for the civilization he spurned thirty-some years ago. His living habits are extremely simple: He neither smokes nor drinks, but he quotes Goethe and Khalil Gibran, reads voraciously, and has been writing a book for years, which he doesn't seem inclined to get to a publisher. He knows how *Life* magazine puts together a story and has turned down a Hollywood offer to film his own life. He is almost childlike in his directness, and at the same time he is sophisticated and suspicious of those who might come to exploit him by taking and distorting his story. There have been some of these.

He was out behind his house until our arrival and hadn't seen us coming. He greeted us as warmly as he had when we sailed in, and he came aboard to welcome us. He had on a pair of red swimming trunks. That was all. His hide was burned to a deep brown with a hint of the patina both human skin and bronze get from years of weathering. My canvas shoes with worn soles were not giving me as much protection as his own bare feet gave him, judging from the way he walked on the abrasive lava stones. He is a bull of a man with a will as sinewy as his biceps.

When Hitler was rising to power, the Angermeyer family could not stomach what they saw coming. Many German families shared the disgust and alarm, but few saw the real nature of the National Socialist movement as early or as clearly as the elder Angermeyer and his sons. It was not easy to get away. But when they did, the violence of the intention generated such momentum that the boys, Gus, Carl, and Fritz, didn't stop till they had come to the end of the world. It was as though in their minds civilization itself was to blame for the creation of Hitler and they needed to be free of civilization. There are few places in the world freer of civilization than where they came to rest.

Because the islands were technically inhabited by a few Ecuadorians and Europeans, the Angermeyers built homes in places almost inaccessible to their neighbors. They do not have a reputation for being unfriendly—on the contrary, they are helpful both to other islanders and to visitors—but they have little desire to be absorbed by or dependent on a colony.

At Gus's house, high on a lava rock wall that runs along the southwest side of the bay, we did our best to keep our boats off the jagged edges as the swell lifted them and threatened to bring them into the wall. H.R. climbed to the top with a line and, from an overhang, hoisted the equipment up piece by piece. Rubber boats are particularly vulnerable to jagged rocks, so we tied them behind one of Gus's small boats, which was riding off between a post high on shore and a stern anchor. Then we climbed into his boat, pulled it as far toward the ledge as it would go, made a leap for the rocks, and began our climb to the top. If you go to Gus Angermeyer's house, you've got to have a strong desire and a good reason to get there. You don't just drop by to chat or to borrow a cup of sugar. But once there, you are treated with warm hospitality.

It's as though he eliminates certain guests by a set of obstacles and then deals only with those who get through. There is a road around the bay, but it stops a half mile from Angermeyer Point and to come overland would be much more difficult than by water.

How long it took him to erect his buildings I have no idea. The house is of stone and mortar. There is plenty of stone around, heaven knows, but it has to be cut or selected and then put into place. The house has rather large windows made up of small panes in neat wooden frames. It is two stories high, and its front terrace arrangement is a concession to his wife, Gus explained, as though apologizing for a feminine touch.

Inside, he offered us tea and a cake he had baked himself in the separate building erected for cooking. We met Anna, a nine-year-old Indian girl orphan, adopted by Gus and his wife. Mrs. Angermeyer was in Ecuador at the time of our visit. Anna showed us some of her schoolwork, and Gus demonstrated that she was learning English and German, as well as Spanish.

Most people, Gus believes, dream of achieving their own independence, but few are equipped to do so. Few have the internal security to face the risks, the hunger, the heavy work, the loneliness. As a result, they dream of the harvest but ignore the necessity of sowing and cultivating. He credits his parents with giving him and his brothers a sense of independence by not only not standing in their way, but by boosting them out of the nest. "Don't ever get homesick," his mother once said.

People who come to the Galapagos to live are of three types. The exploiters, who seek to turn a profit by bringing tourists or colonists wholesale to the islands as a commercial venture; the dreamers, who have little grasp of reality and eventually, disillusioned or frightened, move on or return home; and finally, those who know the price of independence and pay it. These last are seldom people who are merely seeking to escape from something. Instead they have a sense of going to something rather than flying from something. Gus calls this "treasure." He admits his initial motive was escape, but he claims it changed after he left Germany. He could have gone to the United States, or he could go back to Germany now.

I believe Gus Angermeyer is a happy man, but his is not a life for everyone. He has no doctors, no news, no ease, none of the buffers that a large, well-knit community can provide the individual against the harshness of our existence. I say "can provide" because Gus saw in his youth an example of a large, well-knit community that *amplified* the brutality of existence by elevating to official prominence the very worst human instincts and forces, and systematically setting out to obliterate the side of humanity that distinguishes it from other animals. His disillusionment with society is understandable.

But the main message of Gus Angermeyer's life seems to be that happiness is found in independence purchased by work and risk. This can be done in or out of a social framework. He elected to go on his own. Like Rousseau, he functions better in raw, natural surroundings. And like Rousseau, he believes all men would find this the case. In spite of signs of a thirst for companionship in his loquacious hospitality, he is a man who has paid a high price for freedom and feels he got a bargain.

There is an interesting comparison between Forrest Nelson and Gus. Forrest too came to the Galapagos from civilization (Pennsylvania), found it to his liking, and carved a world for himself, exhibiting considerable resourcefulness and self-sufficiency. But where Angermeyer would like to see the Galapagos remain wild with a minimum of humans on it, Forrest would like to share it with large numbers of people through the development of a tourist trade. He is not an exploiter in the sense of an absentee landlord, whose investment money would bring him more money, but rather a willing worker whose investment in labor and planning would provide him with a living and accomplish the larger goal of making his islands known and accessible to visitors. Unlike Gus, he did not leave because the civilization he was born into had turned sour, but because of a pioneering spirit too strong to be satisfied by vacation camping or a sailing trip.

Before we left I made a short side trip through the cactus and the black rocks to the house of the oldest Angermeyer brother, Carl, who was in Europe at the time. Carl is the only one of the three willing even to visit that part of the world. There was scarcely a path between the two houses: isolation in isolation. His daughter-in-law met me at the door and accepted the package I had brought from Mrs. Robert Anderson of Lynnfield, Massachusetts. She had heard I was planning to stop at the Galapagos and asked if I would take a small package to Carl Angermeyer. I was delighted to be a courier. I had sealed it in waterproof plastic covers, and it made the trip intact.

When we left, Gus lowered the equipment boxes on the line after we'd pulled the dinghy in toward the cliff wall. The sun was down and the fast-fading tropical twilight already dimming as we headed back. We had an even chance of getting $5000 worth of sound equipment through the bobsled run of Forrest's entrance into his private lagoon. We made it.

In the evening I made tracings of details from charts of Punto Espinosa and James Bay, where we planned to kill fresh meat on our second day out.

In the log I had set forth some reactions: "This wilderness must be what America was like in its young years. I do not want the life Gus Angermeyer lives . . . For all its rewards of independence, I will not pay the price. I will return to the Big Ice Cream Parlor and pay the other price of compromise and dependence on a society I know to be imperfect in return for the physical and emotional comforts it gives me. But I wouldn't miss for anything living this brief parallel moment, hunting and working in the Encantadas, exploring and discovering among the seals and penguins, the iguanas, the hermits and scientists and pioneers, and the endless black rock and pounding sea.

"SATURDAY, AUGUST 7—Talked to Hal Humphrey on the coast from HC8FN with a phone patch through Jim Smith's station W6RT. The hams of America are a marvelous group."

I'm convinced many of these hams are people whose superior sense of communications enables them to help others to keep in touch; this is their humanitarian motive. The technical aspects of ham radio become merely a means to this end.

When phone patches were impossible due to weakness of our signal, these ham operators would go out of their way to call my wife and relay messages, assuring her that I was all right and offering any help they could. It is difficult to express how much this meant to her and to me.

Back to the log: "Virgil is on the brink of pulling another miracle off. With the aid of Forrest and José Luis, he has put the KWM2 aboard and is getting through. Also has rigged an emergency unit that can send Morse code for contact with U.S.

"SUNDAY, AUGUST 8 . . . Forrest may come with us as far as Punta Espinosa. I'll have to arrange transportation back. It would be worth it to have him along. . . ."

~~~~~~

IX

IT IS 150 miles, as the crow flies, from Punta Pitt on San Cristobal to the west edge of Fernandina Island. Darwin or Culpepper Island is 100 miles north of the equator and Hood Island is eighty-five miles south of it. From almost any of the islands you can see at least one other because of the height of the mountains.

The Galapagos may be some of the youngest large islands on earth. They possibly did not come into existence until the last of the earth's large reptiles was long dead. Estimates of their age range from a few million to one hundred thousand years. There are over 3000 square miles of land area in these islands, almost none of it habitable.

There is a theory, supported at present by growing evidence, that a submerged plateau connecting the island group with Central America was once dry land. Many of the life species show a close kinship with cousins in Central, not South, America. The nearest relations of the giant tortoises after whom the Islands are named are found in fossil form in Cuba.

The treacherous terrain was described by an eighteenth-century privateer as "Nothing but loose Rocks, like Cynders, very rotten and heavy, and the Earth so parched, that it will not bear a Man, but breaks into Holes under his Feet."

This fellow must have landed on Narborough or one of the other islands of recent volcanic activity. It couldn't have been all that bad or the pirates wouldn't have favored it as a place to rest and plan assaults. Melville wrote of Barrington Island: "Near two centuries ago Barrington Isle was the resort of that famous wing of the West Indian Buccaneers, which, upon their repulse from the Cuban waters, crossing the Isthmus of Darien, ravaged the Pacific side of the Spanish colonies, and, with the regularity and timing of a modern mail, waylaid the royal treasure ships plying between Manila and Acapulco. After the toils of piratic war, here they came to say their prayers, enjoy their free-and-easies, count their crackers from the cask, their doubloons from the keg, and measure their silks of Asia with long Toledos for their yardsticks."

But Melville also projects a doleful over-all view of the islands. "Take five-and-twenty heaps of cinders dumped here and there in an outside city lot; imagine some of them magnified into mountains, and the vacant lot the sea; and you will have a fit idea of the general aspect of the Enchanted Isles; looking much as the world might, after a penal conflagration. It is to be doubted whether any spot of earth can, in desolateness, furnish a parallel to this group."

On Monday we met and talked with Dr. Roger Perry, scientific director of the Darwin Station about a mile east of Forrest's.

This station is unique in more than one way. The only truly international scientific organization in the world, the Foundation was set up under the auspices of UNESCO and the IUCN (Internation Union for the Conservation of Nature and Natural Resources). Contributions from

the Royal Society of Britain, the U.S.'s National Science
Foundation, the Audubon Society, and organizations in
Switzerland, Belgium, and Ecuador have given impetus
to work that may yet save many unusual and valuable
species of life from extinction.

We judged Dr. Perry to be about thirty years old, although he has some mannerisms of a much older man.
He spoke in a deliberate, but not clipped, British manner.
He wore a pocketed hunting shirt and an ascot, and he
used a cane because he had injured his leg. His jaw was
clamped on a black-bowled pipe, the bit of which seemed
fused to his teeth. I never saw him without it, or without
the ascot or the hunting shirt or the cane. He was a
pleasant and helpful man. I wanted to charter the *Beagle*,
the Foundation's ship, to bring Forrest back to Academy
Bay from our last stop in the islands before we went on
west. Dr. Perry pointed out that this could be done only
for a bona fide scientific organization.

"But," he said, "you have a scientific interest in the islands, haven't you?" I had. "And you intend to publish
something about your trip, and about the existence of the
Darwin Station and that the Foundation could use more
aid in its research projects?" I did. "Then you are a scientific organization."

I paid the reasonable fee, and a schedule was set with
the *Beagle's* skipper, Fritz Angermeyer, the third Angermeyer brother, who is as laconic as Gus is voluble. I had
met Fritz and his wife at Wreck Bay when the *Beagle* first
brought Forrest there.

Dr. Perry showed us cases of stuffed finches, examples
of each species Darwin had studied, and which had led
him to the theory of evolution. Perry took us to a large
walled compound up the hill where specimens of the island's famous giant tortoises browsed among the cactus,
which they eat, spines and all, along with a supplemental

diet of bananas, fed them daily in huge bunches. One tortoise I saw was fully 4½-feet long and weighed 500 pounds. I tried to upset him with a stout stick, but couldn't do it. They move very slowly and stop with head pulled in when confronted. If one stays behind them they keep going like a tank even if one is trying to overturn them. You don't exist for a tortoise unless he can see you.

The only danger to wild life on the islands, Dr. Perry explained, is man and man-introduced animals, notably goats. The latter are now wild, and they are destroying the giant tortoises when they are young. A stable ecology can thus often be upset by an intruder. Outside of a small rice rat, no mammals are indigenous to the land areas of the islands. If there was a land bridge to Central America at one time, it sank before the Age of Mammals began.

Prince Philip was once a visitor to the islands. He expressed a desire to trek inland on a turtle search. The morning of the expedition, Dr. Perry boarded Philip's ship dressed as he always dresses. Philip appeared on deck in a sport shirt and weather-worn and wrinkled slacks, and after one glance at Perry said, "You're not going dressed like that?"

The scientist's recovery was superb, according to witnesses. "Of course not," he said through his pipe. "I'm on my way to the station to change. Thought you might like to stop there first."

Sunday we sorted laundry and got some of the personal gear stowed aboard in two trips. That afternoon Jerry, Forrest, H.R., Bob, and I went to a point of land south of Academy Bay where there was a deep rift in the cliff and a small sand beach sloping back to the interior. The surge came in with some force, but by climbing the cliff we came on it from a back way. There were volcanic tubes going down seventy-five feet or so. There is a belief that it is through one of these things that a passenger on one of Mike Burke's cruises once vanished. She was a middle-aged woman who took a walk by herself on Floreana Island and was never seen again. There have been many searches for her, all in vain. But of course there are many places where one might vanish. We swam for a while off the beach, being careful not to let the surge send us into the jagged walls on each side.

Monday morning we loaded the mended jib, fresh fruits and bread, and gasoline for the outboards. We now had aboard 275 gallons of water, five drums of fuel, three dozen loaves of bread, soft drinks, the camera and sound gear, another rifle and ammunition I'd bought from Forrest, most of the laundry and personal bundles. I gave Forrest some gin to replenish his stock; he doesn't drink it, but guests such as we do. Eggs were being gathered and would be brought on the *Beagle* to Punta Espinosa.

That afternoon we ran into some unusual activity. Going with Forrest from his place to the Port Captain's office across Academy Bay we heard shots and saw bullets hit the water ahead of us. We slowed immediately and then there were more shots, with bullets hitting behind us. They were coming from the military post on the shore a quarter of a mile away. The National Police, we found later, were having target practice. We went ashore and saw them firing at a large paper target set up toward the bay. The bullets, of course, went through the targets and into the bay among the ships and dinghies. When we called this to their attention they cheerfully told us that when a boat was in line with the target they held their fire! Going back, as bullets sang around us, we prayed they had no cross-eyed police on the line.

The port captain brought our clearance over about six. We would go in the morning (Tuesday). Forrest was going as far as Punta Espinosa, about 100 miles from Acad-

[1] THANE

–under foresail, main and (hidden behind main) mizzen sail

[2] Pete Jackson

[3] Connie Jackson

[4] H. R. Downs

[5] Jerry Galyean

...AND HER CREW

[7] Bob Dixon

[6] Hugh Downs, the skipper, in his "office," shorn but unshaven.

[8] Virgil Bowers

[9] *Thane* dwarfed by her lock-companion in Panama.

[10] The lethal oil drum, now subdued, tamely stands by as the captain snoozes.

[11] Ruth Downs makes friends in the San Blas islands, on Nulanega.

[12] H.D. on the bowsprit as we consider the risk of sailing through Kicker Rock's narrow "slot."

[13] The *Beagle,* Academy Bay in the Galapagos.

[14] H.R., almost lost against the rugged, waterless lava terrain of Narborough Island.

[15] Only the marine iguanas could love the jagged black shards of Punta Espinosa, Narborough Island.

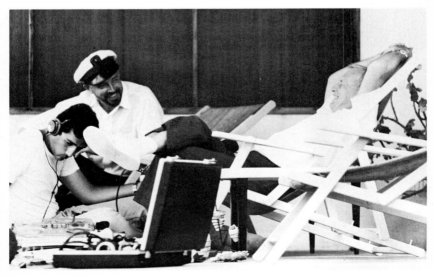

[16] Forrest Nelson, in his do-it-yourself, handmade home, entertains H.D., as H.R. records.

[17] The "ladies" of Plaza Island were gentle and cordial; not so "Big Kahuna," their consort in the background.

[18] Virgil Bowers, peerless helmsman, demonstrates his proficiency, with Bob Dixon alongside.

[19] The feast for the abandoned castaway, Federico, standing next to Connie; background, left to right, are Dixon, Mike Bayles, Hans, H.R., and H.D.

[20] Gus Angermeyer, the self-sufficient recluse-by-choice of the Galapagos, regales H.D. with anecdotes of his strange career.

[21] The famous Mormon Mission of the low-lying shore of Takaroa.

[22] The "church sociable" at the Mission.

[23] Dixon, aloft, pilots us through Takaroa's tricky reef.

[24] Bob, Connie, and H.R. impressed by the exotic beauty of Cook's Bay, Moorea.

[25] Moorea is "your enchanted island."

[26] H.R. and the skipper tour Moorea in primitive, but non-Polynesian, style.

[27] Jerry Galyean and H.D. filming the beauty
of this true-life Bali Ha'i, Moorea.

[28] The famous Moorea bash in the open-air living room, with H.D., H.R., and Larry Nilsen in one of the quieter moments.

[29] The skipper looking half-drowned, which he was, en route back to Tahiti, by the spray of an errant wave.

[30] *Thane* at well-earned rest. We left her in this Papeete berth. Aboard with Pete and H.D. is Marc Darnois.

[31] Jerry Galyean spiritedly haggles in Papeete's fabulous market.

[32] End of the trek—Ruth and Hugh Downs, with appropriate decorations like the traditional shell crown, as we prepare to return home.

emy Bay, and the *Beagle* was to pick him up there Friday.

"TUESDAY, AUGUST 10—Got underway at 8 with Gus Angermeyer and the little Indian girl Anna waving from their house. I promised Gus I'd send pictures if they came out."

We went north along the east coast of Santa Cruz for three hours until we came to South Plaza Island, where we anchored. It is a beautiful, rugged little island about a mile long and 1000 feet wide. The south shore is a high cliff, and the table of its surface slopes down to sea level with spots of beach along the north edge. It looks as though it had been formed flat and then tilted. It teems with sea lions, swallow-tail gulls, boobies, land iguanas, cranes, red crabs, spiders, and cactus. Not a tourist's paradise, but for a naturalist or any seeker of interesting sights, this is a great spot. The two islands together are shaped like the hoofprint of a deer. We anchored between them.

H.R. and Bob and Jerry photographed in the morning and I took lunch to them after our ten A.M. radio schedule aboard. This morning I talked with Carol Florence in my office. Carol had no new word about the equipment that had been sent to Panama.

The state of our transmitting and receiving gear could technically be called functioning, but as Virgil explained it, it was working on one cylinder. More accurately, it was putting out about two per cent of its power. He was getting through only by having friends in the states with powerful receiving antennas beam us on a prearranged frequency at scheduled times, and then boost what signal they got and phone-patch us across the country. Roger Tare, General James G. Smith, Dean Burnett, Philip Schutze, Blair Jones, Marcie Rice, Chuck Bader, and Dorothy Strauber were of immense help in this regard. It plagued Virgil to be operating with such a weak signal when he was used to having enough power to break in on anyone anywhere in the world. Carol told me Ruth was in Michigan visiting Dee Dee at Interlochen, where the already mentioned musical *Once Upon a Mattress* —or *Once Upon a Time*—was being produced. An actress daughter needs a parent in the audience—not a stage mother but an "audience mother."

On South Plaza Island we saw two things we had not seen among the Barrington Island sea lions: a mother with a new-born calf and an enormous and quite unfriendly bull. Both were almost completely fearless and not inclined to let us land or get near them. The bull, whom we nicknamed "Big Kahuna," was more than three times the bulk of the biggest cows: we guessed six or seven hundred pounds. And he was capable of diving directly out of the water and onto a rock shelf five or six feet above the water. (Forrest told us sea lions have been known to dive up twenty-five feet to a ledge.) Once he charged the dinghy with Pete and H.R. aboard. H.R. was recording "ambient sound" with the Nagra tape recorder at the time. So now we have an audio transcript of the bull's approach and the boat occupants' terror. The cow, once we were ashore, would charge us, snapping at our heels, whenever we came too close to her baby. The calf was probably not more than a few days old.

That evening we had a fancy multicourse dinner of fresh food we'd brought with a bottle of wine and candlelight, and topped with a dessert of *baba au rhum*. There was music on the record player, also the Wollensak, which we had repaired at Forrest's.

Before dark, Bob and I took a torch, a thermos of coffee, a bar of Ecuadorian chocolate, and two sleeping bags and went ashore for the night. Big Kahuna was not in evidence when we landed, which was just as well. Pete ran us in and took the dinghy back. We piled up cactus and made a fire as it got dark. We found a clear, flat spot back from the seal rocks and spread the sleeping bags. The moon came up, and as our fire waned, there was clear moonlight.

We listened for a time to the sea lion herd settling for the night. We could hear the voice of the bull, still in the water, barking that agonized sound from deep in the throat as though every vocal effort was his last. If you've never heard a sea lion, imagine a large man suffering from laryngitis being attacked by cutthroats (who just succeeded) and summoning his last strength to retch up one last cry of anguish. Thus you approximate the normal conversational tone of the bull sea lion. It is a cry of such primitive inarticulateness that beside it a great Dane sounds like Sir John Gielgud reciting Shakespeare. The pathetic thing about the bull's almost incessant vocal urgency is that nobody pays the least attention to him. He can bellow a warning to sleeping cows that they are being approached by strange, two-legged creatures, and the cows don't even wake up. In fact, cows seldom even look at him, and when they do happen to glance in his direction, they toss their heads as if to say: "Oh *him!* He does that all the time!" But he never gives up except when he's underwater or asleep. Now the herd was all ashore and bedded down as far as we could tell except for Big Kahuna out there in the dark water somewhere, bellowing his head off.

After about a half hour of this, as the moon was sliding to the western half of the sky, Big Kahuna came out of the water. His barking subsided gradually, and he picked a spot for himself and went to sleep. He was a big dark object in the moonlight, raising his head from time to time to bark a short burst and then sinking down to a snuffle. Before long he was snoring loudly. We threw a torch on him once and saw the unmistakable shape of his big head with the prominent bump above the eyes. Cows do not have this bump, only bulls. We concluded that the bump is pure fat. Big Kahuna had positioned himself between us and the herd.

We took the torch inland and went up the slope to the cliff side to see if we could watch the gulls sleeping. But they are nocturnal and were mostly out feeding. The moon was setting now, and it was really dark.

Now as I write about this island, I can still hear the sounds of those gulls on their cliff ledges. For some reason I think of them first when I think of creatures on the Galapagos Islands. Every night they go out to fish, these beautiful white gulls with their large, round, red-rimmed eyes. And they come back in the black moonless nights, as I heard them then, lying high on the edge of a cliff, their sonarlike clicks guiding them to their windy ledges as the sea crashes on the black, sandless shore below. And as the tireless sea booms and sprays and drips below, the gulls talk among themselves, snuggling and chattering in the dark amidst their eggs and chicks.

At the same time, a world away, an insurance salesman comes back to his suburban home in Pennsylvania or Nebraska to share triumphs and disasters with his wife, or to play with his kids. And somewhere two experts, an ornithologist and a sociologist, isolated from each other and from their subjects, will believe respectively that they know the gulls and the salesman because they have spied on their behavior. The bird watcher may describe the lovely creatures. He may crush one of their eggs and note their reaction, but he will not know them even as well as they know him. And the sociologist may analyze and publish, but he may perish too, and he will not know his human subjects until he weeps for some misfortune.

On the way back from the cliff we found the largest land iguana I've seen yet. He was not a record size, but was possibly two-and-a-half feet, tail and all, with a body about the size of the average house cat. He was dazed by the light, and I was able to pick him up. Land iguanas, unlike their marine cousins, can bite—one took a fingertip off a scientist some time back on one of the islands—but this fellow was so confused by the light that he merely blinked. His head was bright orange in color, and he looked at me across a million years. I suppose I understood him better than he understood me, but only slightly. When I put him down he raced wildly off, still temporarily blinded, and collided violently with a low clump of dry weeds and brush.

Back at the sleeping bags, we were startled to see Big Kahuna lying now about fifteen feet from our camp, still between us and the herd. He snuffled and grunted and on occasion barked a somnolent imitation of his waking yelp. He sounded now like a cross between a harpooned buffalo and a regurgitating drunk. I woke up whenever he moved, but he didn't come any closer to us. My thought was for daylight, when we had to get down to shore to get back aboard, and he might think we were disturbing the herd and get annoyed. We could move faster than he could on land but among the rocks and in the water he could do us in with great skill and little effort. But before dawn, Big Kahuna slipped off into the water, as though he couldn't care less about us.

The log entry for August 11 says: "Weighed anchor 0730. Went north to Baltra in hope we'd get word one way or another about the arrival of the new radio equipment. The word we got finally was that it would not get here. (We were relieved. It would have been too big a deal for the Air Force of either the U.S. or Ecuador to be involved in such a maneuver, even if we were to be totally without radio.) We went on past Baltra to James Bay. Up past Roca Gordon where rumor had persisted during World War II that there was a watering station, past Daphne and Beagle Islands (the name Beagle recurs hereabouts as it was the name of the ship on which Darwin came to the Galapagos), past Rabida, under James Island, and around Punta Socuerizo to James Bay, a run of about fifty miles."

It was almost flat calm, and we used the engine most of the way. Boats need motors in these waters. It is possible to drift around with sails up among these islands and die of thirst: The currents will keep you moving and in sight of land without letting you reach shore. Or you might make shore and more often than not there is no fresh water. Forrest knew of two fishermen in a small boat with a cranky diesel engine that conked out and left them to die on Abingdon Island, eight miles long and bone dry. In books on the Galapagos, there are pictures of others—people who hoped till the last choking breath past a swollen tongue that some passing ship would see their signal. It did, in time to set a photographer ashore to take pictures of their skeletons.

James Island has fresh water. It also has wild goats, and there is a defunct salt company with some rickety buildings and a machine shop, also a diesel Land-Rover. At the time of our arrival, it was inhabited involuntarily by two men. The pair had been left as watchmen when the company went into receivership. Then the last of the owners died, and the bank was apparently unaware of their existence.

When we found them, they had been living on goat meat for some time, the last of their supplies gone except for a hundred-pound sack of sugar and about forty pounds of flour. They were down to three rounds of ammunition and six fishhooks. They didn't seem able to catch fish anyway. They kept a fire going all the time because they had run out of matches. They were attempting to devise a method of trapping goats when we came on the scene.

We came ashore rather heavily armed—rifles, pistols, and newly honed skinning knives. They must have thought the company had not only marooned them but planned to kill them. They were literally trembling.

When we learned their predicament, we assured them we would leave supplies for them and that either word would be taken back to Academy Bay of their plight, or the *Beagle* would come back via James Bay and pick them up. They were much cheered when we brought supplies ashore for them: canned food, cigarettes, matches, coffee, and ammunition for their rifle.

Their story was a saga of frustration. Two months earlier a ship was in the bay to pick up a Caterpillar tractor, presumably at orders of the company's bank. It departed without removing them. Before that a yacht had stopped on its way west. The crew sympathized with their plight and promised to set some stores ashore for them, but instead weighed anchor and left without explanation. They couldn't remember the nationality of the yacht except that it was European. Five days before we arrived a twenty-four-foot sloop put in. This boat, with a crew consisting of Mike Bayles, a Britisher, and a German named Hans, was on its way to the South Seas and was still there. This pair, however, was low on supplies themselves. We met Mike and Hans, and after we'd killed some goats, we all had a feast ashore over a huge barbecue pit. Mike had got the Land-Rover going and told us that the marooned men, Abraham and Federico, had dutifully locked the fuel tank lid every evening. That was part of their duty to the company, and they performed it even in the face of abandonment by their employers. Did they think thieves would swoop down by helicopter to siphon out fuel at night?

They showed us a pathetic letter they'd prepared just after the ship took the tractor, in the hope of getting a mail delivery out the next time a piece of equipment was repossessed. In the letter they said, "We are your children and our lives are in your hands," adding a reminder of the 7000 *sucres* in back pay owed them, and asking for food and supplies. I pondered the difference in thought processes produced by different backgrounds: two U.S. citizens marooned in such a fashion would have prepared a letter threatening litigation and bodily harm when they got off the island.

Some months later, I got word that the men had been rescued. One of them went back to Ecuador and the other to Academy Bay. Mike and Hans did not get off for Tahiti as planned. Hans suffered a leg injury and went to a hospital in Guayaquil. Mike is working in Academy Bay, where as far as I know, the twenty-four-foot sloop still waits to set out into the Pacific.

That first afternoon at James Island we made a curious discovery. We were on deck cutting the goat meat into chunks that would go foil-wrapped into the freezer. Virgil was working the walkie-talkie to Bob and H.R., who were on land a couple miles off on the side of a crater, when he said, "I'm getting someone else."

"Who?" we asked him.

"I don't know. It's faint."

"Has our Robinson Crusoe got a walkie-talkie?"

"No. This is in English," Virgil said, holding the unit close to his ear. "Southern accent."

We came close to him, listening.

A faint voice gave a street address and said, "Call me befoah you leave theah."

It turned out to be a cab dispatcher in downtown Atlanta! Here we were eleven miles south of the equator, almost 700 miles west of South America, picking up a citizen band transmission from Atlanta, Georgia, on a five-watt walkie-talkie unit with a four-foot whip antenna.

"How is that possible?" Connie asked.

"Some of those cab dispatch transmitters are fairly powerful," said Virgil, "and then there's 'skip.' You probably couldn't get this transmission in Panama right now. We just happen to be where it has skipped to."

We listened to the dispatcher for a while. He was a voice from home. Then he faded slowly or skipped elsewhere.

That first evening we showed slides of Forrest's on a projector we were delivering to Tahiti for Louis Palmer, Mireille's brother. These were color photos Forrest had taken in 1953 and 1958 in the Galapagos on his first two visits, and aboard his yacht *Nellie Brush*.

In the first minute of Friday—a Friday the thirteenth—we brought up the anchor and eased out of James Bay, in the light of an almost full moon. To get to Narborough we had to recross the equator and round the north end of Albemarle, which is shaped like the head of a sea horse, then drop back twenty miles into the southern hemisphere to the Bolivar channel between Tagus Cove and Narborough. It is a twelve-hour trip.

We got to Punta Espinosa about noon and anchored in a cove bounded on one side by the channel three or four miles wide and on the other three by the most fantastic landscape I have ever seen: Here indeed is Melville's "ash heap of the world." Black clinker slag stretches in tortured acres clear to the foot and up the slopes of the volcanic cone that forms the central part of the island. This metallic crust takes grotesque shapes both from the way it flowed out of the mountain and the way it broke after cooling. It is as though a billion tons of burnt peanut brittle had been thrown out by an angry god. Wherever you try to find footing, the bubbly black ash alternately cuts shoes and hands, or crumbles under your weight and lets you down through crystal bubble shards onto more jagged pieces beneath. It gleams where the silicates have fused, and when struck, it rings metallically. There is no plant life except a rare mangrove tree near the water's edge and, even rarer, a bright green cactus of a type said to be the first plant life, after lichen, to break down rock into soil.

The volcano was violently active in 1825, so this flow could be only 140 years old. On the other hand Fritz Angermeyer says there are flows in other parts of the island that look about the same, but have been identified as vastly older by radio-carbon dating, which looks about the same. There is so little rain and temperature range throughout the year that the three things requisite for soil creation are virtually absent: water erosion, abundant plant life, and cracking from heating and cooling. In spite of the sparse flora, even this desolate area has thousands of marine iguanas, sea lions, crabs, fish, flies, penguins, pelicans, and boobies.

The island is also the sole home of one of the rarest life forms on earth: the flightless cormorant, which is becoming extinct. Some estimates say that only a few hundred exist, and the Encyclopædia Britannica thinks there may be as few as fifty. We saw three, two of them mating.

Apparently these birds have no natural enemies. They are literally fearless. Their courtship and mating is in the open for all to see. If one moves in too close—four feet or so—it will interrupt the process, and the male will turn with his beak open and shake his head from side to side like a scolding schoolmaster, hissing loudly. But if one moves back a respectful six to ten feet, the cormorant will ignore the spectator and get on with the lovemaking. "That," as the joke says, "is *savoir-faire*." The courtship— and we watched it for more than an hour—begins with a weird, unrhythmic dance with the bird lifting its feet high and stepping sidewise and fluttering the stubby and ragged vestiges of wings. At intervals, the male will pick up a twig or stone or a fragment of crabshell and offer it to the female, who will take it and dance awhile and then drop it. After a few rounds of this, he will go into the water and get a fish and carry it back and feed her. This goes until he gets enough nerve to approach her and rub her neck with his. If she is not too coy, he will proceed with his original intention, after which they are likely to go through the whole procedure again. We noticed that she was depositing his gifts of twigs and crabshells in a ring two or three feet in diameter, which was, we imagined, the beginning of a nest.

With no natural enemies, countless generations of these birds have had less and less need for wings—there's nothing to escape from—and they accept humans as another large but peaceable form of life on the island.

The booby is aptly named. He is a fishing bird whose different species are identified by the color of the feet, which are variously red, blue, and gray. We saw some gray-footed boobies, which can make a pelican look like a dub in the angling department. The booby can spot a fish from enormous altitudes, fold its wings back, and become a projectile, plummeting down like a dive bomber. It hits the water at a frightful skull-jarring velocity. But the booby's beak, head, and neck have apparently been designed by nature to take this shock. Otherwise, I'd hate to think any creature would have to make its living so painfully.

When viewed head-on, the booby *looks* like a booby. Its facial contours are set in a sappy smirk. Further aptness of the name lies in the fact that it supplies fish to the frigate bird, not out of generosity, but because it is being robbed. The frigate bird is unable to land on water so it lands on booby birds in flight, taking the prize from their beaks, or forcing them to drop their fish, which the swift frigate retrieves in mid-air. The piratical frigate thus fishes from the booby bird instead of the ocean: a bit of symbiosis flavored with frustration. The booby fishing fleet sets out, usually hovered over by a fleet of hungry frigate birds. When the poor boobies have fished enough to satisfy these buccaneers, they must then fish for themselves.

The penguins here in these islands are slightly smaller and a little less formally dressed than their antarctic relatives. I saw only two up on the slag, although I saw a flock of them in the water.

Like the cormorant, the penguin's wings are vestigial. There is something sad about wings that no longer fly. Melville said of the penguin that it was a failure in all three elements. "On land it stumps, in the water it sculls, in the air it flops." Like the seal and the cormorant, it is a very skillful—maybe even graceful—fisherman. But why did it and the cormorant give up flight? The gull and the booby and the pelican didn't. Perhaps, like Faust, the penguin made a deal with the devil, and sold its flying rights in return for angling prowess and the dignity of a full-dress suit.

A baby sea lion about two feet long had been left—we hoped temporarily—by its mother in a shallow pool formed by a twig crater on a huge bubble in the slag. It couldn't swim yet, but it crawled along with clumsy swimming motions in eight or ten inches of water. We played with it awhile. Two cows came over and made tentative threatening gestures, but apparently neither was his mother. They may have been aunts doing a poor job of baby-sitting. A big bull bellowed at us for a time, but he turned out to be all bluff. When later we went swimming in the water off his beach, he did nothing but complain.

Radio contact with José Luis revealed that the *Beagle* would be delayed one day in arriving. Forrest offered to stay ashore overnight so we could get away. He meant it. We were to leave him a knife and a water jug.

"You're out of your mind," I told him. "What if the *Beagle* sank? You'd be a dead man."

I remembered an account of a seaman lost on this island in the nineteenth century, who "was brought to such extremes by thirst that at last he only saved his life by taking that of another being. A large hair seal came upon the beach. He rushed upon it, stabbed it in the neck and then throwing himself upon the panting body quaffed at the living wound; the palpitations of the creature's dying heart injecting life into the drinker." He was later rescued.

Forrest didn't want to be the occasion of delay for us.

"It's Friday the thirteenth," we reminded him.

He smiled. "I won't die of thirst before Saturday the fourteenth." But I couldn't accept his offer. We would leave the next night.

The sun set. Except for the presence of our ship anchored in the cove, it could have been a sunset of the year I was born, or a hundred years before, or a hundred thousand years ago.

When Gordon Cooper orbited high above the island, there was such a sunset. The crabs scuttled along the shallow pool's edges, and the seals bedded down under a sky made different only by a new, temporary, fast-moving star.

The same sunset took place on some date in the reign of Cheops, where in Egypt it was a couple of hours before dawn and slaves were being kicked awake to begin another day of sweating and straining under the lash as they inched huge blocks of stone toward the half-built Great Pyramid.

And on the shores of vanished Lake Algonquin west of Duluth twenty-thousand years ago, a stone-age ancestor of the American Indian folded the animal skin he'd been scraping and squatted before the tribal fire as the sun set simultaneously on his forest clearing and this yet-to-be-named island 3000 miles to the south.

All the sunsets are the same—except for one in the year 1825. In that year a square-rigger was preparing to sail out of Punta Espinosa into the Bolivar Channel when the volcano blew. Her English captain wrote later of the rapidly heating air and water around the ship. When the temperature got above 130 degrees Fahrenheit men fainted on the deck. He wrote that he feared at one point they would not live to get out. Only after the superheated gases from the cone began to rise rapidly did enough wind rush in from the east to give the ship way, and they were able to put some distance between them and the island. By then, tongues of yellow-hot lava had reached the sea and flashed it to boiling along the shore. Through great clouds of steam and falling red-hot cinders and ash, they moved out into the ocean, but not before the captain recorded the water temperature near the hull at 147°!

In 1962, during Virgil's first visit to Forrest, a volcano on Albemarle let go. They were sitting in the radio shack on the hill when the sky lit up so spectacularly they both thought it was one of the craters on their own island. It turned out to be one of Albemarle's large volcanoes on the south end, sixty miles away. Nature is still building the islands.

On Saturday, we formed a betting pool on the arrival time of the *Beagle*, which Forrest won. He held the earliest time, 4:30, and the *Beagle* came in at 1:30. We went aboard and talked to Fritz, which isn't easy as he is extremely laconic. The girls, Clara and Marlena, had come along, and we all went swimming off the north beach, where the girls collected shells and played with the baby seal. Connie remarked wistfully that the only time she'd had female companionship lately it had to be dampened by her total lack of Spanish and the girls' lack of English.

The girls had managed to round up several dozen fresh eggs before they left Academy Bay, and we transferred these to *Thane*, settled up and took Forrest and the girls to the *Beagle*.

We reboarded our ship at 5:30, brought the Nautisport aboard, stowed everything, rechecked the stuff lashed down on deck, and prepared to set out. The diesel was running, and at six P.M. we brought up the anchor and moved out past the *Beagle* with much waving.

"Nice girls," Bob said as we slipped by the bow of the other ship.

"Nice *people*," I said. "What's wrong with Forrest and Fritz?"

"They're not girls."

It was a point.

We headed out into Canal Bolivar and then north and finally west along the north shore of Narborough. As it grew dark, a wind came down off the slopes of its great mountain, and we made sail in a fresh breeze, moving at nine knots for three-quarters of an hour. When the island was well behind us, we had a lighter breeze, but we still made more than five knots with just the staysail, main, and mizzen. We were on our way. There were 3300 miles between us and the next landfall.

"ATE AT 6:30," says the log, "and went to bed early. I had the nine to midnight watch with Bob, and then in the changeover I had the three to six A.M. with H.R. Sleep was choppy. Also cold. We are still in the Humboldt Current.

"Now the ship becomes the whole world as far as survival goes for those aboard. Again you go over all the questions you've already answered for yourself. Is the fresh water supply good? Could there be a leak in the main tank? If it should leak or the water prove undrinkable, are the plastic emergency jugs OK? How soon can we stow five of them below in case of a blow that might carry away everything on deck?

"The sound of the bilge pump coming on automatically wakens you in the night, and you note how long it runs to pump out. Slatting of rigging is no longer a part of a pleasant background, but a possible source of chafe, and you check to make sure something doesn't give that can't be repaired underway.

"We are setting out over the deeps from which the moon may have been torn. As night comes on it seems deeper.

"The moon came out of the clouds briefly after midnight and showed us Narborough, fading behind us as though the whole set of islands and our adventures there were a dream or a myth. Only the Pacific is real now."

In a movie called *The Big Country*, Gregory Peck played a sea captain who was visiting Texas. His host, speaking with pride of the great land expanses spread out to their view, asked, "Did you ever see anything bigger than that?"

"Yes," said Peck.

"What?" asked his host.

"The Pacific Ocean," said Peck.

"SUNDAY, AUGUST 15—This whole day glided by in Galapagan style, the weather chilly, damp, and calm. With all sail up we managed 5 knots. But again it was ghostly.

"Jerry was the substitute cook, so we all ate at 'Galyean's in the Main Salon.' It was rather good. A sign on the bulkhead invited all to cocktails at 5 in the cockpit. ('Canapes on the Poop,' the sign said.)

"We dressed for this occasion in ties and ascots and socks and shoes and jackets—finery that looked ridiculous on board underway. We hoped a liner would come by and see us. Lucky it didn't, I guess, or it would have taken us in tow and delivered us over to the Happy Farm.

"Wind still down but we glide along. Every foot counts . . ."

It was not quite so chilly that night. The night watches, when the breeze blew off the waters of the Humboldt, had taken to putting a sleeping bag in the cockpit and crawling into it in turns when not at the wheel. H.R. would don a hooded sweat shirt, put the hood up, and pull the drawstring until the face opening was shrunk to a hole for his nose, and then crawl deep into the sleeping bag. Now the helm could be his own lookout, there being nothing to look out for. Each watch at night made one forward check to see if the running lights were on (they can't be seen from aft). Every watch had to record course and speed, weather, and wind and any unusual condition or event encountered during the watch period. This went into the waterproof (!) wheel log, kept in a plastic bag under the seat cushions along with a flashlight and pencil. We found that an ordinary lead pencil was the only writing instrument impervious to salt water. The course logged was always a compass reading. Between here and the Marquesas the magnetic variation is a pretty consistent 10° E (actually 9° in the Galapagos). This means that if the compass showed a heading of exactly west (270°), the ship was really going a little to the north of west. Magnetized needles do not point to true north everywhere in the world. In fact, there are many more places where they don't than where they do.

"MONDAY, P.M., AUGUST 16—H.R. and I had a long talk on our nine to midnight watch about life, careers, time, parenthood, marriage, love, war, politics, death, and taxes. Then we spoke of serious matters such as rock-and-roll music and who'd go below to get us both some coffee.

"TUESDAY, AUGUST 17—Still boiling along at 7 K. plus. . . . The trade winds are steady, and we are ahead of schedule."

The daily position report and the mark on the large Mercator Chart of the Pacific kept in the salon showed our progress. Seven knots seem intolerably slow to a mind set for automobiles and jet planes—it's about eight miles per hour. Sometimes when you're on a turnpike going ten times that fast, slow down where you can safely do so to less than eight m.p.h. and it will seem as though you have just about stopped. The sense of speed is relative. If you have been conditioned for weeks to traveling at a speed a shade faster than a brisk walk and then pick up to seven knots, you feel as though you're really moving. We were now in the fringes of the southeast tradewinds. When you don't stop for lunch or dinner or to sleep, the mileage mounts up at any speed. We made 194 miles in one day (twenty-four hours).

"THURSDAY, AUGUST 19—Little to log this day. This far from land no news is good news. Increasing periods of sunshine. We drive on in excess of 7 knots and the sea is only moderately rough. Levels of swells are considerable, perhaps 20 feet, but they are spaced with such majesty that we ride up and down them without slamming around."

We had no more of the kind of beating we took in the Caribbean, but when the wind dropped below where it would keep sails full we were concerned over damage from slatting. Over long periods of time, this loosened and strained the standing rigging, also the sail seams and shackles.

"FRIDAY, AUGUST 20— . . . the normal chores keep one tired. The good thing about this is that sleep is easy no matter how the bunk pitches. I think we'd stay asleep even if thrown clear out of a bunk."

This entry must have been written during or after a squall. I don't remember feeling tired except on occasions of fast turn-around, watch changes, or special conditions that caused a missed sleep period.

There is an entry in the log on Saturday the twenty-first noting that we stumbled on another gift from Al Startz, our friend in Fort Lauderdale who had supplied us with prodigious amounts of mangoes at the start of the trip. It had been handed aboard during the loading at Fort Lauderdale, and stowed without notice automatically. It was a dozen harmonicas. The plastic wrapping was not intact, and we found that many of them had mercifully rusted. All of them were damaged. But by distributing those which could still sound in part of their range we managed, in the fashion of Swiss bell ringers, to thread our way through some old favorites, mangling them painfully. "After they'd been heaved over the side, three of us dreamed we heard harmonicas playing in the night. Spooky," the log adds.

The next day was Sunday and my turn to cook. I didn't log and don't remember what the fare was, but I recall distributing folded menus wrought in a fine hand and attempting some fanciness, for we'd taken to trying to top each other on meals. We were running out of fresh stuff; the remaining bread was beginning to spoil. I recall promoting the idea that the moldy parts of the bread were the choice parts. "Like a fine aged steak or certain cheeses," I said.

"Or like an old violin," said Jerry, "a moldy Strad will bring more than one where the wood is sound. Any day."

There was the usual Sunday cocktail hour at 1700 with, today, a can of mixed nuts, Boston brown bread and cream cheese, and of course the best-stocked floating bar within a radius of twelve hundred miles (unless a cruise ship lurked over the horizon). I also had a surprise. I had brought along a stereo tape of railroad sounds, recorded by Audio Fidelity for rail buffs, which I had set on the Wollensak. Now at full volume an unseen steam locomotive pounded down on us. This, in the middle of the Pacific Ocean, has an effect that is difficult to describe!

Navigating and cooking on the same day are a challenge. Perhaps, like drinking and driving, they don't mix. I shot star sights after dinner but then did the dishes before I got around to working the shots into a position. The interruption made the figures a little cold.

This day also we had another minor diversion. A squid about ten inches long flew into the cockpit and hit Jerry. This ferocious beast was like a miniature special effect out of a Disney space movie, except that it was quite transparent, like a specialized jellyfish. Squid can apparently jet propel themselves some distance clear of the surface. This may be a protection against pursuing predators, as with flying fish. They are not of course trying to get aboard, but have the misfortune to be jetting just as a sailboat comes into their flight path.

In rough seas flying fish, unable to sense just where the surface is, also shoot out of swells at odd angles. We've had some of them hit halfway up the main and drop on deck.

"MONDAY, AUGUST 23—This morning I spoke to my brother Paul in San Francisco by phone patch Virgil arranged with an amateur operator on the Coast. Quite a network of hams are tuning us in now.

"Later in the morning we rigged a bosun's chair from the gaff of the main for 'ge-dunking,' a sport that involves swinging out from the lee side of the ship and partially into the water while underway. Dixon rode in the chair but was slammed so hard into the side on two occasions that he risked fracturing something. We called a halt. At 1400 miles from land, our margins are cut down and extra safety is called for."

We had had a bright sunshiny morning with relatively little wind, seemingly less than there actually was because we were running before it, and the decks were dry and hot. Some laundry rippled under the main boom and on life lines. After lunch the wind came up a bit, the sea continuing heavy, and some bulky cumulus clouds came up from behind us.

I was readying a sun sight with the Plath sextant. Virgil was sitting on the wheelbox.

"What is the prize," he asked with great casualness, "for sighting a ship?"

"It's for sighting Fatu Hiva," I told him, "and it's a martini in a chilled glass, served by six stewards."

"Isn't there a prize of some sort for sighting a ship?"

"Not that I know of."

"I think there should be. Something like an extra dessert."

There was a silence. Pete was on the wheel. "Seems reasonable," he mumbled, his attention mostly on the compass.

"OK," I said, "an extra dessert for the first person sighting a ship."

Virgil then directed our attention off the port beam, where a ship appeared about three miles off each time we rode the crest of a swell and disappeared when we troughed. It looked like a freighter. As we watched it awhile, it became apparent it was not underway. Virgil went below and tried to raise it on the marine radio, but either we didn't have common crystals (even the distress frequency got nothing from them), or they didn't speak English, or they didn't see us, or they didn't give a damn.

The sun went under a heavy cloud. A couple of gusts of wind came across, and we picked up speed a little. Suddenly Dixon noticed a distant object off the port bow. It stuck up a little from the water—a flag on a pole. A raft? We made for it. Now the gusts were tearing the tops off some of the waves as we changed direction and came up more into the wind. The whole day changed. The sky got darker, the sunlight was veiled, the bow began slamming heavily into the swells, drenching our decks. Hastily we closed the hatches and fetched our foul-weather gear. A light rain added itself to the dampness. The wind now whistled through the rigging.

There it was. A flag on a pole, bobbing along 1400 miles from anywhere and apparently attached to nothing. It was a red flag, solid red with no markings. All sorts of wild ideas went through my mind. There should be 1800 fathoms depth here, but every so often a new shoal is discovered or reported. Did this mean a shoal and a rock awash, discovered since the last Notice to Mariners was published and marked hastily by a Japanese fisherman or a vessel from the Hydrographic Office? We run at night without thinking of such things, watching the compass rather than what lies ahead. What if we'd hit it at night and next morning found a red flag on deck and a broken piece of pole? We would have had a fascinating mystery for the rest of our lives.

We speculated that it might be related to the ship we could still see, and may have marked one end of a fishing net they were stringing out.

"TUESDAY, AUGUST 24—Spoke this afternoon with Harry Ecklund, an NBC Chicago engineer with whom I worked many years ago. There's getting to be quite a crowd on our ham network now. What a strange harvest electronic communication yields. I have visited Chicago many times since I lived there, but my path didn't cross Harry Ecklund's until I went far from the U.S., more isolated than I'd ever been. We reminisced of old times, remembered many faces, many days."

The sea tends to punish smugness. The relatively languid pace of travel sometimes lulls unseasoned sailors into unawareness of the devastating speed with which conditions can change. An incident this night, for example, brought us quickly from tranquility and security into danger and depression, even though what happened was fortunately not disastrous.

After a delicious evening meal of chili and asparagus tips, and *baba au rhum* (which Virgil had two portions of: no problem, as H.R. doesn't care for it), we sat in the salon till late, enjoying coffee and tobacco and conversation. (We may have lived ruggedly at times, but we never lived simply, and often we were living high considering where we were.) We took our leisure in this fashion almost until the midnight watch. The conversation dwindled finally, and some of us began to read. The sea was moderately rough, but the wind had come up enough to offer some steadying influence through the sails (the worst condition for a sailing ship, barring all-out storms, is a rough sea and winds too light to steady and give the ship way). While we were pitching, we were rolling less, and were getting along toward Polynesia at an encouraging seven or eight knots. I finally went to my cabin, wrote some in the log, and got into my bunk. I read for about a half-hour and turned out the light a little after 12:30.

At 12:43 the ship rolled heavily, and a sequence of sounds brought me up out of a mist of dreams. I heard a loud flapping of canvas, a thump from the deck as though it had been struck by something that sent a shudder through the whole ship, then a continuous ringing of the ship's bell and a call from the helm for all hands. I got out of my bunk and put on a harness and handed one to H.R.

On deck a frightful sight met us, illuminated by the high spreader lights. The main was down by the throat, the halyard having parted. The ship was now bucking into seas that had moments before been following, and the bow occasionally dipped under, putting hundreds of gallons of water on deck to wash through tangled lines and cables and folds of sail. I had Virgil take the wheel to keep her into the wind and to free Galyean and Dixon to get the peak halyard loose and the mainsail furled. Pete was below setting switches to get the engine going. We began to lose way quickly, and falling off would have made furling the main impossible. The noise of the wind and sea and flapping canvas was so great that we could barely hear each other. It seemed that in seconds a majestic, helpful sea had become a screaming, monstrous demon, bent on devouring us all. If anyone had gone overboard, it is unlikely he'd have been recovered.

The gaff of the main was swinging wildly. Just before we got it loose, something gave way that made the steel cables in the starboard main rigging twang a deep, doleful sound, like the lowest note on a grand piano, and a shroud rung came loose at one end in my hand. I thought a backstay had gone, and if it had, we had enough headsails up to carry away the mast itself in this blow.

The ship had now lost way completely, and the helm wouldn't answer. The mizzen was sheeted so loose that it could jibe any second. Moreover, Virgil was under it— and it had a tradition of coming down on top of him!

But now Bob and Jerry were getting the main in slowly. On my hands and knees, I crawled through the slashing water on the lee side of our slanting deck to sheet in the mizzen. Virgil was trying the starter, and I remember seeing Pete coming back on deck just as Virgil got the diesel started.

Everything looked peculiarly colorless. The foamy water washing on deck was dead gray. The whole scene had the look of a faded old photograph. Pete fought his way forward on the windward side. *Thane* was slow getting way, and the mizzen was still threatening to fill from the wrong side and jibe. All I could think of, besides praying that nobody went overboard, was being dismasted and dependent on the current to get us to the Polynesian Isles. I may have been eight seconds getting back to the cockpit, but in that brief time I thought of the following things in roughly the following order: My NBC contract (so help me) and how I could make the company believe I was not goldbricking in not showing up on October 11 as agreed; how I could get H.R. out of this mess even if I didn't make it; and how I could get word to Ruth and Deed not to worry. At no time did I feel despair, only annoyance at the delay these events could cause. I had no doubt that if the ship were actually foundering (which of course it was not), the company would all end up in the rubber boats with fresh water and some food and a compass and sextant and flares, and we would either be picked up by rescuers or make our way to the Marquesas.

For some unaccountable reason, as I crawled aft over tangled lines awash in sea water that scuppered off too slowly, I also thought of one early summer morning in the midwest when I walked along a railroad track four miles west of Lima, Ohio, with a cousin. He was fourteen and I was eleven, and we had .22 rifles and were after crows, which were very cagey and kept just ahead of us and out of range. We followed them off the right of way through some plowed fields, where we found Indian arrowheads. It was not so much the events of that expedition that came to me as it was an intense mood—the whole flavor of that time and place burst on my consciousness with all the original colors and smells and feelings. I was able for a brief moment to recreate and illuminate this vision of my early childhood. It was as though the super-awareness that one develops in moments of crisis produces energy sufficient to electrify dark compartments of the mind's catalog.

About the time I was getting the mizzen sheeted in, Virgil had *Thane* headed back into the wind and the main was beginning to come down as the loosened peak halyard was worked. The furling was not too difficult with her head to the wind. The hatches were closed, and we took no water below. The main, finally furled sloppily but securely, was left till the next day, and we continued under power.

Back on course, *Thane* rolled more, but otherwise behaved the same as before, the Pacific once again majestic and helpful. Prospects of full repairs within a day were reasonable. I went back to my bunk. But this time I did not sleep well.

I recall that I was plagued once again with morbid thoughts, darting at me out of the dark like fragments of bad dreams: going overboard, abandoning ship (and hope), reports to surviving relatives, hearing my own will read. I could only dispel this gloom by going over again in my mind all the positions of the safety equipment, procedures in fire-fighting and transmitting May-day distress calls—thoughts less morbid only by virtue of being useful and positive.

"Wednesday, august 25—We took a leisurely start this morning at making repairs. I must say things looked less dire in the daylight, and the damage was light considering the wild flogging of last night. The fabric of main was not ripped. We need to rig a new halyard for the throat, and a new line is needed through the perls on the mast collar. H.R. whipped a cord of three-strand nylon, which proved too big for the purpose, so one strand was removed and the remaining two made into a necklace string. Pete went up in a bosun's chair to reweave the halyard through the block. As we were still rolling, it took some effort for him to hang on. The main was back in business and the engine off after eleven hours.

"On the big Mercator we keep in the salon, I plotted the area where our trouble occurred. The whole area and the distance covering our slightly altered course for those hours was scarcely a blip. I make a dot with a ball-point pen as small as I can to give each day's noon position. It occurred to me that the ship we saw a few days ago, way off on the horizon, had to be inside one of those dots with us, or we would never have seen each other."

Whereas at noon, August 24, we were at 6° 42.8′ south latitude, 117° 21.7′ west longitude, thirty-four miles south of our track, and had made 140 miles in the last twenty-four hours, leaving 1305 miles to Fatu Hiva, our intended landfall; at noon of the next day we were at 7° 07′ south, 120° 10′ west, sixteen miles south of our track, and had come 171 miles in twenty-four hours. It was now only 1116 miles to Fatu Hiva. It was good. But the sea is so vast.

> *"And what is the sea?" asked Will.*
>
> *"The Sea!" cried the miller. "Lord help us all, it is the greatest thing God made! That is where all the water in the world runs down into a great salt lake. There it lies as flat as my hand and as innocent like as a child; but they do say when the wind blows it gets up into water-mountains bigger than any of ours, and swallows down great ships bigger than our mill, and makes such a roaring that you can hear it miles away upon the land. There are great fish in it 5 times bigger than a bull, and one old serpent as long as our river and as old as all the world, with whiskers like a man, and a crown of silver on her head."*
>
> (R. L. Stevenson, from *The Merry Men*)

On August 26, in spite of the total loss of our main antenna in the mishap of two nights back, we got a report through to Jim Smith on the West Coast and a message from Connie to her parents. The report estimated our earliest possible arrival in Takaroa as September 4. Otherwise the day was without incident—though my log entry was not exactly brief:

"THURSDAY, AUGUST 26 . . . In one thin track across 3100 miles of the Pacific up to this point, I have either watched the surface drift by this hull or had it glide by within a foot of my face as I slept. And yesterday's flying fish look the same as those 10 days and 1500 miles back. And they do not know each other. Today's porpoises are as friendly and playful as their cousins north of the Galapagos, and I don't know their names anymore than they do. Do they have need of names? Do they thirst for identity? If not why do I fancy it is important to have identity and a name? This imagined need may be at most an encumbrance. I am taught that a label is necessary because I have a soul. Very well. That is either true or untrue. If true, then I possess this thing called a soul and we'll give it a unique name and sew a label in its collar so it won't be confused with someone else's. But what is the 'I' that possesses this thing? Would 'I' not be just as important possessing another soul or none at all? Where are the names of the dolphin and the flying fish? Where are the tags that identify each drop in the Pacific? If there were names but no drops there would be no ocean. If there are drops but no names the ocean is here. I may be as nameless as these real things. But I am as real as these nameless things. And so I think about them. I am, therefore, I think. Descartes might have said: *Sum, ergo cogito.*

"This meandering is the result of a relatively uneventful day for which we're thankful. We strive to make our lives dull reading. Good weather, safe passage, pleasant sunshine, easy work, swift progress. That's what we hope for and work for. Great living, dull reading."

Sometimes the daily noon position report to the ship's company, issued on legal-size yellow tablet paper, got so wildly embellished that I caught some of the crew looking at me as though I were on the brink of cutting out paper dolls. Here's one:

"August 27—Noontide comments, Containing Facts, Poop, Scuttlebutt, Lowdown and Sundry and Divers bits of Intelligence, not to mention Tips and Verities Concerning the State and Condition of the Good Ship *Thane,* as

well as Position, plus and including Speculation on Abandonment of Fatu Hiva as a Landfall, and Not Ignoring
such Prospects as Making Straight Way for Ye Tuamotus,
together with Calculations on Time of Arrival at Ye Pleasant Port of Takaroa:

Position at noon: Lat: 8° 49.5′S.
                         Long: 124° 05.0′W.

Miles in 24 hours: 102
Course Averaged: 232 Mag (242 T.)
Track to Fatu Hiva: Now 74 miles South of track
Bearing of Fatu Hiva: 263°T
         Mileage: 864
Bearing of Northernmost Tuamotus: 255°T

"Should Fate and Ye Winds drive us so much Southward as to cross ye 10th parallel before we are within a
day of Fatu Hiva we will, rather than beat any to the
North, give up sighting this worthy Island and stand
forth straightaway for the islands of the Tuamotus group,
bringing up Napuka, nearest of Les Iles du Désappointe-
ment, probably named by people who were also unable
to sight Fatu Hiva. Napuka is 141° 10′W. and 14° 10′S.,
and Lies now a Span of 1055 Miles from us. From Napuka it is but 210 miles to Takaroa in a direction 266°
True. Two days would do it."

Bob Dixon, in one of our conversational sessions, com-
menting on Hollywood's influence on our perceptual set,
observed that in movie scenes of men at sea—Humphrey
Bogart, John Wayne, Gregory Peck, and Errol Flynn—
none of them ever leaned, lurched, bumped, staggered,
or fell while underway as we all continually do. In Hollywood's shipboard scenes, the lamps sway, the same as
our lamps, and the tables rock on their gimbals the same
as our table, and on occasion, books, dishes, and cargo
spill forth chaotically, as do our books, dishes, and cargo.
But the heroes always manage to move with unbruised

dignity and suave assurance. They don't even have to clutch handrails and rigging but carry on such routine duties as quelling mutinies and rescuing maidens without a hint of the vertigo and disorientation that send us smashing into bulkheads and flying out of our bunks.

We know from well-publicized evidence that the real-life Errol Flynn on his real-life yacht sometimes vaulted *into* many of the bunks aboard, whether or not he ever pitched out of them, but on the screen he put us all to shame with his superhuman sea legs. There is no such thing as sea legs aboard a sixty-five-foot ketch in heavy seas. But eventually one develops sea hands and sea knees and elbows and even a sea seat, which becomes chapped, calloused, and bruised from salt water and inadvertent sudden sitting on decks and other surprise surfaces.

I find in the wheel log of Saturday, August 28, a notation not transferred to the ship's log. Dixon and I were on watch 0300 to 0600: " . . . 0340 sighted satellite eastbound, descending right past the star Al Nilam . . ." I was not aware at the time that this was Gemini V, launched August 21 with Gordon Cooper and Charles Conrad aboard.

Our noon position report on this date shows 740 miles to Napuka, the new landfall. "Calms in this region in these months," says the Pilot Chart, "are unknown." That may be true. The calm we ran into today was certainly totally unknown to me. I wasn't even fully aware of its presence until the ship had lost way entirely and wallowed and milled and slatted about like a lost elephant. We can't summon up a wind by wishing or cursing, and our fuel reserves are not sufficient to get us to the nearest land. The picture came to mind of a future revised Pilot Chart note saying, "Calms in this region are rare. The massive calm of 1965, which lasted five months and during which several people in a small yacht died of thirst, is an exception."

"SUNDAY, AUGUST 29—H.R. cooked. Another windless day, milling about in oily swells. Started the engine with an eye to investing about a quarter of our fuel in seeking a wind elsewhere. Left sail up to trail. In one hour found a light breeze and shut down the engine. Continued under sail until after midnight . . .

"Shortly after midnight, the mainsail had to be taken in because a seam had started to part. It would have to be resewn in daylight. Wind so light it was a good time to run the engine. The engine started up all right, ran briefly on fuel in the line, and then quit. We spent the wee small hours unclogging the fuel line, while we wallowed miserably and the sea walked aboard through scuppers and over rails alternately from one side and the other. Not too much progress was made through the vasty brine toward our destination."

Julianus, prefect of Roman Egypt 2000 years ago, said of a sea captain, Mygdon by name, that he "went to hell in his own boat, having no need for the ferry of the dead." At night you think of things like that when a fuel line clogs and a mainsail starts to come apart and you're 700 miles from port and the chart notes deny that the wind can behave as it is behaving. But always it becomes better in the daylight. Clouds had balked star sights the last few evenings, but I could almost always get some kind of shot of the sun at noon and morning and afternoon sights.

Wheel log entries are traditionally formal and brief, but sometimes ours contained more than the sparse information required (course and speed, wind and condition of sea). For example: ". . . despite superb seamanship, difficult to hold course of 235." Or, "Well, here we are logging out again. Course held a little south of 235.

Sea like ground glass. Blagh!" Or, "Quartering sea, wind fair. Discussed the esthetic sensitivities and legend of Juanita Mae Schlossenheiler (a college girl at an American university whose nymphomaniacal proclivities led to the boast of an eighty-two per cent conquest of the student enrollment and nine per cent of the faculty.)"

An August 23 entry reads "1800–2100. HRD-GAL. Steered 240°. Wind light and caressing sea balmy as it slaps side of the hull. Had an inspirational songfest of forgotten melodies of yesteryear."

Two of the lengthiest entries reflect the dreariness of certain hours and conditions. The first one, written in a simulated child's hand, reads:

My Watch, by Bob Dixon.

"You can't imagine the thrill I felt when I was told my friend Jerry and I had the 2100 to 2400 watch. We went up on deck a few minutes ahead of time, first making sure to put on our red foul-weather gear. Was it ever dark! Soon we got used to the darkness and could see the many stars and the faintly luminous sea. We talked to our friends Hugh and Pete for a little while, but they soon wished us a good watch and went below. I steered first, from 9:00 to 9:45. Jerry and I talked a lot about all kinds of things. The boat rocked quite a bit. Jerry steered from 9:45 to 10:30 and had lots of fun. I steered again from 10:30 to 11:15, all except for five minutes when I went down for coffee. Finally, Jerry steered the rest of the time. All in all, we steered about 245°, because, try as we might, the sails would slat if we went any more west, and we were afraid of hurting Peter's ship. All in all, Jerry and I agreed we had a lot of fun, and we are looking forward to standing watch again."

The End.

The next morning these two drew the 6 to 10, and Jerry wrote:

My Watch, by Jerry Galyean.

"Boy was I surprised when Hugh woke me at 6:00 and told me I could have the 6 to 10 watch with my friend Bobby Dixon. This seemed too good to be true since I had the watch with Bobby not more than six hours before and had had so much fun that it was sad when we had been relieved by our friend Virgil. Boy! Can he steer a boat! Wow! When I came upstairs (or topside as the real sailors say) there was old reliable Peter steering the boat right on course as he always does. Sometimes I think he can steer a boat even better than Virgil. He told me how beautiful everything was, as he always does, made fun of me, as he always does, and then went downstairs, I presume to sleep, as he always does. Then Bobby and I steered the boat about 235-240 because there wasn't very much wind. The boat rocked back and forth so much that I got sick and puked over the side and decided that I never want to go on watch ever again."

The End.

The next watch logged:

Our Watch, by Virgil Bowers and H. R. Downs.

"220°."

The End.

My log of September 1 devoted a lot of space to a personal evaluation of the trip so far. There had been a number of minuses—disappointments, frustration, worry, physical discomfort—but on balance, I felt that the pluses far outweighed them: The venture had been more rewarding even than my expectations. It occurred to me that one of the many pluses was appreciation of the fact that the distance had been covered, not by taming, but by harnessing the great beasts of sea and air: the water made to float the hull, the air made to move the sails to where the sailor, not the wind, desires. This was part of the joy this trip, but still not the prime factor. Was it the symbolic laurel of having brought off something unusual and perhaps glamorous? Did it lie in the attractions of the end of the journey? The safe harbor, the exotic lagoon, the palm-lined strand, the simple natural life of the tropical paradise? Well, there would be pleasure in the safety of the harbor, relaxation in the lagoon, and perhaps life would be pleasantly simple for a moment. But if it were for that alone, I would have flown to this part of the world and had more time to spend in it.

"In my mind," I wrote, "what tips the scales decisively, what makes sailing here worthwhile and makes me wish to do this again sometime is something extremely difficult to define. It has to do not with the land but with the sea. And it can be glimpsed only once in awhile, on deck at night when there is nothing as far as the eye can see but stars and waves. It can be felt in the breeze, and there is no word for it. To name it is to miss it. The best poets prove only that they have felt and heard it and can evoke a feeble echo of it in their lines. It whispers something and you turn your head to answer, giving it sudden and joyous attention you realize has been long asleep, and then you lose it. While you are straining to hear again, the stars spell it out in a flash of unfamiliar beauty, and then become once more the distant punctual lighthouses sending their guiding messages in prose. In the garish light of your focused effort, it retreats a thousand fathoms down in the black waves and waits for the periphery of your mind. Sometimes in the noon heat you see it add its color to the bleached deck like St. Elmo's fire and you know why you came here to the middle of nowhere and why you would come back. It is the World, or the World's heart, somehow less eclipsed here in the solitude of the wide wet waste than in other places.

"There are these fragmentary sightings of something

indefinable. And there is the understanding that throughout the attrition of all other material, the human body withstands; it does not chafe or mildew or crack or spoil or part under ordinary stress. It builds calluses and muscles and it yields and recoils and counteracts and adapts. And unlike water and fuel reserves, which dwindle, human hope and cheer draw from some secret inexhaustible supply. There is the growing appreciation of the truth that man is part of nature and not an observer of it and that there is no need to try to escape from civilization into nature because it is all the same thing: The boats and skyscrapers he builds are as natural as beaver dams or the nests of trap door spiders.

"It is for insights like these, and whatever else their source might yield, that I would attempt another venture of this kind."

The *Sports Illustrated* writer Hugh Whall put it well in a July 4, 1966, piece in that magazine: "The things that drive a man to ocean sailing must be pretty much the same as those that drive him to drink. For of all sports this is the most habit-forming, the most expensive, the most exasperating, the most exciting, the most soothing, the most strenuous, the most uncomfortable, and the most fun."

According to some authorities the southeast trades blow constantly year round at force 4 in these waters. During the last week we had fitful zephyrs from northeast to east-southeast at less than force 2. And we were still out of fuel range and had to wait for a wind unless we swam ahead.

At this time I had an uncanny sense of land near. Possibly it was psychological, deriving from chart orientation, possibly some subtle message nature sent that did not get to the level of conscious analysis, but was there.

I looked for the signs Columbus got, but he was closer

to land when floating weeds, birds, and cloud formations told him he was near. I saw no birds, the color of the water and the shapes of clouds were no different than they had been 1500 miles back, yet I felt closer to the landfall each day.

"FRIDAY, SEPTEMBER 3—Now we are on the chart which shows the Tuamotus. Starting tomorrow, night watches must keep alert to spot reefs and land as exact position can't be known because of currents and wind drift. Celestial gives good fixes but dead reckoning in between can be slightly off. And 'slightly' could be seriously.

"We all feel tomorrow will bring a wind. If it comes up, we sail into Takaroa; if it doesn't, we'll turn on the engine and burn one-third of our remaining fuel in the hope of picking up any wind among the islands. A prolonged calm is impossible. (This use of fuel was not mere impatience. Our fuel would dwindle even if we never ran the main engine, because we had to run the generator a certain amount of time even if the ship stood still.)

"Nights are now warm and starry. The moon is half full and the sea calmer and warmer. Here is the ocean of coconut islands and outrigger canoes. Far different from the murky, cold, equatorial ocean around the Galapagos and different also from the mid-Pacific deeps a thousand miles west of the Galapagos. Now the water is blue in the daytime, and at night there are reflections of stars in what looks like liquid obsidian. Less than 400 miles now . . . No water crashing aboard . . . Occasional light fresh rains . . . Pleasant sailing.

"All projects other than the voyage itself have suffered some. The oceanographic work is a total loss. The first few days I got almost nothing, because of improper speed. I had thought if I got ahead of schedule I could slow the ship some during the dark-of-the-moon towing hours, but never gained the time. The darkest hours are the important ones, as plankton shies away from light, sinking more than 400 feet in daylight hours, and rises at night. If there is no moon they will come clear to the surface. As it happened, the few successful tows I got were not during the dark of the moon. It is clear that while this project can be accomplished from a small yacht, it would have to travel at controlled speeds and remain in a specific locale until all conditions were right. One understands the need for research vessels specially outfitted for these projects.

"SATURDAY, SEPTEMBER 4—Coming so far south now that we cannot bring up Napuka on this tack. So heading northwest now with an eye to slanting down directly to Takaroa. Don't want to come on any of these islands in the night. They have no lights and are only about ten feet above sea level and are simply not visible even in clear daylight until you are on them. Proceeded back up to 13° 02′ S. latitude. Noon fix shows we're OK if lookouts look alive through the latter part of tonight. There is some worry about the current setting us south. We're supposed to pass well to the north of Napuka and its little companion island Tepoto. (Oddly there's another island called Tepoto far to the southwest—don't know how the islanders distinguish between them.) Wind coming up fine now. Perhaps we can make Takaroa before dark Monday."

At Wreck Bay a month before, we had purchased a quantity of large bars of that fine Ecuadorian chocolate. Now we found that small white worms crawled through the remaining supply. Usually around the edges was the feeding ground and by breaking the bars into pieces we could eliminate the wormy parts. But every bite carried the risk of discovering half a worm left. "Weevil roulette," H.R. called it.

Some of the unusual items we carried aboard deserve comment. We had a supply of paper sheets and pillow cases, sturdy and disposable. The used ones made excellent waste for dusting and wiping grease. You could make up a bunk with them, use one side and then reverse them for another use by turning the sheets and turning the pillowcases inside out. Jerry Galyean suggested we get still further service out of them by erasing them and starting over.

For washcloths we had a disposal product sealed in individual plastic packets, called by the proprietary name "Wet-naps." They were sealed in astringent and aromatic liquid. They saved us some fresh water and much laundering.

Once we were comparing our life at sea with mariners of a century ago.

"Their biscuits were weevily," I said.

"Their rum was warm," someone else put in.

Jerry Galyean said, "And their 'Wet-naps' were dry."

We had been making good progress lately. The swells were not as regular, showing a hint of confusion as though reflected off land somewhere, or shoals. Saturday night I had stayed up through all the watches; I couldn't sleep because of uncertainty as to how close we were to Tepoto. There is a saying that if you hear breakers when the wind is behind you it's too late to work off the reef. We heard nothing and saw nothing. But in the morning a sun line gave a longitude position fifteen miles past Tepoto, and the noon sight gave a fix which, joined to a previous position mark, made a track showing us to have passed within eight miles of that little rock. In daylight we might have seen it. The current was apparently stronger than I'd supposed. Now we were clear for the 200 miles to Takora. If the visibility just held . . . !

"SUNDAY, SEPTEMBER 5—Dixon cooked again. Has it really been six weeks? He stretched a length of nylon rope across the door to the salon at dinner (noon) and met us with a napkin over his arm and a beret, asking in a French accent if we had reservations. He served our last bottle of wine with as fancy a meal as could be arranged in view of our being by now completely out of all fresh food.

"The now routine Sunday cocktail hour was held at 5, again in the cockpit, the weather being fine."

Once in the middle of the night Virgil and H.R. reported seeing a "moonbow." Rain in a squall coming on from the west caught moonlight and made a bow. It was less colorful, they said, and thinner than a rainbow, but unmistakably arcing over a big part of the sky. Perhaps in night rains there are "starbows" too faint to be picked up by the eye.

Laundry aboard was an interesting challenge. During the short legs of the journey it was possible to hold personal laundry and find a laundromat ashore. But west of Panama this wasn't practical, and fresh water could not be spared. Standard operating procedure at sea is to wash clothes in a bucket of salt-water soap solution, rinse them in clear sea water and hang them on rigging and life lines to dry. Pete, Connie, Bob, and I did this. H.R. put pieces of salt-water soap in the pockets of garments and trailed them on lines in the sea. When the soap had dissolved after a million gallons of water had passed through his laundry, he hung it out, running unmentionables up halyards as "discourtesy flags."

Virgil's laundry system was the most drudgery-free of the bunch.

Once I said to him, "How do you keep that T-shirt clean? I've never seen you do any laundry."

"I deep-six everything," he said simply.

And that was his system. He had stowed aboard an enormous store of underwear, slacks, socks, and Bermuda shorts. When it was laundry time, he heaved the dirty ones overboard and broke out new ones. Since they were all alike and new, it gave the appearance of his having access not only to a superb laundry but also to a dry-cleaning establishment.

"I had an uncle who did that with neckties," I told him. "Bought cheap ones, wore them once, and threw them away. He wasn't on the Scotch side of my family."

"I've got a necktie with me. I've worn it four or five times."

And the shirts he wore it with? He'd buy them in port and dump them at sea. On a line between Panama and the Tuamotus you might find a string of the best-dressed dolphins in the Pacific, fitted out in hand-me-downs.

"MONDAY, SEPTEMBER 6—It was after 10:30 that Pete spotted Takaroa on the horizon dead ahead. . . ."

After sailing for twenty-two days and more than 3000 miles, it gives a triumphant feeling to have a landfall straight ahead of you within an hour of the prediction. It was fifteen minutes after Pete first saw the palm trees that I in turn saw them for sure. All these islands are very low lying, and when you strain your eyes for details on a wave-broken horizon you will often imagine you see trees. At length I was certain, and I went below to prepare the prize martini. All of us ceremoniously presented it to Pete. The swells were more like waves now, but we ploughed on under power with fair steadiness. The sun was hot and the decks dry.

We set about the tasks of approaching port. We brought logs up to date, cleared away fishing gear, readied the anchor and mooring lines, wiped and tidied the deck, started straightening bunks and cabins, bundling laundry, readying flags, papers, sealing up liquor and guns, compiling lists of needs, setting the security watch, etc., etc.

Our decks looked pretty clean. Hundreds of miles ago

the last of the diesel fuel in the drums lashed on deck at the mizzen mast had been put in the ship's fuel tanks and the drums pitched overboard and sunk by pistol and rifle fire. Now we looked like a yacht again instead of a barge.

At one P.M. we were approaching the village and the pass, which are on the western end of the island. We hove to, lowered a boat and had Pete and H.R. go out to scout the entrance to the pass. We watched them with binoculars. They found the pass, a long straight channel that looks man-made but isn't: It's cut through a massive protective reef ringing the atoll, under about two feet of water at low tide. We saw Pete and H.R. come up to the dock at the town and lost them. Among the buildings of the town, I could spot the Mormon Mission, which I recognized from photographs I'd seen.

About a half-hour later Pete and a pilot came out from the town. H.R. had gone to the Mormon Mission in search of his sister and the Palmers, Mireille's family.

The pilot was the chief of the island. His name was De De Mervin (pronounced Day Day Mair-van). He is a cousin of Charles Palmer. Mireille was born on this island.

De De Mervin was short and stocky, bronzed deeply by the sun, and probably in his late forties. He was wearing plain maroon swim trunks with a buckled web belt and a narrow brim straw hat—no shoes. Shoes are the last item a Polynesian takes to. Neither was I wearing shoes, but I'd get them on before I walked the crushed stone streets of the village.

Getting into the town dock is extremely tricky. The cut is straight and eighty yards wide, but tide current runs over the top of the reef and can set a ship off to one side in no time if it loses way. Mervin crabbed it in and got us safely alongside. There was a language barrier with Mervin since he didn't speak my one language and I

didn't speak any of his three, French, Paumotu, and Tahitian, except of course for my carefully memorized
phrase asking to be led through the pass, now superfluous.
I did try out the last part of the phrase, informing him
(I hoped) that "my ship draws nine feet."

His eyes lit up for a moment, and then he snowed me
under with rapid-fire Paumotu.

"Sorry, that's it, Buster," I said to him. "Unless your
ship draws nine feet, I can't understand a word. You've
just heard all the Paumotu I have." He already knew I
was unable to carry on in any French more complex than
the whereabouts of the pen of my aunt, so we made do
with sign language.

De De Mervin was most helpful. He had known we
were coming and tried to explain that neither Palmer nor
my daughter were on the island. I didn't find out why
until later and wasn't sure I understood that they weren't
there until we docked and I was able to talk to H.R., who
by then was certain they were not on the island.

Mervin's sister spoke a little English, enough for me to
establish with Mervin that I'd like to use the radio station
on the island to contact Ruth, who was surely in Tahiti
now, and that if he had any diesel fuel we could use some.

H.R. had gone directly to the Mormon Mission to try
to find Dee Dee, although he had a pretty good idea she
had not arrived or she would have been at the dock. On
his way, he encountered a friendly-looking chap seated
on a low wall. "Pardon me, but do you speak English?"
H.R. asked him.

"Yes?" he replied, inclining his head and saying the
word tentatively as if it were a question.

"Is that the way to the Mormon Mission?" He pointed.

"Yes?" said the other.

"Do you happen to know if a young American girl is
here on the island?"

"Yes?"

H.R. says he had a flash of anticipation that we'd yet find Deed here. "She is? She's my sister. Is she at the Mission?"

"Yes?"

"You don't have any idea what I'm talking about, do you?"

"Yes?"

"And you are a complete idiot."

"Yes?"

"I thought so. Thank you very much anyway."

At the Mission he met Elder Garcia, who spoke English. Deed was not there, of course, but Garcia proved to be an enormous help to us. Elder Garcia is not very elder, maybe twenty-five years old. But he has a rank in the church which carries that title, and he heads some youth work at the Mission. He is dedicated to the work and the Mormon faith. Born in Havana, he has lived most of his life in California, and came recently to the islands as a missionary. There was an entertainment scheduled that evening in the recreation hall next to the church and he invited us to attend, provided we didn't smoke while we were there.

The entertainment was most interesting and brought forth more talent than I'd have guessed existed in such a tiny community. People played native music and sang songs that had originated on Takaroa and the neighboring island of Takapoto, and performed some Polynesian dances. The dances ranged from local folklore to Bora Bora, to New Zealand. One little girl who couldn't have been more than thirteen did an absolutely fracturing dance, wearing a flowered lei that covered her only about forty per cent of the time she was in motion.

There were group dances and more solo dances and one grandmothers' dance in which two middle-aged

190

women went through a relatively sedate bit of choreography, punctuated by suggestions of hip movements that recalled more ardent efforts of earlier years, and which each time produced convulsive laughter in the audience. Far from being dismayed, the participants were pleased by the amusement.

At one point, Elder Garcia joined a young girl named Victorine in a chorus of "Moonlight Bay." One of Victorine's parents was English, the other Polynesian. And she had a figure that went right against the grain of the missionary teaching she'd been getting.

Victorine was "a good girl," we were told, and took her religion seriously, respecting all the strenuous taboos. (She was slated to go to the States on a church project.) Pretty nearly everything was taboo. The irony of Victorine's situation was that it would be so much easier for her to follow her chosen life if she were fat or ugly or unfeminine—but she was so young and voluptuous that some stress attended being near her, particularly in men, three of them under thirty, who had been out of sight of land for what seemed like years.

I turned to see the reaction of the audience. Behind us there was a boy of about ten or eleven, who grinned and made an incredibly obscene gesture. I frowned at him, and thought he'd be thrown out, but I guess it was all right: He wasn't smoking.

The next day Virgil arranged for Elder Garcia to communicate with his parents in California. He had been in the islands for ten months and had not been able to be in touch with them at all. We were pleased that this could be done. There may have been some question of the legality of firing up that electronic rig in French waters, but Virgil is never happier than when he can put people in touch with each other.

The log reads: "TUESDAY, SEPTEMBER 7—Hard to get

used to land. But it's welcome. For all the weak and capricious winds we got in the third week of the trip here, our luck was incredibly good. Today a fierce wind blew from the southeast and brought heavy rain with visibility of less than half a mile. The island schooner *Vaitere* stood off outside the pass for four hours waiting to get the right current, during much of which time she was not visible due to the rain. They made one try about two P.M. and gave up after nearly running on the reef. Yet she has an experienced captain who has come here many times from Papeete. If we'd arrived one day later, this is what we'd have faced. We will not attempt Tahiti from the island until the weather improves, though I had thought at first of leaving this afternoon since Dee Dee isn't here.

"The 8 mm. has given up. Salt water corrosion. Hope the film I got thus far has some value. Took some here in Takaroa but with difficulty. Lens ring and trigger are stiff and granulated.

"There is one store with a funny attitude toward commerce. The sales person, a young woman, settled for less than the named price in francs for some soft drinks because she didn't have any change. Then a record in a display case caught my eye, and she put it on a little phonograph she had on the counter. I liked it and said I'd buy it. I thought she didn't understand, but finally realized she didn't wish to sell it because she liked it too! So she put it back in the display case. Next there were some fresh-caught fish we wanted to purchase. She indicated they were not for sale. I was beginning to wonder if this was a store or a private house when she *gave* us the fish. She wouldn't take any money and seemed to think it was funny that fish would be bought or sold: Fish are free in the lagoon, so they were free to us.

"H.R. tried to photograph a child. He wanted something candid but the camera made the child pose self-consciously, so H.R. decided to settle for a portrait. He lined the kid up, and as he squared off for a waistshot, an elbow appeared in a corner of the viewfinder, so H.R. stepped back and refocused to include a little girl who wanted to be in it. By that time, two more had come into the frame and he stepped farther back. When he finally took the picture it was a group shot of half the children in the village.

"I wish we had brought a 16-mm. projector and a French feature film. There are no commercial movies on the island. We could have entertained in return for the hospitality we received.

"We did witness some history. The schooner *Vaitere*, which finally got tied up behind us at the quay, off-loaded a lot of material, heavy lumber and cement, and building supplies for expanding the meteorological station (a general program throughout the islands because of French nuclear testing), and among the lumber and oil and kerosene drums was a small Citroën truck—the first automobile to grace the atoll. It created a sensation. If it has a collision, it won't be with another motor vehicle."

There were almost thirty passengers aboard the *Vaitere*, most of them seasick. She had come from Tahiti, and I thought Deed might be among those getting off. She was not. Among the arrivals, however, were two young Australian chaps, Buddy and Roger. Buddy had one leg missing. They had brought diving equipment with them and intended to spend a month diving in the lagoon. In Papeete they'd made arrangements with Elder Garcia to live with a family on the island. Although they were not Mormons, Elder Garcia had been a great help to them too, as he was to anyone who needed help. Buddy had lost his leg as a result of a motorcycle accident. He had been riding behind Roger, and they went off the road and got badly smashed up. Buddy's mangled right leg had to be amputated above the knee. He did not use an artificial limb, didn't think he needed one. He got around well with metal crutches. He said his diving wasn't hindered in the least. We were all going diving together in the morning of the eighth, but we never made it, because of a small unhappy incident.

The day it rained I got wet and stayed that way for some hours. This was nothing new: I'd been wet for long periods aboard. But the rain was cold, and I ended up with a stiff neck. It was not severe and not particularly painful, but I couldn't move my head freely. Late the afternoon of the *Vaitere's* arrival I went aboard to talk to the captain. I took an area chart and showed him my planned route between the islands. He told me how the currents run and showed me an alternate route to the west of Apataki. He thought it might be a safer route if the visibility was down. (I didn't tell him that if the visibility was down I didn't want to try at all. I'd wait.) I thanked him. When I left his cabin, I noticed the gangplank was crowded with workmen unloading material. So I climbed over the rail and jumped to the dock. The ship was within three or four feet of the concrete, and the drop was not more than six feet or so, but when I hit I seemed to have dislocated something in my neck. I got a bad pain in my left shoulder and down the arm, and I gradually lost all feeling in my thumb and forefinger. I found out later a disc had slipped in my neck. (I had probably damaged four discs in my spine, one in the neck and three farther down, when I went overboard in the Caribbean. The surgery I underwent later in the year did not involve the disc in the neck, which gradually went back into place with the help of a supporting collar I wore for some weeks. The pain in my shoulder and arm and numbness came from the squeezing by the disc of nerves leading to the arm from the brain.) I went back to the ship and stretched out on my bunk. I learned in the next days that I could put the fire out in my arm by relaxing on my back. Sometimes after holding my head still this way for a long period I began to get feeling back in my hand. But I couldn't spend the rest of the trip in my bunk, and right now I had to get through on the island's radio to Ruth and find out why Palmer and Dee Dee weren't there.

I finally got a cable through to Ruth with instructions to go to the cable office and talk to me direct via Takaroa radio. Our set on shipboard was useless for that short distance.

While waiting for word on why Deed hadn't made it here and whether she and Ruth had even made it to Tahiti, we visited an uninhabited island immediately to the north. We got to it by wading across about 400 yards of reef averaging knee-deep water at low tide. Several similar islands in a circular chain make up this atoll. The one we visited was a typical desert South Sea Island, idyllic even in bad weather, but I'd hate to be marooned on it. Coconuts are hard to open, and we couldn't find any breadfruit trees.

We took the two Australian boys out in the Nautisport to the lagoon to scout diving locations and saw here some absolutely beautiful under-water scenery. I could see it from the boat with a hand-held glass-bottom viewer: coral heads up to within three feet of the surface and coral formations like castles with bridges, cliffs, exotic plants, animals, fish showing off as though auditioning for a South Sea Isles movie. There were pearls down there, but no pearl fishing was permitted this year—the government opens it only often enough to take out surplus. Without this conservation, pearls would have vanished by now from the island waters. There were dozens of types of bright-colored reef fish, the shellfish tridacna, lobsters and crabs, crayfish of the kind the Portuguese call Langostina. And down to a depth of sixty or seventy feet the water was still clear and brilliant in color under the high sun. This scouting took longer than I thought it would, and the tide was pouring into the lagoon at about six knots when we started back. It boiled over the reef on each side of the channel like rapids, and we had trouble making way against it with the boat loaded. I felt as though I needed to lie down when I got back. Buddy joked about my useless arm and his missing leg and said between us we'd make about one and a half divers. He was being kind. He was a good diver even with a leg gone, but I knew I was luckier than he whatever discomfort I was undergoing. Back at the ship I stretched out on the deck until the pain in my shoulder subsided; it didn't really take long. I was lying there when the man from the radio shack came to the dock, saying he had word that that evening at eight I could talk directly with Charles Palmer and my wife. They'd be at the cable office at the Papeete airport. That was a load off my mind. Even if the call didn't come through I now knew she was there. And the weather was clearing. We'd leave tomorrow for Tahiti.

The wind was still strong. We had a military kite aboard, and we flew it from the quay, to the great amusement of the village children. They couldn't figure out why we were flying it. Truthfully, neither could we. It was designed with self-inflating louvered fins and had a high angle of attack relative to the wind. It flew almost straight up. It was called the "Slim Jim Parafoil," and its inventor designed it to fly an antenna wire for transmission from liferafts.

We had dinner aboard at 6:30. We had invited Chief Mervin and his wife and sister but they declined, although the chief had had lunch with us once. Perhaps he felt he'd have had to reciprocate—and there were seven of us. Later I gave him two cartons of cigarettes, and he promptly gave me a shell necklace, which was several cuts above the tourist-trade necklaces one buys at the Tahiti airport. What started as a gesture of gratitude had turned into a formal exchange of gifts.

The Australian boys, however, did accept our invitation to dine aboard this evening, and over coffee we speculated on whether a dictionary of Paumotu existed. Buddy suggested that one of us compile a dictionary and phrase book for tourists and yachtsmen. We concluded that, with a yacht coming here once every six months on the average and charter ships moving through the islands every month or so, we could sell enough to get all of twenty-five cents a year in royalties. As the party loosened up with the hospitality, we began to make up useful phrases to go in our phrase book. Among the more noteworthy suggestions for the island phrase book were: (At the bar:) "Madam, you are standing on my neck." (At the laundry:) "Don't starch my loincloth." (General:) "Which direction is the club car?" (All purpose:) "Your attitude is un-American." (At the doctor's:) "May I please have a pre-frontal lobotomy?"

Hatches were always wide open for ventilation while we were tied up here. One night when we were asleep, a cat wandered in and panicked when he couldn't find his way out of the after cabin. The poor thing began bouncing off walls, then scrambled across my chest and fell on Jerry's head, Jerry being in a settee bunk just below my bunk. Sound asleep, Jerry stated clearly and matter-of-factly: "That hurts." Later he disclosed that he was having a dream about a pain experiment. The people conducting the experiment had attached a device to his head and began closing it until pins on the inside stabbed the skin of his face and head. He was to tell them when it began to hurt. This dream must have unrolled in a split second. Jerry, however, thought not, and that it was a coincidence that the cat landed on him just at the moment the pins touched him.

"WEDNESDAY, SEPTEMBER 8—We will leave today. It's more than five years since I first studied charts of the Tuamotus and decided the best time of day to leave Takaroa for Tahiti (5:00 P.M.). The distance between Takapoto to the southwest and Apataki is a safe, deep, night run. Daylight is needed to thread our way among the next set of islands and the following night will again be clear of islands and reefs. Weather is clearing nicely . . . Even in ideal weather, it is possible to come to grief unless the navigation is sharp and cautious. There are many accounts of ships that cross the Pacific without mishap and end up wrecked on a reef in these islands. The reason, I'm convinced, is that one gets the attitude: "Well now I've got it made. I've crossed the big stretch. Now this local stuff is duck soup. I can relax now." The truth is there are comparatively few dangers in the broad expanse of the Pacific. The dangers are many here in these low islands. The currents are strong and variable. The weather and winds are less consistent. The reefs are often barely submerged and sometimes out of sight of land. I'm determined to be more cautious now than when at sea in the long crossing. And I need the visibility for sun and star sights and keeping track of where we are at all times. Since Takaroa is the god of wind and sea, I trust our stay here bespeaks the reverence he is due and that he'll reward us with safe passage to Tahiti. Now that Charles Palmer is not here to go to Tahiti with us, we will need the smile of Takaroa."

The radio call finally came through. I talked to Palmer and Ruth and Deed, who were all gathered at the cable station between Papeete and the airport. Now I learned the reason they hadn't met me in Takaroa: Palmer's commercial schooner had recently been wrecked off Etearoa and was in fifteen fathoms of water.

Without particularly striving for punctuality, we had started to move away from the quay at exactly five P.M. The moon, nearly full, had risen exactly forty-seven minutes earlier. There was a crowd at the docks, some of them working on and off the *Vaitere,* but most of them there to see us off. There were a few young men and women, but mostly they were middle-aged or older, or children under fifteen. As in all small communities in today's world, the young adults found no reason to stay in this village. If they had talent, like Mireille, they might go half-way round the world. There were jobs in Papeete for those with more moderate abilities, and at the very least, a girl with reasonable looks and youth could be assured of income in Tahiti if she were not too severely indoctrinated with missionary morality.

The sun went behind a low bank of clouds as we were casting off, softening the deep colors of the island and the lagoon beyond the town. The red roof of the Mormon Mission took on a maroon shade. I looked for Elder Garcia in the crowd, but couldn't see him. But we were to meet again, although I didn't know it then.

The tri-color rattled stiffly in the breeze on the flagstaff over the weather station as *Thane's* bow swung out into the narrow pass. The tide at that moment was still pouring out of the lagoon as from a giant mixing bowl. As we turned to head out, we moved sideways past *Vaitere* at four knots, the stern clearing by only a few feet.

Bob Dixon was aloft and piloted. He could see the underwater walls of the channel far out to the open sea. With just enough power to give control to the helm, we glided by the quay at what seemed great speed, borne along by the current of the island's emptying lagoon. The children waved.

The sun was down, and the low silhouette of Takaroa blended with the horizon as the wind strengthened and we heeled stiffly to starboard under main mizzen and staysail and watched the moonlit outlines of Takapoto's palm forests to the south. Then it too slid behind us and with our lee rail down to the water we took up a course of southwest for the night. At dinner the gimballed table stayed in one position: tilted as far as it would go to port. Tahiti was 300 miles away.

It is difficult to grasp the sparseness of the scattered islands of the Pacific. The Polynesian islands are scattered over four million square miles of water, yet their combined inhabited land areas are less than four hundred square miles.

How did people get to these islands?

Te Rangi Hiroa, a Polynesian on his mother's side, is an anthropologist who became Sir Peter Buck, and was once Director of the Bernice P. Bishop Museum and Professor of Anthropology at Yale University. He supports this theory, widely held by professionals.

Man must have originated somewhere near the Middle East. Whether in Africa or Asia, his original home was on that side of the world. Many thousands of years ago, through endless migrations, he had spread over those continents and to the new world via the bridge between Northeast Asia and Alaska, walking across the ice between the Diomede Islands. The feat seems prodigious, but the distance from Mongolia to the southern tip of South America could be covered at an average rate of tribal migration of two miles a year within thirty thousand years. This is, of course, a small fraction of time in the life of man. Thus man apparently came to live on both shores of the Pacific before he occupied both Atlantic shores.

Human stock had developed very early into three main types: Mongoloid, Negroid, and Europoid (Caucasian). It was the Mongoloid type that migrated the farthest. They were the ancestors of the Incas; the Japanese (except the Ainu); the Patagonians; the Siberian and Canadian Eskimos; the Huns; the Seminoles, Iroquois, and Apaches; the Malaysians, Tibetans, and Georgians; the Mayas and Aztecs; and the Koreans, Chinese, and Vietnamese. Long before any seamanship was developed, these people covered every large land mass but Europe and Africa.

An Oceanic Negroid type appears to have been forced by peoples behind them down the Asiatic corridor of Indonesian islands into the Pacific. But they did not come as far as Polynesia.

The Australian aborigines moved down the corridor later, crossing to the Australian continent from New Guinea. While the primitive animals of Australia, the monotremes and marsupials, arrived at a time when the continent was connected to the Asian mainland, the land bridges had long vanished before such higher mammals as cats and deer or rabbits and monkeys had evolved. Man, then, certainly had to arrive by boat. Wood Jones says the Australian aborigine with his women and dogs arrived at Australia "not as a castaway, but as the navigator of a seaworthy boat." Navigation, like man himself, is older than we tend to think.

It's likely that up to this time no people had reached any of the Polynesian islands because of the enormous ocean distances involved. At some point another wave of Oceanic Negroids moved through the corridor, probably completing the evacuation of the Australian aborigine from that path, and moved on to the Solomon Islands and

Fiji, part of Melanesia. Those who came this far are known as Melanesians; those who ventured no further than the southeast tip of New Guinea are called Papuans.

Where did the Polynesians come from? They arrived late in the world's history. They are neither Mongoloid nor Negroid. And they did not come through the Solomons and Fiji.

Thor Heyerdahl tried to prove they had come from South America by raft. He proved the trip could be made by doing it himself on the famous raft he built and named *Kon-Tiki*, but few anthropologists credit his theory. The Polynesians are not Mongoloid, as were the ancient peoples of South America.

While the term "Europoid" seems to be a catchall category into which are placed those human types neither Negroid nor Mongoloid, and it is an admitted oversimplification to try to force pure racial identity on a pure Polynesian, or a blond Scandinavian, the fact is that the Polynesian people are Europoids. Europoids can be blond or brunet, tall or short, dolichocephalic or brachycephalic in cranial type.

A branch of Europoids with probable ancestry in India moved east, according to anthropologist Buck. There may be traces of the Mongoloid in the people who arrived at Polynesia, he says, but they are only traces. And they came, not through Melanesia, but through Micronesia, the group of smaller, more scattered islands north and east of New Guinea (the Carolines, Marshalls, and Gilberts). And, considering the equipment available and the facts known about the universe, they were the greatest navigators the world has yet produced.

They arrived comparatively very recently. Tens of thousands of years after Mongoloids had come to the plains of the American midwest, the ancestors of the Polynesians were still three thousand miles west of Polynesia.

They may have come to Tahiti as late as A.D. 200. They probably were not there when Homer was singing the Iliad.

Because the sweet potato grows in the Polynesian islands, and because it comes from South America, some anthropologists believe the island navigators had spanned the Pacific at its widest part, hundreds of years before Columbus crossed the Atlantic. If one can get to Easter Island from Tahiti, it's no trick to get to South America.

We read they accomplished these feats in "canoes." The word canoe is a complete misnomer. The expedition of the explorer Captain James Cook chose to call all the native craft "canoes" and the name stuck. *Thane* is a ketch sixty-five feet overall and about fifty-three feet on the waterline. The Polynesian ocean "canoe" was a double-hulled vessel (the ancestor of the catamaran) up to seventy-five feet long with four times the deck area and more than five times the interior volume of *Thane*. It carried whole communities with livestock, plants, and soil, as well as great quantities of prepared foodstuffs and fresh water. W. S. Kals, in an article in the August, 1965, *Motorboating*, claims the voyaging canoes were a third longer than Cook's ship *Endeavour*. This would give them a length of more than 130 feet. The Polynesians were not exactly "small-boat" sailors.

Granting them the seamanship, how did they arrive at distant places and then come back to their starting points? We locate ourselves by mapping land and water areas and imposing on the globe a system of polar-coordinated grid lines. To the Polynesians the sun rose in the east and set in the west, and most of the stars traveled set paths; a few, along with the moon, wandered, but very early they noted the patterned behavior of the moon and its phases and locations in the sky. It is possible that by the time they came to Hawaii in the north they were aware of the curvature of the earth.

A very sophisticated navigation can be developed without knowledge of the true nature of the universe. A compass can be made without a magnetic needle by marking the bearing of the sun's rising and setting through a year-round pattern. A calendar can be made with accurate seasons marked by counting days and noting when the sun rises farthest south of east and north of east. This marking device can be carried to sea. Both north and south of the equator, whole groups of stars, instead of rising in the east and setting in the west, are seen to move around a point in the sky. In the northern hemisphere that point is so close to Polaris that the ancients considered it a pole star. (Its precise location is just enough off the pole point to make a landfall error of fifty-four miles either side of an island in running down a latitude, but this was not crucial in returning to islands like Tahiti or the Marquesas, which can be seen from that far away.)

Running swells in open ocean distances are consistent for long periods of time even in temporary shifts of the wind. By trimming the sails of a craft to the wind and then checking direction changes by swell direction and star and sun risings, long distances can be traversed with a reasonably certain heading.

Currents must have puzzled the old island navigators. (They can puzzle a twentieth-century sailor: I can vouch for it.)

It's worth noting, again comparing *Thane* to man's earliest large ocean vessels, that with a well-designed hull and ballast keel, rigging of nylon, dacron, and steel, and well-cut dacron sails, *Thane* can do 9½ knots in a stout breeze and average between five and six knots, and the Polynesian voyaging canoe is estimated to have averaged seven to eight knots.

Kals claims that the Polynesians may have carried with them species of birds that cannot land on water. When released, these birds will climb high and make for land if there is any in sight. If not, they will return to the ship.

Whatever their methods, the Polynesians spanned the Pacific from Asia to South America, and maybe to North America, long before the Vikings ventured out of sight of land, and possibly before the Phoenicians were plying the coasts of Europe and trading dye and pottery for tin ore in the British Isles.

The art of Polynesian navigation collapsed along with their religion, their happiness, and independence, soon after the explorers Wallis and Bougainville and Cook separately visited the islands in the eighteenth century. The stone tools, the shell-craft, much of the folklore, and the seamanship, soon vanished. The big carved idols expired in weed-choked groves, the great canoes rotted, and the temple drums and shell trumpets sat silent in the museums of strangers. In place of these things they were given Christianity, venereal disease, gunpowder, and European responsibility. According to Diderot, one old Tahitian chief, seeing the islanders crying when Bougainville's expedition ended and the French sailed away, told his people, "You should have wept, not now, but when they arrived . . . our customs are wiser and better than theirs . . . we knew only one disease—old age . . . they have stained our blood . . . (with) the ravages that follow their wretched caresses."

Are the South Pacific islands ruined? Of course they are. Anything is ruined when it changes if conditions preceding the change are used as a standard of judging.

The islands have been changing since they were first formed and thrust up out of the ocean. They are ruined now that the French are doing their nuclear testing there. Up to that moment they were unspoiled. They were ruined by World War II. Up to that time they were Paradise. They were ruined by the time the painter Gauguin got there. Prior to that they were perfect. They were ruined by the arrival of Oriental traders. Up to then they had been free. They were ruined before that by the arrival of Cook. Up to that moment they were idyllic. They were ruined when the Portuguese navigator Quirós spotted them in 1606. They were ruined when worship of the god Oro was imposed by force on Polynesians by Polynesians and the violent wars between Oro and the older god Tane were fought through the islands. Up to then they had been orthodox. They were ruined when the old god Takaroa was retired in favor of his son Tane. Up to that time the faith of the ancestors was observed. They were ruined, if you can look at it that way, when men first came and the coconut crabs and reef fish and the birds felt the first impact of a strange and crafty intruder who promptly set about to change the appearance of the islands by felling trees and spearing and netting edible creatures who had owned the lagoons since the beginning of time.

But in another way, they will never be ruined. They are there, and the sun rises and sets and the tides pour in and out and the winds blow and the stars look down on all the coral and volcanic rock and the vegetation and animal life. A man is merely a small part of this, whether he was born here or is just visiting, whether he is the recipient or author of happiness or unhappiness. He may find himself here or he may ruin himself; he cannot really ruin the islands. Whether he brings a new god or an antibiotic, an automobile or a business, an atom bomb or syphilis or cynicism, he will see, if he looks closely, that the islands are as they always were: in their steady, beautiful, timeless state of ruin, beckoning and awaiting the next intruder with promise still capable of fulfillment and with benign resignation.

"THURSDAY, SEPTEMBER 9—About 9:30 sighted Apataki, the N.E. tip called Point Teonemahina. Current seems negligible according to D.R. Glided past Aavere, Parao, Tekomapao, Tamaro and Totoro, beyond which was the wreck of a large vessel run on the reef long enough ago, and marked on the British Hydrographic Office Chart. What a way to be immortalized!

"Lost sight of land about noon and made to Faro, easternmost island of the atoll Kaukura. Spotted this at 3:30 P.M. and passed within a mile. From here in a straight line to Tahiti it is open water. Made south through the night with some cloudiness but generally good weather. Light winds. If wind not better for S.W. course, we'll tack tomorrow.

"FRIDAY, SEPTEMBER 10—Open sea all day. Bathed on deck. Water quite warm. Air moist and tropical. Not terribly hot though. Did some photography. Worked on assembling stuff to go ashore at Papeete.

"Virgil and I talked with a ham operator named Guy aboard Destroyer Escort Calcera, headed for South Pole for Operation Deepfreeze. They are 2500 miles northeast of New Zealand. The ocean is not crowded . . .

"In the evening a full moon rose behind us (we had tacked to west at 2 P.M.) and a clear sky tops a warm light breeze out of the N.N.E. Tomorrow by dawn we should be in sight of the high mountains of Tahiti. We are now south of latitude 17° S. by about 5 miles (noon sun line). I will have the midnight to 3 watch tonight."

The next morning we kept looking to the west and a little south where Tahiti should appear. We were moving along at just under five knots, but we had not gone as far during the last two days as we had intended. A morning sun line gave a rough longitude a little to the east of our expected position. This delayed our sighting. It was hazy-clear but still possible to sight tall mountains like Tahiti's for 40 miles or more. Nothing.

"I wonder if it will look the same from a distance as when Cook first saw it?" one of us asked.

"Which direction did Cook approach from?" I asked.

"The south," said Dixon.

"How do you know?"

"If you're talking about the *Endeavour,* his first ship, he came west on about nineteen south latitude and then came north onto Tahiti. I saw a map of his track here."

The sun climbed higher. There were two or three of us standing in the bow constantly, straining our eyes for a first glimpse.

I went below to get the Plath for a noon sight, which I took perched on the doghouse. Virgil had given me a radio time-tick before my morning sun sight. (We were getting them now from Hawaii. From the beginning of the voyage through the Galapagos, we had gotten them from Washington.) I made a couple of sights and found the sun still climbing. Astronomical noon deviates from twelve o'clock depending on where you are in your time zone. It comes when the sun is at its highest point regardless of what your watch might read. A person standing ten feet away from you to the east or west will have a different noon from yours. At that distance, it's a negligible fraction of a second, but it is still different. You can calculate the exact time of astronomical noon in advance only if you know your exact longitude. Now, crossing a noon sun line with the morning sun line moved as far as the ship had moved since morning, we would get both the longitude and the latitude determined by the maximum height (noon) of the sun.

Between shots I kept looking over my left shoulder off the bowsprit to see if Tahiti was visible. As the sun neared its maximum height, I noticed something about the sky ahead that gave me an idea why no one had seen Tahiti yet. It was clear of clouds but hazy. I didn't want to miss the moment when the sun was at its height, but I didn't want to say anything yet.

Expecting to hear "land ho!" at any minute I went on until I got the noon sight and wrote the time and elevation. Then I went below and put the sextant back in its box.

When I came on deck and looked again, I was fairly sure of what I was seeing. Well above the horizon, there was a change in color along an irregular line. The gray-blue of the sky seemed to come right down to the water, but at this serrated line it became a shade more neutral and just the faintest bit darker. I had been looking much closer to the horizon for a sign of land. So had the others.

"Land ho," I said as softly and matter-of-factly as possible.

☆ XII

~~~~~~~~~~~~~~~~~~~~~~~~~~~~~~~~~~~~

PETE WAS TRADITIONALLY the first aboard to sight land. "Where?" he demanded incredulously when I made my statement. "What do you see?"

"I see mountains. Big ones."

Virgil was the next to see them. Then everyone traced the faint ragged edge of Tahiti-iti and beyond it to the north the high peaks of the main part of the island. Instead of appearing on the horizon, it had materialized out of the haze, its towering peaks now within thirty-five miles and becoming more distinct each minute.

Well, there it stood.

"I guess we made it." I grinned at H.R.

"Not yet. That might be Martha's Vineyard. And we might sink yet."

"I'll paddle us in the dinghy from here. Or we'll swim it."

"What are you going to do first when you get ashore?"

"You have to ask?"

"I'll tell you what I'm going to do second: get drunk at Quinn's."

"Yes, and eat a washtub full of green salad. That's third."

The wind dropped. We turned on the engine and took in sail.

The palm trees on Point Venus rose out of the water, and late in the afternoon we glided by this northern tip of Tahiti and down Matavae Bay to the entrance at Papeete. It is well marked. There are range towers lined up with the narrow cut in the reef, and just before sunset we turned into the harbor.

A cutter came out. The harbor was almost mirror smooth as we turned east along the low, red-roofed buildings lining the waterfront. On board the approaching government craft were three women, all looking Tahitian with straw hats and shell leis, and skin darkened by the sun. Two thirds of them were mine. The other third was a friend of Dee Dee's, the daughter of Walter Grande, member of Parliament and, as it turned out, our landlord, since he owned the house Ruth had rented.

The launch came alongside, and three harbor officials helped the ladies aboard. Dee Dee stared at my beard for a second as though she was not sure it was her father and then shrieked, "You look wonderful!" Her eyes shone, and she said, "Your beard makes you look younger!" That stopped me. And then I realized that the reason I have always felt a beard made a man look older is because, when I was young, old men had beards. Today young men have beards; middle-aged and old men are clean-shaven.

Dee Dee's friend's name was Hinano. She was an intriguing mixture of Polynesian, French, and German Jewish, quite good-looking and sixteen years old. It was busy on deck getting lined up to back into our berth, but none of us could help staring at our guests. Ruth told me about their house and how they'd watched from it all day for us. I went below with the government people.

Our French flag was already flying, and this puzzled

harbor officials who thought we must have entered in the Marquesas. I was tempted to tell them we entered at Mururoa where the bomb testing was being set up, but that might have caused difficulties. It was hard enough for them to believe we had entered at Takaroa, since that is not a proper port of entry. But we had got a cable by radio from the French Governor General permitting it. It hadn't impressed De De Mervin the least. But the Chief has never been overwhelmed by bureaucracy.

They assigned us a berth among the two dozen or so yachts tied up stern-to along the street. Anchored off the bow, and with crossed stern lines springing the ship into a forward position from bollards made of old cannon buried muzzles-up in the ground between the curb and the concrete sea wall, *Thane* rode between the forty-five-foot ketch *Monsoon* on the starboard side and *Heather*, a little sloop of twenty-eight feet, which had been sailed there single-handed by a South African named Larry Nilsen.

We were careful to set the anchor dead ahead of the bow since there were so many anchors out in a row that fouling risk was heavy. Larry Nilsen later told us of a scuba diver who lived there who used to eke out a living by clearing fouled anchor lines. He discovered a way to create work for himself: when he submerged to unfoul one anchor he drifted down the line and fouled two others. It was a long time before the yachtsmen caught on to him.

It was completely dark when the paper work was finished, the coffee drunk, and things enough in order to go ashore. I had as yet not set foot on Tahiti.

I stood on the stern for a moment. Ruth had gone ashore earlier to bring the car up. The lights of motorbikes and scooters and cars and trucks streamed by with their big-city sounds. Out toward the harbor entrance the marker buoy flashed. The range lights were on now, but there was enough glow in the west to see the north outlines of Moorea's mountains rise into a cap of clouds. The mooring lines creaked. Pieces of cardboard carton and small boards and scum had gathered under our stern and against the wall. A French soldier ambled by between the yachts and the street. There were trees at intervals nearer the street than the sea wall and one of these half-shaded a nearby street lamp.

Pete came on deck. "Ruth told us where there's a good restaurant."

"Yes. She'll be here with the car in a minute." When Connie came on deck they decided to walk to the restaurant. Dee Dee and Hinano and three of *Thane's* crew were already at the place, two blocks beyond the post office and up a side street.

"It isn't what they say it once was," Pete sighed, watching the traffic.

"You didn't really expect the canoeloads of bare-breasted girls?"

"No, but this is just another city." He helped Connie off the stern of the boat.

We said we'd see each other later.

It was a city, but not just another one. It has its own character, and I was not grasping it at the outset. The only things I'd heard before arriving were that prices are relatively high, inflated by the great surge of tourism in the last five years, and by the presence of the French military in large numbers; that pure Polynesians were scarce in the city; and that Americans were not particularly welcome.

The first of these is true. Imported things are beastly high in price, and island items have followed the upward trend to the extent the traffic will bear. There seems to be little effort on the part of the French to curb a crippling inflation.

The second is also true. Pure Polynesians, whatever that originally meant, seem relatively scarce in downtown Papeete. But actually few of the islands, I learned, have what can be called "pure" Polynesians now because the idea of racial exclusivity is usually not a part of the culture of a people cut off from other races. If they tended to stay to themselves as islanders, it's because no one else really came there until European navigators caught up with their skill and arrived from the east.

The third idea I'd brought with me—that Americans were not welcome—is false. My impression derived from the fact that the American Consulate on Tahiti has been opened and closed a number of times because of ambivalent feelings by French officials (in Paris, not Polynesia) who struggled between the attraction of the American tourist dollar and the complications of NATO and French independence, plus regard for security in France's nuclear testing in the islands. The Polynesians, the Asians, the mixtures, the French businessmen, and officials in Tahiti are all really most cordial to Americans, we discovered. And the tourist bureau is doing a splendid job to make things as pleasant and rewarding as possible for Americans or any other visitors to the islands. Their regulations and rules are reasonable and relaxed and their information is accurate.

Ruth pulled up in the little rented Simca. I threw the duffle ashore and jumped to the ground.

After loading the car and explaining why I held my neck that way (I was still learning the hard way not to jump) I drove, at her direction, to the little house high on a mountain overlooking the harbor and the town. I knew that I would appreciate it even more in daylight but the view at night was spectacular.

We went back to the restaurant where we formed the second shift. Dee Dee and Hinano had established a beachhead and ordered for the boys, who arrived after their chores and promptly pounced on someone's salad. I explained to the girls that these men were suffering from scurvy and beriberi, and that piracy of salads was a symptom.

Virgil found a hotel near Point Venus. Jerry and Bob and Pete and Connie continued living aboard for a few days.

Later that night, some of us wound up at the legendary Quinn's. There are times when Quinn's is quiet: 7:30 in the morning, for example, or five minutes of noon. Otherwise it is not quite believable even when you're inside watching what's going on.

Quinn's Tahitian Hut, as it is called, bills itself modestly as the "happiest bar in the South Pacific." Its fame is worldwide. It has a sturdy frame of hewn beams underneath an exterior of split bamboo and pandanus panels, built somewhat in the manner of Tudor exteriors, the bamboo appearing to be embedded in pandanus and the whole façade painted bright yellow and blue.

When the activity is at a minimum, there are only half a dozen motorbikes parked outside. When things are swinging, the sidewalk is choked with them. Once inside, it's like a painting by Hieronymous Bosch. You start to back out, convinced the place is on fire and that others are trying to get out too. In the dense pall of smoke, people seem to be caroming off the walls and exploding in and out of doors at the back. The crowd at the horseshoe-shaped bar is four deep, and a huge mass of flesh of approximately two sexes dances to recorded music of ear-splitting volume. Everyone acts as though things are like this all the time. And so they are.

But somehow people get served, people get acquainted,

people dance, and after a while benign smiles transfigure their faces and they order still one more round in what they now agree is indeed the "happiest bar in the Pacific."

The only coeducational public toilet I ever saw is at Quinn's. The men's area is farther from the door than the ladies', so technically you go through the ladies' room to get to the men's. There is not only no lock on the door, there is no door. I seem to remember a beaded curtain or some such in the opening. One might think such an arrangement would cause trouble, but with so much trouble going on out front all the time, it didn't really matter.

One night a fight broke out at Quinn's, during the course of which closing time arrived. The head bouncer whacked the bar with a bung starter and made himself heard over the din to announce the hour. Everything came to a standstill. Then combatants and spectators all moved to a bar up the street with later closing hours, and the fight was picked up where it had been broken off.

A single road rings the entire large part of Tahiti, with dead-end side roads leading inland for short distances. The small part of the island (which would be a separate island if the Pacific were 100 feet higher) has roads on two sides, but they do not join. These roads dead-end and leave the tip of Tahiti-iti pretty much as it was a hundred or a thousand years ago.

Sitting at Vaima, a sidewalk cafe on the main street, you see Papeete go by—on its way to work, on its way home to lunch and rest, or so, and again at quitting time.

The most beautiful girls on the island are the racial mixtures. Different proportions of Oriental and Polynesian and French ancestry have produced some of the loveliest sights imaginable.

Mireille arrived on the twelfth from the States, and there was a great reunion with her parents the Palmers, her sister, and her brother Louis. For years Louis had been in the French army and had been imprisoned for over a year and under a death sentence, in Algeria, until he was able to escape. Also present was Bob Thornton, owner of the Mai Kai restaurant in Fort Lauderdale, who came to Tahiti to update his Polynesian review at the restaurant and to acquire material for new costumes. He helped in the bringing off of the big birthday surprise for Ruth. I had been planning this one, with Mireille's help, for more than two years. I never planned one as far in advance, or had one come as close to total disaster as the 1965 Birthday Surprise.

This yearly event—Ruth's Birthday Surprise—evolved from the original attempt to surprise Ruth on her birthday about three years after we were married. At first it was not a "yearly event," but roughly every other year, until it mushroomed into a monster under the challenge of trying to top myself each successive time. In the twenty-three years we've been married I've attempted eighteen of these bashes with varying degrees of success. There've been a couple of out-and-out bombs, but I'd say fifteen of the parties have been successful and fun. It gets more difficult each year to come up with something surpassing, but I'm trapped in the tradition.

Ruth knew that in 1965 she'd be in Tahiti over her birthday, but she didn't know exactly what to expect.

The original plan I'd worked on with Mireille involved an enormous *tamuré* (like a Hawaiian *luau*) to be held on Bora Bora, with war canoes and leis and roast calves and pigs and almost the entire population as guests. But it seemed very far out to me, and although the estimated approximate price was not out of line, it was all too big. Finally we made it a little less ostentatious and moved it to Moorea and then to Tahiti itself.

But it very nearly never happened.

It was to have been the nineteenth, a week from the

Sunday Mireille arrived. She had set it up with her first husband, a man with the unlikely name of Hiro Levy, owner of the Princess Heiata Hotel and producer of excellent *tamurés*, to arrange with the owner of a piece of land on the neck of the island south of Atchoun's famous place.

All would have been superb except that a heavy rain started the evening before and didn't let up for three days. I couldn't get hold of all the guests to make sure they knew it was postponed for a week. I had to keep the more complex details secret another seven days. I was naturally disappointed with the change of plans, and I couldn't find Hiro. All these things made me behave in a very un-Polynesian way: I worried. I cursed the weather. Then gradually I learned that those I hadn't been able to reach were not in the least distressed—some assumed the weather washed out the affair, others traveled out to the place and discovered the obvious cancellation. In either case they took it in stride. The Polynesians don't worry. You took life as you found it. (*When* will we be able to teach these backward people to develop ulcers and heart disease, to get apoplectic about little things! How have we failed?)

The first weekday we were there, H.R., Deed, Ruth, and I drove around the island. The flowers are incredible —as though some association of florists with unlimited resources had arranged them along all the mileage of the road—the small gardenia called *tiare Tahiti*, frangipani, Bougainvillea, and hibiscus. There were neat patches of growing taro, coffee, or vanilla, and coconuts. Mango, breadfruit, grapefruit, and avocado grow between the road and the swift-rising tangle that hides the "rotten rock" of the base of the mountain. There is a memorial to King Pomare V, the last king of the island. He drank himself to death with Benedictine and a large stone-carved Benedictine bottle tops his monument. There are grottos and waterfalls, the bridge where Edgar Lateeg, the artist, was killed on his motorbike, the house Marlon Brando rented while he was filming *Mutiny on the Bounty,* the ruins of an ancient temple, private homes ranging from large, thatched, one-story mansions with neat palm groves and manicured landscaping to small, thatched, one-story huts with sand and coconut husks for a yard. But it is the same sea behind all the dwellings on the waterfront, the same view of the open ocean, of Moorea rising abruptly and majestically from the horizon to display its many moods and colors depending on weather and the time of day.

At the end of the circular road, out the little dead-end stretch to Tautira, we stopped at a house where Robert Louis Stevenson is said to have lived. A talkative old Swede now ran the place. Apparently the house hadn't been changed much since Stevenson was there. Kerosene lamps lighted the way to a bath not adjoining any rooms, and guests might, if they wished, fix meals on a primitive cooking facility.

Beyond Tautira Point where the road ends, there is a path part way to Vaionifa Pass. From there on, it is rugged going on foot. There are two anchorages beyond Aiurua Pass to the south, but they afford little shelter since the prevailing wind is on-shore. H.R. and I went to the end of the path where we saw some net menders who looked at us as though we might ask them directions into the ancient past. Then they resumed work.

Gauguin's home and the Gauguin museum were quiet places. We were the only ones in the museum at the time. Many of the painter's valuable effects have been assembled and arranged to tell the story of his life, but nowhere on the island—not even in the museum named for him—is there a single Gauguin painting.

Next day we ploughed through accumulated chores: assembling and filling out forms to mail back film, taking stuff to the dry cleaners, trying to get the passports back with extended visas for everyone, taking the rifles and ammunition to the harbormaster's office, as we had promised when we came in, sending off some letters and cables, contacting M. Gilloteaux, the head of tourism, for permission to film, checking the airlines for space out on October 4, setting up an interview with Governor Sicurani, off-loading last-minute items from the ship and leaving those necessary for Pete and whoever came out to sail *Thane* back, trying again to get in touch with Hiro Levy about the *tamuré* (now scheduled for *next* Sunday), without Ruth's finding out. (This I finally left to Mireille.)

At the police station, a bureaucrat fixed me with a baleful glare. He had all our passports in his clenched hands, and his attitude indicated they'd never come back into my possession.

"Where did you enter?" he asked. He had a British accent flavored with French, and would have been good in the movies cast as a bureaucrat in a Tahitian police station.

I told him we came in at Takaroa.

He'd never heard of it.

"Why didn't you come in at the Marquesas? That's the port of entry, you know."

I told him we'd cleared into Tahiti, which is also a port of entry.

"Yes, but you stopped before you came to Tahiti. At Takaroa." He looked at a list of islands, scanning it with his pencil tip for some time.

"Takaroa," he said ominously, "is restricted."

Takaroa had gone on some kind of list because of the weather station going up there. I didn't tell him the governor knew I came in to Takaroa. So now I was a spy. I let him stare at me for a while and then I said, "So?"

"Furthermore," he went on, "you plan to leave Tahiti by plane."

"That's right."

"All but one of the people whose passports I have here are reserving air passage out of the island. You can't do that."

"Oh?" Now I looked at him sharply. "I thought the big fear was that people would come here and not be able to leave the island."

"Yes. Precisely. You cannot come in on a ship and disband the crew. There has to be a guarantee the ship can be sailed out of here."

He had me. We were all crew. I had put up bond for everyone, but hadn't thought of this hitch. He was going through the passports. He isolated Pete's.

"If Mr. Jackson is left here, can he sail the ship away alone?"

"No." (Even Connie was flying back.)

"So you are in effect stranding him in the islands. We get this excuse all the time, Mr.–uh–Downs." Here he took my passport and looked at it. He looked at the photo and then at me. He exuded suspicion like sweat. Usually one's passport photo looks like one, however unflattering. Mine had been taken more than a year ago and showed a smiling beardless face topped by a conventional haircut. What he was confronting in person was a dark-skinned, bearded man, thinner (and certainly older-looking in spite of my daughter's theory about beards), and topped by a short, ragged thatch of faded, almost bleached, gray locks, growing in not too well at the front. I hadn't even been to a barber for a trim.

I felt slightly embarrassed.

At length I said, "The ship will get away. The owner is

sending men from Washington to help sail her back." I held out my hand for the passports.

"I'll keep these until some satisfactory guarantee is offered that you aren't leaving Mr. Jackson."

I was on the brink of doing something stupid like asking to speak to his superior, but I checked myself. To humiliate a man like this would create a string of red tape sufficient for a ticker-tape parade. We didn't have the time. There was no real problem. The authorities at the top knew without affidavits that Pete Jackson was not a potential ward of the state and that *Thane* would leave before the expiration of visas, properly manned and outfitted.

When I went back two days later I smiled and held out my hand. He gave me the passports without smiling, and darned if he didn't ask me again, this time almost conspiratorily, why we came into Takaroa.

I couldn't resist. I said, "I'm interested in your methods of tracking fall-out." And I left.

M. Gérard Gilloteaux, head of tourism, proved most helpful and reliable. He manages a French schedule and way of life in a paradise of lotus eaters, and he does it without a single ulcer or any abnormal blood pressure.

He cleared our photographic equipment, listed points of interest, didn't try to encroach on our editorial freedom, and even got harbor charts for all of Tahiti and Moorea. Eric Cridland, his assistant, was also most resourceful and helpful. Arrangements were made for an interview with Governor Sicurani for Wednesday, September 29.

Five days after we had arrived in Tahiti, we sailed to Moorea. Ten minutes out of the harbor and it was like old times. Pete seemed more cheerful: We now had two passengers, Ruth and Deed.

At the mouth of the harbor, just before going out the

narrow break in the protecting reef, we saw a shark. It was the first shark any of us had seen on the whole trip. We had somehow come through eight hundred thousand dolphins, millions of flying fish, sea lions, tuna, and everything else to be found in the deep and had not until that moment seen a shark.

My daughter was in high spirits—and a bikini—when we started, and she detailed the shark sighting in a lyrical and highly unnautical entry in the wheel log: Five minutes later she was seasick.

The map of Moorea looks like a child's drawing of an island. It's a triangle with the point down and with two fingerlike indentations in the east-to-west base. The easternmost indentation is Cook's Bay. With a high, jagged skyline on each side, yet with a strip of beach and flat groves all along the water's edge, it is protected and beautiful. Cook sailed in here on his first visit and saw, on the shore where the Aimeo Hotel now stands, the massed warriors and canoes of the Mooreans. They were setting out to fight Tahitians, but Cook, misunderstanding, made a judicious decision not to try a landing and sailed away.

Moorea is the "Bali Ha'i" of Rodgers and Hammerstein's *South Pacific*. From the sea, one sees no evidence of man except thatched huts. These "huts" are two of the most sophisticated hotels to be found in the tropics, but their appearance doesn't mar the landscape. On the island, there are two jeeps and a truck, enough traffic for a collision, but not enough for a jam; but there is no pavement, no structural steel visible, and what glass there is on the island is bottle-shaped and discreetly helps furnish three well-stocked thatched bars.

We anchored off the beach west of the Bali Ha'i Hotel. The whole group ate ashore that night at the Bali Ha'i. There was an Indian movie company staying at the hotel. India's total motion picture output is number two in the world. Only Hollywood tops it in quantity. While the quality of many Indian motion pictures is less than grade B, there are a number of excellent pictures produced for the international trade. The industry works feverishly as though to overtake Hollywood and become number one. They are the Avis of the motion picture world.

Next morning Ruth and I got one of the jeeps for a half day and made a circuit of the island. The side toward Tahiti is not quite so fresh as the north shore. There are some tide flats and swamps in places, and the road is a bit rugged. However, there are good bridges over the rivers and ravines. On the west tip of the island is the Club Méditerranée, a unit of a franchise system of hotels, international in scope, but catering more to European than American clientele. A long stretch of beach leads south from the club frontage. About a half-mile along the sand, past several homes, I saw a sublime adaptation of an alien and imported device: an outhouse. It had been erected just inland of the beach, but instead of facing the woods, it faced out, and instead of four walls, it had three: the entire front was open to the sea. Here was the finest example I'd yet run across of good sense accommodating to puritan pressure. The occupant of this box-like, wingback chair could serenely contemplate the coral sand, the surf, the ocean and birds and clouds to a distance of fifty miles.

This eminently sensible adaptation of an incomprehensible custom is parallel to an event said to have occurred in Samoa when the missionaries uncrated great bundles of cotton T-shirts and distributed them to the women to cover themselves. This made sense to the women. Cloth is valuable, the apparel was surely in fashion in the civilized world, and there were advantages to being possessor of such a fine and gleaming white garment. But the fabric irritated their nipples. This proved to be only a momentary problem which the natives solved with a direct resourcefulness often missing in conformist cultures. The next day the donors were horrified to see the T-shirts defaced with two large holes in the front through which the forward parts of the chest fitted proudly and comfortably.

We got back before lunchtime, and while I was returning in the jeep, Dee Dee came running to me with the news that she'd been asked to be in the Indian movie, and could she please, *please*, accept because it was her big chance and because a great, glamorous, artistic, wealthy future stretched out from this piece of good fortune if I would just for once avoid being stuffy about school and all the things I get so stuffy about all the time. I waited until she had settled back to within a foot of the ground. Finally she had to take a breath and I got a word in.

"What kind of a role is it?" I asked.

"Oh, it's a very good one—he said it would take about three weeks and it's to be in New York—they're coming there because this picture is about an Indian couple who go around the world on eighty cents a day and when they come to America they meet this girl in New York who is Indian. I mean she lives in the States but she's Indian even though she's American and that girl would be me if I can take the part he says I *look* Indian and Oh *please* can't I? I could go to school in the evenings and not miss anything!"

Another breath. This girl may have an operatic career if she can sustain vocal tones this long without breaking for air.

"And it's all planned that you're to go to his room tonight to study the script. Is that the schedule?"

"Oh no, nothing like that, Daddy; he wants to talk to you; he said it can't be a real offer unless he talks to you and gets your permission."

"Who is 'he'?"

"The producer, Mr. _____."

"Dee Dee, don't get your hopes up, because this can't be done. You're going to a new school that isn't in New York and your schooling comes first. But I will talk to Mr. _____. It sounds as though it might be a bona fide offer. If it is, there'll be others, which you'll be wise to decline until your training is farther along."

I could see from her face that my stuffiness had hit a new high. Every emotion, every mood, every thought and feeling my daughter has, washes across her face like an infinitely sensitive system of signal flags. She'd make the world's worst poker player. As I looked at her I picked out the following information: (1) She believed the offer was real and knew herself to be sharp enough to spot a come-on. (2) She'd expected resistance from me and was not surprised, hence not really as hopeful of bringing this off as she'd have been if my reaction had not been anticipated. (3) Deep down she knew she was too unseasoned to plunge into a film career at the expense of schooling, part of which was an excellent drama workshop. This all was so apparent that I looked at her with new pride. She was, thank God—though female, good-looking, and sixteen years of age—a girl of sense.

Still a part of her wanted this with the consuming desire characteristic of the young. Now that she had stopped talking, her eloquence increased. She turned on a look that made me feel like a butcher holding his child on a chopping block with a cleaver aloft. I hoped my gaze hid my momentary wavering.

"I'll talk to him," I said. "Where is he? Maybe they'll be doing a picture sometime in New York and you could be in it when it won't interfere with school. The more you train the better you'll be."

The moviemakers were set up on the shore in front of

the hotel huts. They were doing a sequence in which the Indian couple on their eighty rupees a day, or whatever, were apparently hitching a ride on a small native catamaran used by the hotel as a garbage scow. This vessel had been built by an American nut who intended to sail it to Hawaii. It looked just about seaworthy enough to get to the other side of the reef and back without sinking. It had an eighteen-horsepower outboard auxiliary now which could possibly make one knot against the current and three with. The trip to Hawaii had been attempted but ended prudently while Moorea was still in sight, in what may have been the only burst of common sense the dreamer-builder had in him.

The scene was a strange one. Turbaned Zanucks were giving directions in a British accent to a Polynesian canoeful of girls in *pareus* and saris, *lava-lava*-clad Tahitian crew members, and a hotel manager in Bermuda shorts. They ground away at this floating United Nations for a few minutes and then took a break for a couple of hours. I went over to where Mr. ———— was having a lemonade in the shade of a coconut palm.

"My daughter says you think she ought to be in pictures."

"I do," he said. He offered me a cigarette. "I'd really like her to be in this one. Let me show you something. Maria!" He called to the Indian girl getting off the catamaran. "Run get a sari—the one we tried on the girl this morning." Maria raced off to one of the huts. "We do everything on an opportunity basis," he explained. "Even casting. We'll be shooting in New York in a few weeks and we'll find someone for a part we have in mind, but she'd be perfect, your daughter, if she could do it."

I explained why she couldn't. He gave me his card, and hoped she might be in India sometime. He was always making a movie and apparently she would be welcome

in any of them. Like many directors he was not the least
concerned about talent, and also like many, he had the
scripts to these epics largely in his head. If he seemed like
a hack, at least he didn't appear to be sinister. Deed
came down to the beach looking more shy than hopeful, if
it is possible to look shy in the eight square inches of
a bikini. Maria then reappeared with a sari, which they
draped around Dee Dee and, by George, she could have
passed for an Indian Princess. She looked more Indian
than Maria, who even had a caste mark. Dee Dee's eyes
are more Mediterranean than Indian—and like her
mother, she is taken for Greek, Italian, Spanish, Near
Eastern or a certain type of French—but in a sari she
was right out of an olive grove in Hyderabad.

"Perhaps next time," Mr. ——— smiled at her. "You're
very beautiful."

Her disappointment was assuaged by the compliment,
and her pleading this time was only perfunctory. Maybe
she was even relieved. At least the offer had been real,
and there was glory in that.

Three trips with the dinghy got everybody back aboard
the ship. The trip back was not so rough. There was no
seasickness but it took a little longer.

It was dark when we came into Papeete harbor for
the second time. The excellent range lights make the approach easier at night than in daylight, but it's scary to
glide through that opening in the reef without being able
to see when you've passed it. You know only that if you
keep the lights lined up you won't run aground. The harbor was flat calm. The city lights gleamed and the traffic
streamed, and somewhere over the noises of cars and
scooters and bus horns, a strain of recorded Tahitian
music floated across the water. The nightly activity was
beginning. The shops were shut up, and before long, even

the waitresses would be through work and would start
to live.

As we tied up, we saw film director Frank Bibas on the
quay waiting for us. He had arrived that evening for a
week or ten days of work on the filming in and around
Tahiti. He had brought along some raw film stock and
some ideas, among other things.

H.R. and Bob stayed on board for an hour or so to
check for personal belongings and certain project items.
The rest of us sat outside at Matavoi for some dessert
and coffee. After a while, I went down to the waterfront and found the boys and the car gone. I was puzzled.
They wouldn't have used the car to go to Quinn's. I
walked back to the restaurant and sat awhile longer.
They showed up at about the time the place was ready to
close, and each ordered a large drink.

"Where've you been?" I asked, wondering if the drinks
were gilt on an already golden lily. But they were cold
sober.

"Wait'll you hear. . . ."

They had been working below deck when they got a
distress call from a bearded fellow who was crewing on
a yacht down the line. The owner, a New Zealander, was
ill and had to be got to a hospital. Bob and H.R. rushed
down to find the stricken man in severe convulsions. They
thought it might be epilepsy. They helped two other men
get hold of him and stuff a cloth in his mouth, to keep
him from biting his tongue badly.

The ill man was very strong, and the seizure had not
really subsided even after they got him up to the car. As
they were trying to put him inside, a Peugeot swung in
beside them and a young fellow in jeans and a striped
T-shirt jumped out. "I know the way to the hospital," he
said. "Follow me." The man struggled some on the way,
but the three of them kept him from hurting himself and

in ten minutes they were at the emergency entrance behind the Peugeot. The young man joined them, and the five of them took the stricken man into the hospital emergency ward. The T-shirted stranger disappeared, but Bob and H.R. waited; from time to time they inquired for details of a nurse at the desk. She could tell them nothing.

After a few minutes the young Peugeot driver reappeared from within, removing a white gown. H.R. said he wondered if it were a Tahitian custom for a good Samaritan to accompany emergency cases brought into a hospital.

It turned out that the young man was a Dr. Thooris, one of the best medics on the island, who just happened to be passing at the moment they were trying to get the unfortunate yachtsman into the car. We learned later that the victim recovered from the seizure and returned to New Zealand.

On the seventeenth Deed had to fly back for school. Farewells at the Faaa Airport are sentimental affairs, for no one leaving can ever be going to anyplace more beautiful than Tahiti. Departing guests weep and stagger under massive collars of shell leis. (The tradition used to be flower leis, but plant materials cannot be taken into many countries and insects can't be shooed out of pressure-sealed aircraft, so now it is shell leis.) If fifty people are departing Tahiti there will be 500 at the airport. Deed's departure entourage exceeded the average. What with her friends and Mireille's relatives and *Thane's* company, the scene resembled—and in a way was—that of a movie star taking queenly leave of the scene of her triumph. She wore a white travel suit and twenty pounds of shell leis that looked like a regal collar of fat ermine. We waved and smiled and threw kisses and as Deed carried her flight bag and make-up case out to the ramp,

Ruth clung to me as though the gesture would propitiate the gods of flight and weather. I noticed the tears on her cheeks.

"Is it because she's leaving," I asked, "or because she's grown up?"

Now THERE was one less of the convivial and motley group which had comprised our private convention in the paradise isles.

Two days later there were two less. Virgil returned to Long Island and to his endless communication with the world on electronic equipment undamaged by salt water. The night before he left he invited us to a dinner at his hotel on Point Venus.

He was clean-shaven and dressed somewhat as I'd seen him when I first met him in New York. I'd got my beard trimmed and had carefully combed what hair I had, and had donned a tie.

"Seems odd not to have the deck pitching under us, doesn't it?" I said during the evening.

"Or to see you drinking a martini out of stemware."

We discussed the fact that, the whole first day ashore, the ground had seemed to move constantly. Virgil told us of a man who suffered seasickness for weeks and finally got over it only to get landsick as soon as he stepped ashore.

There was much rehashing of the events of the voyage. I was glad Ruth had got a chance to get better acquainted with this man, whom I was proud and lucky to have got for the trip. His temperament and ability make him a wonderful sailor. These are attributes that count more than previous nautical knowledge. If I ever do it again, I will ask for Virgil Bowers.

Next day it rained. We photographed some interiors aboard, stuff too difficult to get while underway.

Frank Bibas made a deal with Larry Nilsen and Pete Munch, a yachtsman and half-owner of the *Windwagon*, a ketch en route around the world and in Tahiti for some weeks, to help out in another sail to Moorea, to free *Thane's* crew for photographic purposes. He also bought a lot of heavy lumber and clamps and with Pete's help made an outrigger platform for Jerry to stand on while photographing *Thane* from an otherwise impossible angle.

We had met a French parachutist named Malau, who was to go with us to Moorea with his camera (and a proneness to *mal de mer* as bad as Dee Dee's. Fortunately the trip is only two hours, or I think he'd have died. He's a good diver, a good parachutist, a good photographer, and a game guy, but an unlikely sailor). This second trip to Moorea was not due until the day after the *tamuré*, which was still a secret from Ruth. Parachutist Malau was invited to attend however, when it finally came off, and became the twenty-sixth person entrusted with the world's fastest-leaking secret.

Early Sunday, we went to the market. This is one of those teeming *souks* where every vegetable- and fruit-grower, fisherman, and two-bit wholesaler brings his catch, yield, produce, or harvest. Private citizens mingle with shrewd restaurant buyers from five in the morning until about eleven A.M. to noon, when every vestige of their wares has been removed and sluiced away with firehoses. The market area is an immense, shed-roofed, concrete platform without walls, with gutter ridges running at intervals through the whole area. At five A.M. on a Sunday morning, it's crowded and it smells of fish. You can buy milk in plastic bags, flowers, shell crowns, octopus, yams, any species of fish, beef, pork, vegetables, tripe, and horoscopes in French—it's all there till that early-day closing time. Then no ghost of it lingers in the clear, hosed-down concrete.

It had rained, and I left the market dejected and wet, thinking of the difficulty I'd have telephoning everyone that the party was off for another week. I went back to the house in a black mood and lay on the floor. That was the only place I could find relief for the now frequent pain from the slipped disc. I could no longer even lie in a bed or sit in a soft chair without a great deal of discomfort, and I had to harden the car seat and back with boards. Yet I thought that coddling myself was bad, and I continued to jump off the stern of the ship when coming ashore, and jump down from the high running board of Walter Grande's Land-Rover. On Moorea, during a climb in the hills, I had pushed myself thinking I might thus loosen up and help cure the difficulty in my back and neck. This amateur diagnosis was probably making things worse. As the doctors told me later, it may have worked to fragments two already herniated discs, and caused further damage to two others.

One time in Tucson, Arizona, I watched a tableau enacted several times a day at a place called Old Tucson, where a very realistic gun fight is staged by stunt men, with special effects that make it look for all the world as if live ammunition is ripping up the place and people are really dying. One fellow "dies" high on a storefront, drops to a shed roof, rolls off it onto the street, and hits like a sack of fresh steak. His wrists and ankles are reinforced and he is slightly padded but otherwise he is without protection. As we talked between the shows, he told me that once he had a bad back—could barely walk, and was in constant pain.

"That must have put you out of commission," I said.

"Oh no, I had to go on workin'," he said.

"You went on working? Falling off that roof with a bad back?" My mouth fell open.

"Yep. Sometimes I'd lay there with tears in my eyes and thought I was like to faint, but it gradually got better."

Either he was tougher than I or he hadn't busted up his discs in falling.

Now Mireille left. I said good-bye to her Sunday night although her plane was not due to leave for a couple of days. We, however, were going back to Moorea and would not return until after she'd gone. She said she would make one last check with Hiro about the *tamuré* but of course she wouldn't be there when it came off. And Dee Dee was gone. Maybe by the time it came off there would be *no* guests, and Ruth and I would have to row the war canoes and wear all the flowers and eat all the roast calf by ourselves. OK, we would. (I was thinking more like a Polynesian every day.)

Monday morning I took Ruth to the seaplane base at Faaa, whence she left for Moorea. We got away in *Thane* about ten o'clock with our lumber and extra help. Twenty minutes out, our friend Malau turned green and hung over the rail for a while. Losing his breakfast didn't seem to qualify his cheerfulness. He grinned as he demonstrated his familiarity with American idioms.

"I toss my cookies, no?" he laughed.

"Very thoughtful of you to do it on the leeward side," I told him.

Anchored at Moorea, Frank supervised the building of the camera platform. It comprised padded two-by-eights clamped athwart the rails fore and aft of the cockpit and a cockpit for Jerry to stand on, out from the hull a good eight feet. He was dry and high on the port tack, but his feet were under a couple of times on the starboard tack when *Thane* heeled in the wind. Ruth took the flying boat back to Tahiti, and the rest of us went exploring. We found we could borrow a couple of horses, through the help of the islander named Paul who had been cooperative on our last visit. H.R. and I rode them along the beach and into a wooded area. Along the way we met a young Moorean who demonstrated his adeptness at opening coconuts. It takes an expert to get into them easily even with a heavy machete, but the Moorean could do it with the much smaller diving knife. He could also walk up the trunk of a slanting coconut palm to loosen the cluster nuts. Frank and Jerry and Malau photographed his prowess, while H.R. and I discovered that we could ride the horses well out into the water, which was only about knee-deep out fifty feet or more. There was very little tide action.

In the still sunlight only two things were intrusive in that memorable natural scenery: horses, which weren't introduced there until the eighteenth century, and the metal collars on most of the coconut trees, which weren't introduced till the nineteenth century. The collars are for the purpose of keeping rats from the coconuts. (Rats were introduced by European ships stopping at the islands.)

Paul drove us up into the hills in his jeep, which was really loaded. There were Paul, the jeep owner, Frank, Malau, H.R., Jerry, and a girl we'd picked up whom we nicknamed Samantha. She wore a *pareu,* one of those garments which always looks, when fastened around the top of the chest and hanging loose like a very short-skirted sack dress, as though nothing else is being worn.

There are many farms up away from the shore. At one

coconut grove, which had cattle in it, there was a fence with a typical western barbed-wire range gate. Except for the coconuts we could have been on a ranch in Wyoming. A little beyond this farm was as far as the jeep could go, and we continued a way on foot. Again there was that still, high, palmless, tropical forest I'd seen in Tahiti.

We backed the jeep down a way, and returned through the Wyoming ranch. As we closed the barbed-wire gate, a man of forty-five or fifty in a white cotton undershirt and faded jeans came up to us. He was barefoot and carried a thick-bladed machete.

"Hi!" he said. Not "Ha'i," as in "Bali Ha'i," but "Hi" as in standard U.S. lingo.

"Do you speak English?" I asked him.

"Yeah. I was in the States for six years. But I came back." He smiled as though anyone would of course come back if he had ever known Moorea. It was his farm, and he had seen us go through and came to thank us for closing the gate each time so his cattle wouldn't get out. It was like a scene from a TV horse opera. I guessed aloud that in the States he had probably lived out West. No, he told us, he had spent most of the six years in New Jersey.

We took a different road back. I had to stand up in the jeep, holding onto the frame that supported the cloth top when it was in place to cushion the shocks and spare my spine, which hadn't been helped by the horseback ride.

Before leaving the foothills, we found a beautiful mountain stream with a swollen place that formed a pool. H.R. and I waded across it at the narrow end. The bottom was hard, black gravel, and the edges were overhung with flowers. The water was icy. Malau picked some flowers and gave them to Samantha with a courtly bow and then unfastened the knot of her *pareu* and took it away from her. She had on a bikini of flowered material. He asked

her in French if she'd like to swim and let us take pictures
of her. She was agreeable. The wide end of the pool was
quite deep, with a sudden drop-off. I was upstream a few
yards when the others discovered this, and they tried to
lure me toward that end as I waded. My jeans were wet
only to just above the knees. The girl was now lying con-
tentedly in that icy water, stretched out along the bottom,
her long hair streaming in the current, and she moved
slowly to over the deep part, floating then but pretending
still to be in shallow water. I waded on innocently. "If
you come out over here," Jerry called, "you won't rile up
the upstream water." He was all set to record on film
my plunge into the deep pool.

It didn't work. Too many people were smiling too
much, too many cameras obviously poised. Suddenly I
sensed there was no next step. "You *fiends!*" I said. "You
missed shooting me going in the drink at Great Inagua
and in the Caribbean and now you want to stage it in
fresh water."

We tried to get Samantha to take off the top to her
bikini in the interests of perpetuating a traditionally Polynesian and eternally commercial photographic cliché, but
she demurred. It was difficult to understand her shyness
in view of the fact that she had unselfconsciously demonstrated some mannerisms that could be called either
"naturalistic" or "lusty," depending on one's point of view.
Once she clutched H.R. so unmistakably that he jumped
into the ditch. This set off a burst of general merriment
in which Malau said, "I do not understand you, 'Asch.'
('Asch' was Malau's French rendering of 'H,' as in 'Asch
Air'.) You are on ship for t'ree month and now when
chance comes you leap in ze wrong direction!"

There were some baby pigs at a small farm down near
the end of Cook's Bay. We tried to run a couple down
along the road. They led us into a side path, where we

were suddenly confronted by a ferocious sow. We gave up; the little shoats were safe under her massive flanks. The people in the farm house, who had been watching, laughed uproariously, and pretty soon we were all friends. Paul and the girl interpreted for us. The lady of the house was enormous and jollier than a department-store Santa. Everything was funny to her. She had two little girls about eight or nine, one of whom looked like Ava Gardner. I asked if the girls were sisters. They were half sisters. The grandmother pointed to the one who looked like Ava Gardner and said, "American," which I took to mean that her father was an American. I couldn't get the girls to smile. I think it was my beard. I found it hard to smile myself whenever I looked in a mirror. The husband was about as tall as Mickey Rooney and half as wide. I'm sure his wife was four times his weight.

We dropped Samantha at the store at the end of the bay. She had a *tiare Tahiti* blossom in her hair, and she looked long and unsmiling at us when we thanked her for going along. In her eyes was a flash of that patient wisdom I've seen in many Polynesian faces and which I interpret as a mixture of puzzlement and pity. How could they understand a people who come to such a place and drag their own world with them, their machinery and electronics, their cameras and motorcars, their preoccupation with work that leaves no time for play, their analytical approach to life that keeps them forever outside it, these poor, serious, pale-skinned men with the power to change others, but so rigid they cannot change themselves.

The entertainment at the Aimeo Hotel was superb. A dance troupe with torches performed against the backdrop of the bay and its jagged skyline—the *otea*, the *aparima*, the *paoa*, a songfest with lyrics made up on the spot like calypso and ripe with double meaning. The drums and laughter echoed across the bay.

Paul had set up a party at a private home, which started after the entertainment at the Aimeo ended. There was a rather long eating house (Polynesians traditionally maintain separate structures for eating and sleeping), and I wondered whether our host had a large family or was in the business of giving 'private' parties. This was not a tourist affair. The owner had torn down a whole wall of the house so that no door was needed for entry or exit. The panels were leaning against the side and back of the house and would be nailed up again when the bash had ended. Dancing went on outside the house; although the weather was threatening, it had not yet rained. There were several guitars, which nearly everybody played at one time or another, and a set of "native" bongo drums (made in France!).

A young mother was there with her infant, who surveyed the whole scene with mild interest and then slept soundly amid the growing bedlam.

Wine and beer were served around in enameled pitchers with curled flint chips exposing dark areas of metal, and then poured into plastic tumblers.

After an hour or two of frenetic dancing and several gallons of drink, the party began to liven up. The feeling grew that we'd all known each other for a long time. The language barrier cracked and then crumbled away. We laughed at the funny lyrics of the local songs when *they* laughed, not just to be polite, but because they *were* funny, understood or not. They laughed at ours.

I sang one chorus of "Venezuela" after an elaborate introduction by H.R., and then Larry Nilsen asked if I could accompany him on the guitar. "Can you play the chords to 'Waltzing Matilda'?"

I said I could.

"Play it," he said.

I played it, and he stood on the table and sang a set of rollicking lyrics. Not exactly off-color. More like filthy. Six and a half of us spoke English (the half was Malau), and we fell into such a laughing fit tears streamed down our faces. The Mooreans found it just as funny and were convulsed also.

Two and a half liters of wine banished the discomfort in my neck and back, and I'd have been tempted to the indiscretion of one of those dances except for the fact that I don't dance even when there's nothing wrong with my back.

Seated to my right at the long table were two very young girls, one of them rather pretty. They were shy about joining in the dancing; each danced once with the host but came back to the table where they giggled and nudged each other and called me *le capitain*. I managed to find out from them without the aid of an interpreter that they were fifteen years old, they were not sisters, and they went to the school in the town of Temae. They were learning French, they liked parties, but I gathered that they limited their activities to singing and watching and listening to the merriment.

Malau came over, took the pretty one by the arm and started to lead her out to the dance area.

"Malau," I said to him, "dance with her but bring her right back here. I am her father."

Still holding the wrist of the girl, who trailed behind him giggling, he came back to poke a finger in my chest.

"You," he said, "are worse than Asch." And he dragged her into the lighted dance area. But he brought her back at the end of the music and delivered her to me with his courtly bow.

Another liter of wine and ten songs later, I needed to

go into the dark by myself, and hoped I could negotiate it without stepping, or worse, on anyone.

As I was returning I heard a word whispered and then spoken to me. "Brother," it said. It was our host, and he was using the only word of English he knew. From his repetition of the word and the solicitous tone, I thought he was concerned for my health or my ability to navigate in the dark, but finally I realized that he wanted me to follow him. I did. He led me to the other house, the sleeping house. We went through a dim anteroom into a pitch-black inner room. My host struck a match and lighted a kerosene lamp. He gestured for me to sit down and spoke earnestly in Tahitian. From a table drawer he took a ballpoint pen and a scrap of note paper. I looked around and saw that the only place to sit was on an unmade bed, with blankets bunched at one end. As I was about to settle myself the blanket seemed to move. I sat down cautiously and then reached over to the blanket and pulled it open.

Under the first layer of blanket was an infant not more than three or four weeks old. It lay happily on its back. Its eyes were coal black. It made a sighing sound and kicked its legs and then tried a smile, biting its lower lip with a ridge of pink gum. My host paused, then continued writing.

I tried to think of something to say and finally came up with, "Gotta be careful where you leave your children, Jack. Strangers could sit on them."

He replied cordially as though accepting the advice and then handed me the paper. It was his name and address. Through sign language and here and there a word of French he got across that he'd like copies of the pictures Malau and H.R. had been taking. Would I send him some? Then he made it clear that the child was his daughter's, and she was the little girl who had sat next to me so patiently telling me about her school, and who had danced once with Malau and on whose virginity I'd have wagered.

He made signs that seemed to mean he was offering the infant to me, or to my son, along with the mother if we would take them back to our country and provide for them. The baby was a little girl. They were *both* little girls, for God's sake. Suddenly this whole silly situation became poignant and sad to me. What lay ahead for that girl and her child? Unless she married the young man who could hack coconuts with a diving knife (he was at the party but paid no attention to her), she would probably go on watching more parties and dancing with more strangers like Malau and have more children. Or in a couple of years she might drift across to Quinn's Bar to become part of the economy of Papeete. My little schoolgirl studying French at the Temae school! She'd learn French a lot faster at Quinn's.

I thanked our host—my Brother—and promised to send him the pictures. No, we couldn't accept his daughter and her child but wished them well. I got out and found H.R. We had to get back to the ship anyway. The party was thinning. We signalled Paul that we were ready to go back. He told us he'd already taken Larry back and Pete Munch and Frank. On the road back I remembered to stand up in the jeep even though my back felt fine. I told H.R. of our gift, which I'd declined. I couldn't see the expression on his face, but I heard him say "Good Lord."

At the Aimeo we found two of our group sleeping heavily on the dock. There was a narrow plank leading off the stern of *Thane* to the pier. It took superior coordination to traverse it in the daylight, cold sober. In the light of a half moon and the wake of a blowout like this one, it took enormous good luck as well. Malau and H.R.

tight-roped it successfully, wearing their cameras. I sighed with relief and started aboard. For some odd reason I, too, made it safely.

I went up on deck and smoked a cigar. Malau was asleep already in the cockpit under a sailbag. I went around and checked the ship, although Pete Jackson had undoubtedly done the same thing before he turned in. The moon was high and the anchor light shone steadily like a super-nova. Even the ship was asleep. No pump, no generator sound. Green frogs or some large insect droned metronomically in the palm groves. I reflected that tomorrow we'd ruffle the waters of the bay momentarily in sailing this ship away from Moorea, and in ten minutes it would be as if we had never been there.

I was anxious to get back now to contact Hiro Levy about Sunday's long-awaited *tamuré*. Now I had an alternate weather plan because there could be no further postponement. It was already three days after Ruth's birthday. On that day I had wished her a happy birthday and explained that her gift was the trip here and that she certainly understood there could be no surprise party this year. This subterfuge was pretty weak, since I'd said "there would be no surprise this year" on other occasions.

Next morning we were up at dawn after a good, solid night's sleep of about an hour and a half. We sailed back in a brisk southwest wind. *Thane* heeled and scooted; the decks were drenched as she bucked stiffly into seas that sent up great plumes of spray. This wind was like the one we'd had the first night west of Punta Espinosa. We made nine knots.

At Papeete there was a note from Mireille saying goodbye and explaining that I should get in touch with Hiro just to reconfirm. This meant she hadn't been able to find him either! She had given me lengthy instructions to help me trace him and even gave the name of his partner in case Hiro and I missed contact. She had put down the name of someone who could supply flowers, a map showing the location again, and several other details. She said she hated to miss it after all this time spent planning, but that if she were the type who could ignore her obligations in the States in order to stay, she would still be living here, and not in Tahiti but in Takaroa.

Friday it rained again in the morning but finally cleared up. H.R. went around the island again to build up his portfolio of photographs. He had made arrangements with an attractive girl to enhance the scenes by posing in his shots. H.R. has a good deal of skill at posing amateur photographic models. He waits until the pose is slightly uncomfortable, and when the subject momentarily relaxes, he gets his shot before the person stiffens again in a self-conscious pose. Some of his pictures were later published in the *TV Guide* article on our trip, and he sold one to an encyclopedia.

That night Larry Nilsen, Bob Dixon, Ruth, and I dined at a balconied upstairs restaurant on a side street. We discussed everything from apartheid to beard styling. Nilsen's was well trimmed, and he told me the secrets of the art. For one thing, the neophyte grower usually lets the adornment get somewhat too long; it should be kept trimmed short. At its nether tip, it should be slightly peaked (too much peaking gives a slick Mephisto look, particularly in a black beard) and combed forward. There should be a quarter-inch break between the ends of the moustache and the upper points of the beard on the chin. It should be shaved down from the lower lip between these points, leaving a center peak immediately under the middle of the lower lip and cropped along the sides of the jaw, tapering to a point on each side well below the sideburns. "If these instructions are followed,"

245

Larry said, "you become Robin Hood. Unless you are a lady—in which case you join the circus."

We ordered a variety of appetizers and entrees. I happened to specify antipasto and roast veal. For some reason I got my roast veal first. Thinking the waitress had forgotten the antipasto, and deciding I didn't need it anyway, I started on the veal. The Tahitian waitress then appeared with the antipasto, set it down and hit me sharply on the shoulder. "You suppose to eat t' appetizer first!" she scolded. I was bug-eyed, and the rest of the table sat in that crackling silence that precedes a collapse into laughter. I reached around and poked her lightly on the shoulder and said, "You suppose to *bring* t' appetizer first!" Larry slid right off his chair under the table. Dixon fell forward in his soup, and Ruth exploded into hysterics.

The waitress walked off with neither pique nor embarrassment and was cordial during the remainder of the meal, in spite of the fact that we picked up the bit and took to belting each other for the tiniest infractions of table etiquette. It got a little rowdy for a while, but no one in the place minded.

No waiter or waitress in Polynesia displays the obsequiousness we've grown so used to in the European tradition of service. Nor is there any tipping anywhere. When a Polynesian serves you, even on a commercial basis, he is your equal, and any courtesy he shows you is genuine because he likes you. In an experienced European waiter, obsequiousness is completely phony and masks arrogance. It is a suave ritual of seeming to acknowledge a formal caste barrier between you and him. And he will act the same whether you are cordial and generous or cranky and stingy.

The Tahitian waiter or waitress, on the other hand, may be your host or hostess at a private party the next night, and the attitude will not be any different. It is not unusual for a waitress you know to sit down with you during a break and chat while sharing coffee with you.

Larry Nilsen was thirty-four years old. He had been a builder and contractor in Durban, South Africa, where he was born. He is the holder of the Queen's Medal, South Africa's highest civilian honor, an award for bravery, which he received for rescuing a lifeguard who'd been attacked by a shark off a beach at Natal. In 1963 he got hold of the *Heather*, the twenty-eight-foot sloop tied up beside *Thane*, and sailed it single-handed around the world. At the time we met him, he was on the last leg of the trip, headed west from Tahiti to New Zealand and thence to South Africa. He'd been in Tahiti about a month. On a previous trip around the world he'd been in Tahiti for ten months, working as an extra in *Mutiny on the Bounty*. That trip had taken some time. He had to get enough money to maintain and provision a boat, and he spent two years in New Zealand. He calls himself a vagabond sailor, but claims it's a means to an end. He wants to see the world and can't afford to book passage on a plane or ship. He says he hates sailing, but it's the only way he can get from place to place.

When Malau, standing on *Thane's* higher deck, had first looked down at Larry's sloop, he said, "He sailed from South Africa in that coconut?" And when we told him Nilsen had done it by sailing west around the world, Malau shuddered.

My interview with the governor, which took place about this time, provided some useful background to understanding of the island. His Excellency Jean Charles Sicurani, Gouverneur de la Polynésie Française, was born in Algeria in 1915 and had been a career man all his adult life. He had been Director of Political Affairs and Information in Indo-China and the Sudan, and a cabinet minister in France. He came to Tahiti as governor in January of 1965. With apparent ease, he straddled the ambivalent French policy that seemed to want to develop tourism in French Polynesia but at the same time qualified its own efforts by opening and closing the U.S. consulate in Tahiti in alternating fits of secrecy and coldness and warmth and welcome. He reported directly to General de Gaulle, and I would guess that he was the kind of man who would be frank in his advice to *le bon Charles,* and that in turn the advice would be respected but probably not accepted. A UPI release in May had called the closing of the U.S. consulate in Papeete the latest in a series of measures restricting the free movements of Americans in Tahiti. Many believed it had to do with the scheduled bomb tests. But as the French are quick to point out, Mururoa, site of the atomic activity, is farther from Tahiti than is Hawaii from Johnston Island, where the U.S. exploded a bomb. Both the governor and M. Gilleteaux, head of tourism, forge ahead with plans, with no apparent fear that De Gaulle might shoot down the whole tourist structure on a whim. They told me only a very few islands, uninteresting from a tourist standpoint in any case, are closed, for the safety of travelers, and that French Polynesia still welcomes all. (Indeed they are so loathe to see visitors leave that a five-dollar departure tax is levied at the airport.)

The governor's mansion is a relic of colonial architecture. As the symbol of governmental authority, it is, of course, large, with well-kept grounds. The Polynesians have a voice in their government, but Polynesians are not politicians, and the rules are European. Many of them feel that the disadvantages of civilization would be minimized and that tourism would benefit native residents more if Tahiti belonged to the U.S.

The *tamuré* finally came off on Sunday the twenty-sixth. It was highly enjoyable in spite of the fact that I never was able to reach Hiro and there were no war canoes, or animals roasted on spits. It was hastily improvised with the help of Pauline Morgan at the Tahiti Hotel, who came through with a great abundance of flower crowns and leis and a good dance troupe, and it took place at Faratea, where an excellent buffet meal and drinks were served. The weather cleared, and eighty per cent of the guests were able to make it, among them Mireille's father and mother, and her Uncle Paul Doucette and his wife, and their son and daughter-in-law, and it had a genuinely Tahitian flavor. The impact of the surprise was dissipated, of course, because of the week's delay: Ruth didn't know exactly what was going on but knew that something was. No matter, it was a good party.

Later in the evening, a group of us stopped at Uncle Paul's place. Uncle Paul has a town house in Papeete and a Tahitian house on the ocean a few kilometers west. From here we watched the sunset on Moorea across the way, seeing it fade from gold to purple to black and then almost disappear in the dark.

Suddenly Malau's sports car wheeled into the drive. Malau jumped out from the right side and, throwing himself down in mock terror, kissed the ground, exclaiming, "Asch drove!" Asch had a big grin on his face as he climbed out, and I was annoyed. I mentally composed a speech about burning up these winding roads to impress a French parachutist. But it came out, "Watch it, Buster!"

H.R. interpreted my look, however, and said to Malau, "You've met Captain Bligh, who took the breadfruit to Jamaica?"

Next day we were guests on *Valrosa*, a beautiful, black-hulled schooner belonging to Marc Darnois. Ninety-nine feet in length, she had been built for an Italian countess, and was sumptuously appointed with wood carvings and ivory inlays. Marc took charter parties through the islands. He had pulled *Valrosa's* port shaft for overhaul (she had two diesel auxiliaries) to refit her for what, as it turned out, was her last charter. She rode easily between her big anchor and her stern lines to the bollards of the yacht section of Commercial Quay. We had drinks on deck and talked and set up a recorded interview.

Marc had lost a leg in the French Army in World War II. It was gone above the knee, but he had an artificial leg, which he wore only on shore. Aboard, he didn't bother with it, carrying out his duties as master without feeling the least handicapped. He was lean and bronzed, with sharp aquiline features and iron-gray hair.

Aboard were Darnois' Tahitian wife; Des Kearns, the mate; and a beautiful French girl, Bikki, who was hostess aboard *Valrosa.*

A few nights before I left, we all went to Uncle Paul's town house for dinner, and afterward we visited the Mormon church with Mr. and Mrs. Charles Palmer. There we saw our helpful friend Elder Garcia again, and we discussed the work of the Mormons in the islands with him.

In Punaauia we went to a cockfight. The Polynesian cockfight is not the bloody affair that they used to stage in Cuba: here they don't put steel spurs on the birds. But an enormous amount of money changed hands at this one. The arranger was Chinese. He held the bets and scheduled the individual matches. Whenever any two bird owners agreed to a match, it was scheduled; agreement was reached by a hand weighing of the birds by both parties—the weight had to be about equal. Conditions for mutual agreement required that both parties believe their bird could win. Optimism and pride inclined an owner to this view; caution and shrewdness made him seek matches in which his bird had some pronounced advantage. As a result there was far more weighing and arguing than there was cockfighting.

There were about seventy-five men in this arena in the large yard of a home not far from the site of Gauguin's home. Behind the house were palm groves, and in the bright sunshine, stretching up in progressive steepness, were slanting farms, terraced garden areas, lush green foothills, and topping everything, the mile-high, jagged peaks of Mahutaa, Aorai, and Diademe. Across the road was a thick palm grove, and beyond lay the sea.

The cocks, plucked of superfluous feathers and looking a little like escapees from a poultry market, stood around in the yard, each tied to a stake by one foot. One, momentarily neglected, had got tangled in his tether and was exhausting himself trying to pull the stake out. We looked around for somebody official, either an owner or the Chinese referee, but nobody seemed interested. Jerry untangled him, and immediately the bird lit out, to be brought up short at the end of his string and slammed down on his beak. He fluttered and squawked some more. I asked Jerry and Frank if they'd ever seen a chicken hypnotized, and I set about to calm the excited unhappy rooster by mesmerizing him. Any poultry farmer knows this old trick, but it impresses people who weren't brought up around chickens. I held the bird firmly by the feet and caressed him down onto his port side, holding my other hand on his starboard wing so it wouldn't flutter. After he quieted a bit, I very slowly withdrew my hand. Then I picked up a twig about the size of a short pencil. Still using very slow movements I took away my other hand from his feet, substituting the twig for it. There he lay with no one holding him, with the twig lying on his crossed feet. In a moment I slowly took away the twig and eased myself to a standing position.

"Will he just stay that way?" Jerry asked.

"Not indefinitely. He thinks he's still being held."

A few men had gathered to watch the end of the operation. Suddenly the owner burst on the scene and became very upset, assuming some harm had come to his bird. The onlookers hollered back at him as he picked up the cock, which once on its feet was perfectly normal. I became the object of the discussion and the target of black looks from the owner, who now understood that I was responsible for the trance. The crowd was growing, and I was in the spotlight. Even the smiling onlookers of a moment ago now began to adopt the attitude that this obviously foreign intruder was in sinister employ. The owner shrilly demanded something of me. I could tell it was a question because of the upward inflection of the ending. I felt obliged to answer, but even if I'd told him my boat draws nine feet he wouldn't have understood; he was speaking Tahitian and, as is widely known, Paumotu is *my* second language.

"Get Ruth in the car," I said to Jerry. "I'll try some kind of delaying action." I was amused in spite of the awkwardness of the situation: the poor guy thought I'd put a hex on his chicken, and I didn't want to be around if he lost with his whole bundle on it. We still had an opening behind us, but it was closing as the crowd grew larger. Jerry started to laugh.

"It's not funny," I said out of the side of my mouth, but I couldn't keep a straight face either.

A diversionary tactic was called for. I pointed to the first onlooker I'd seen watching my Svengalian performance, and I told the owner that he'd obviously become the butt of a joke authored by *this* fellow. "Practical joke," I said, and then tried, *"Practical joculaire Tahitian,"* although no French was being spoken (not even by me). Soon others began to chuckle and point to the same fellow. I had shifted the target. The Chinese promoter elbowed his way through, spoke rapidly in Tahitian, and extracted money from everyone, ignoring me until I got across to him that I wanted to bet fifty francs on the cock I'd put the spell on. This further appeased the owner, and things began to return to normal.

We left after the second match, before my contestant was scheduled. Unless you're betting heavily or have an emotional attachment to one of the birds, it isn't terribly exciting. They swat each other around and what few feathers they have left will occasionally fly, but there's more fire in the crowd outside than in the cock pit itself.

In the car, Ruth had not been able to witness the altercation.

"Hugh was magnificent!" Jerry told her on the way back. "Several of them pulled knives, and one guy who looked like Sydney Greenstreet . . ."

"*Was* Sydney Greenstreet," I corrected.

"Yes. Greenstreet himself—pulled a pearl-handled revolver out of his hat and trained it on Hugh and . . ."

"Tell her about the speech I made. You know, when I said he could shoot me if he let my friends go. About how I'd had a good life and had known the love of a good woman . . ."

"I'm getting to that. But before that, when you took the gun away from him and emptied it all but one cartridge and threw it back to him and said, 'You first.' That took nerve!"

"So you've known the love of a good woman?" Ruth said. "I never thought you were like that. I thought *I* was your moll."

I left some things on *Thane* for its trip back: the courtesy flags, dye markers, Very pistol and parachute flares, the remaining dry cell batteries, medical supplies, ammunition, tide tables and light lists, charts, all of the safety equipment, and some navigating supplies. But I took my two sextants, the Plath and an old English sextant Clayton had given me made in 1845, two pistols, the New York

Yacht Club burgee, one set of walkie-talkies, enough cigars for two days, the photographic gear, what was left of the oceanographic equipment, the contents of the strongbox, a hand bearing-compass, binoculars, the log books, and one or two books out of the library.

I gave Pete the receipt for the rifles locked up at the harbormaster's and all the Panama Canal papers and forms. Then I wished him luck. He thought he'd get away toward the end of October. Connie was going to stay until then and fly back.

At the house, Jerry and Frank were packing cameras and film, and Ruth was finishing her personal packing. H.R. had walked up the hill to return some dishes and pots to Walter Grande (who had kept giving us eggs and other goodies).

I lay down on the living room floor and listened to the sounds of work around me. That's much more pleasant than doing it.

Bob Dixon came in. Seeing me supine he said, "You lie around on floors more than any sober person I ever knew."

"Good for the back," I told him.

"I'm staying," he announced abruptly.

Since we'd all said that from time to time I didn't realize at first that he was serious.

"I think I can get a work visa, and I want to start a magazine in English about Tahiti. There's a market for one."

"Well," I said, staring at the ceiling. "There's a lot of red tape . . . the tourist officials don't think it's an easy matter to stay on. And there's a police captain who'll give you fits about it."

"I've already talked to the governor about it. I'll stay."

And so he did.

Monday, after much kissing and leave-taking, staggering under our sentimental burdens of shell leis, we mounted the steps to the deck level of a Boeing 707 jet, and waved the last time to the people who had come to see us off: Walter Grande and his wife, and pretty Hinano, the Doucettes and the Palmers, Malau, Larry Nilsen and Pete Munch, M. Gilleteaux and Eric Cridland, Bob Dixon, and a dozen people I didn't know, including some good-looking girls who had either come to see off H.R. and Jerry or else just liked kissing and found this a good place for it.

The real end of the voyage came when the door to the 707 was locked. We were now in a jet plane and at an airport, and this scene is the same all over the world. I was instantly back home. The few palms still visible could have been Florida.

I smoked my last cigar thirty miles off California's Catalina Island and didn't smoke again for months.

When we landed, Ruth, H.R., and I stayed in Los Angeles; Frank went on to New York; and Jerry went to San Francisco.

I made one television appearance on the coast. I came on the Johnny Carson Show the night of October 4, and both Carson and the audience did a double-take (the producers hadn't told Johnny) as I walked out, bearded and crew cut and completely out of context.

October 11, I was back with "Today" in New York and fell quickly into the pattern of the familiar routine. But by November 19, I knew my back needed more medical help than lying on floors. In early December, unable now to walk, I went into the Harkness Pavilion at the Columbia-Presbyterian Medical Center for surgery. I came back to work in late January without a cane, and in six months all traces of weakness had vanished. I was hale and symmetrical and grateful to Drs. Frank Stinchfield and Lester Mount, an orthopedic-neurosurgical team, who said I could play football by August—a miracle, I said, unable to resist the old gag, since I couldn't play football *before* I had back trouble.

Jerry Galyean went to Africa on a government photographic mission and is back home in the States as of this writing. Bob Dixon stayed in Tahiti, married a Chinese girl, and founded *Reef Magazine,* in partnership with Marc Darnois. Its features and photo-essays are an attractive way to keep in touch with the islands, and a valuable guide to anyone planning a trip there.

H. R. Downs joined the Navy (as though he hadn't seen the sea); Virgil Bowers lives serenely (but not quietly—his voice is heard literally all over the world) on an island at Latitude 41° N., Longitude 73° W. It's called Long Island, N.Y., and it's marvelous for getting away from all that tropical lushness and comfort.

Thane sailed from Tahiti, October 25, with Pete Jackson, Don Null, a Pittsburgh photographer, Dr. Bud Hartle of Saginaw, Michigan, Chuck Popenoe, a physicist from Washington, D.C., writer Mark Gross of New York, and a camp director named Wally Smith.

They were plagued by storms and a great deal of seasickness, heavy damage to sail and rigging, and the loss of their generator and diesel auxiliary.

They were not allowed ashore at Rapa Island and tried for Pitcairn Island, but were blown far southeast of it by a typhoon. Abandoning that plan, they made for Easter Island, which they reached in December. From there they radioed via the South Pole to Miami and Pittsburgh to advise that they were all right.

That was the last that was heard of them for some time. The doldrums near Panama treated them brutally. Null said in a newspaper interview, " . . . all I wanted was to see my wife, Lee, and the two kids . . . We were in a prison without walls. Just ten minutes out in the hot sun was like a slow fry, and we felt as limp as the sails looked. I was afraid we'd become mentally disturbed."

After nearly two weeks of this they were dangerously low on water and without radio or enough fuel to reach any land. They did "some fervent praying."

A Colombian freighter sighted them, and on January 10 they were safe in Balboa, where the ship was re-outfitted. As of this writing it is the owner's plan to send her to Connecticut.

Even so *Thane* fared better than *Valrosa*. Two days before *Thane* left Tahiti, *Valrosa*, with a charter party aboard, was sailing west through the Tuamotus on the way to Bora Bora. *Reef Magazine* gives this account of the end of a beautiful ship: "[She] was running before a stiff wind . . . at 4:20 A.M., Mate Des Kearns was on the *Valrosa's* great wheel, and Captain Marc Darnois was napping lightly in the deck cabin. Suddenly Des cried, "No, Marc, I don't believe it!" Captain Darnois awakened to find Des spinning the wheel to port, and a second later the black-hulled yacht shivered from stem to stern as she slammed into the reef at Tikehau. *Valrosa* hit broadside and heeled up onto the reef, the strong surf crashing against her seaward side. Passengers and crew stumbled onto her crazily canted deck, and thence down onto the coral, making their way to the beach only a dozen yards away. Captain Darnois thought of freeing his ship for a fleeting instant, but as she rolled on the reef, the deck buckled under him and he heard the awful agony of the ship's frames breaking. *Valrosa* was finished. She broke up into matchwood in less than two hours."

So, the trip on *Thane* was now history. And the dream that had started to grow many years ago in the Midwest, unnoticed at first, had reached a very pleasant and rewarding peak of fulfillment. But it has not ended, because this kind of dream has no end. I'll go back—again and again, if I can. If not through the Pacific and to Tahiti, through other waters equally timeless and mysterious, alternatingly friendly and ominous; if not to Tahiti, to other landfalls, equally exotic or grim. And if they are not so lushly attractive as that corner of the world, it won't matter, because the game is in the sailing, not the destination.

For this is a lifelong love affair. It has its heights of passion and its planes of near-despair, but it is undying.

☆ *Appendix I*
General Preliminary Planning

~~~~~~

IT IS POSSIBLE to jump into an adequately provisioned sailboat on a sudden whim, sail across an ocean, and arrive somewhere, sometime.

But to achieve this feat in comfort and reasonable safety, arriving at an intended destination close to an intended time, considerable planning is necessary. In the narrative body of this book I have suggested or detailed various aspects of that kind of planning. Here in these appendices I am organizing that information and other details in practical form for those readers whose dream of sailing the ocean, as mine did, is beginning to approach feasibility.

The matter herein is not presented as rules, nor as definitive; and certainly it has no official status. It comprises merely the procedures and materiel that I used, after much research, advice, and consideration, for our trip from Florida to Tahiti. Adapted to your requirements, it should prove useful in your own planning.

Most of the people who have published data on ocean voyaging have more experience therein than I. But there is one advantage in being a neophyte: One is very conscious of and thorough with details. More experienced people sometimes slight or overlook items, either because they are too much "second nature" to be readily articulated, or because to the old hand they seem too obvious to mention. It is better to build a footloose voyage on methodical planning than to be forced to improvise methods of coping with the situations arising from lack of plans.

In this section, I will start with very broad generalities, and in the subsequent appendices we'll get down to specifics.

About the broadest generality is *where to go on your trip*. Time is the decisive factor here of course. If you have unlimited time, you can decide on any destination that intrigues you that money and the boat available to you can command. If your sailing time is limited, you are confined to destinations that can be comfortably reached therein. Now the size of boat, route, time of year, etc., become important variables.

A useful rule of thumb for estimating the travel time factor is this: Once you have decided on a proper sailing route, figure distances on a straight-line basis, inflate the figures by twenty-five to thirty per cent and count on making an average of five nautical miles per hour. Figure the time you want to spend at each shore stop and add four days to this for each stop.

As far as the best time of year is concerned, if this is a free choice with you, a careful study of ocean pilot charts, sailing directions, and sailing-ship routes will be extremely rewarding. The first of these will plot wind force and direction for each area for the different months, averaged over a period of years; the second will give detailed conditions for approaching and leaving all ports, and the last will list the best tracks to follow for getting from one part of the world to another. While a sailboat can be made to go against the direction of the wind, it takes lots longer to beat (go against the wind) than to reach (go across the wind) or run (go with the wind).

The next broad generality, again assuming free choice here, is *what kind of boat to use*. It's possible to cross a large ocean in a power boat. I would discourage anyone contemplating this, however, unless the boat had a minimum keel length of 130 feet. Even then, without the steadying effects of sail, there can be discomfort from rolling in beam seas. There is also more danger of broaching and capsizing than in a ballast keel sailboat, and if the engines quit, you are dependent on what help you can reach by radio. Also it takes a boat of 130 feet or larger to carry sufficient fuel for the cruising range necessary without giving up living space to auxiliary tanks. A sailing ship is only out of fuel when the wind stops. In most places in the world, it blows most of the time. It appeals to my parsimonious Scotch blood that the winds of the world supply an inexhaustible, free source of power.

Many people have made it from England to Tahiti in sailboats of thirty-two feet, thirty-five feet, thirty-eight feet. Some have gone across an ocean single-handed in much smaller boats. Robert Manry crossed the Atlantic in a 13½ footer. A sailing ship of 100 feet or more requires a sizeable crew, and if you can afford to pay and/or feed them—fine: It's perfectly safe to cross the ocean in a large ship.

For the maximum *feeling* of sailing, and the maximum safety and comfort with the most sensible price tag attached, the optimum boat length is about forty-five to sixty-five feet on the waterline, ketch or schooner rig.

As the text has discussed, you can charter or buy your boat. If you are a fourth-generation oil magnate, or have just tripped over a mother-lode of jade on your property —in other words, if money is no object to you—you will have no trouble buying a boat on the day you first decide to buy it. Almost every boat afloat has a price, because almost every boat owner is anxious either to upgrade the size and luxury of his yacht or to unload a burden he cannot afford.

But if keeping costs down is a consideration, in either buying or chartering a vessel, you will want plenty of time to find the right one at a price that can be called reasonable. With luck, it is possible to find a distress sale, wherein vital need for cash requires the owner to dispose of a boat for a good deal less than its true worth. A factor in the value of any material possession is the intensity of its possessor's need to turn it into cash. This seems particularly true of yachts. Time can be on your side.

Although charter prices less often reflect any "distress" character, it is possible to benefit from long-range planning in getting the right boat at the right price.

On chartering a single long ocean voyage it is not unusual to be charged an amount close to the purchase price of the boat. But keep in mind that if you were to purchase and resell the boat, you would suffer the enormous depreciation incurred during the voyage, you would pay the equally enormous insurance, you would pay the broker's fee on reselling, and if you had to sell it immediately after the voyage—in other words a distress sale—you would lose heavily.

Experts contend that charter is generally better than purchase for single voyages.

I recommend the services of a yacht broker. There are many good ones, and they earn their money. They get it, not from you, but from the seller. But those brokers with established reputations will work just as hard for you as for the party providing their fee, because when you become a buyer you will almost certainly become a seller at some point, and they would like to continue a relationship with you. Brokers can also be enormously helpful in arranging a fair charter fee and contract. This is such a specialized business that unless you've been close to it all your life you should not try to handle it by yourself.

Next general point: planning *whom to take along*. The number of people you want with you is largely determined by the size of the vessel—how many can it comfortably sleep? If the ship is planned right, it will comfortably sleep somewhat more than are required to handle it.

Selecting a ship's company involves considering ability and personality, both of equal importance. By that I mean that a candidate deficient in either of these attributes should be eliminated. He will almost certainly prove a liability. Start with general ability and a list of those who would be capable of making the trip from the standpoint of pulling their own weight, of health, of knowledge of sailing, or in some cases, of having a special talent you feel it's important to have aboard, then weigh each in the personality balance and eliminate those you couldn't stand to be cooped up with for a long period of time. Better to be ruthlessly frank at the outset than to look for replacements at Panama. I've covered in Chapter II those things I felt were potential dangers to morale and a cheerful passage.

Now comes the generality concerning *what you take along*. Voyages can be seriously marred because you have forgotten something. A small but annoying crimp can be put in a day's sail because there is no bottle opener; a life can be lost because first aid and medical supplies lack some simple item. Once afloat, the ship must be your drugstore, your firehouse, your grocery store, your place of business, your doctor's office, and your home.

Appendix II, which follows, presents schedules of suggested material, in various categories. They represent the result of a score of years of reading about voyaging, five years of specific planning, and several small and one long, voyages. There will be sailors who will scoff at some of the things I carried aboard, and there will be others who would list things I have omitted. All I can say is that on the entire crossing of the Pacific I had no occasion to say "I wish I'd remembered to bring such and such."

Provisioning and outfitting a ship involves three large categories: 1) the hull and completed interior with living space, plumbing, machinery, and fittings; 2) the masts, sails, and rigging, standing and running, plus deck, dock, and ground tackle; and 3) everything you put inside to take along.

The hull of course must be sound and seaworthy. You will not assume this: it is a dangerous assumption. There are many beautiful ships, afloat and in service, that are unsafe to take on a trip out of sight of land. Get a marine surveyor (he'll charge a reasonable fee) to go over any boat you are interested in chartering or buying, and give you an opinion of its seaworthiness, with recommendations as to what ought to be done and how much it will cost. You will think of him when you are a thousand miles from shore, and you will sleep better.

In the category of mast, sails, and rigging, basically the standing rigging is what keeps the masts upright and the running rigging is that which positions the sails. A ship is seaworthy only with good standing and running rigging and enough spare line and parts, but I do not inventory these down to the last detail in the following schedules, as they vary from one rig and one ship to the next. Certain basics in deck, dock, and ground tackle are worth listing. I have grouped them into one list, along with bosun's stores and engineer's supplies. You can use them whether you have a bosun or engineer aboard or not. The rest of the schedules in Appendix II take care of practically everything else that falls into category three, above.

~~~~~~

Schedule 1—Bosun's stores; deck, dock, and ground tackle; and engineer's supplies.

Lifeboat oars and step mast and sail. (The ship will be equipped with at least one dinghy or lifeboat. If there are two, the second can be a light, fast launch. A "Boston Whaler" or similar type is an excellent boat for this purpose, but the deep-ocean lifeboat should be built as a ship's boat or surfboat. In it should be stowed survival kits with food rations and fresh water, the oars and sail arrangement listed, plus a cache of dye markers, flares, a steering compass, and if possible, a cheap sextant, some large-area ocean charts, almanac and tables, and hand-cranked distress transmitter. Or all these things can be stowed with a rubber life raft if one is aboard.)

In addition to two dinghys, both of rubber and powered by outboard engines (a Johnson and an English Seagull), *Thane* had a Winslow self-inflating life raft capable of holding eight people. The military rubber boat and the Nautisport were each capable of holding the entire company. (We had nine in the Nautisport once and it showed no signs of swamping.)

Fire extinguishers (The two above-deck extinguishers should be stowed at the wheel and in the deck cabin or doghouse. In addition, a jet pump is recommended. There are high-speed pumps available that serve the dual purpose of pumping out bilges in a hurry in case of a large hole and, by putting the intake over the side, throwing a hefty stream of sea-water on a fire. We had one aboard, powered by the generator.)

Life preservers (One for every member of the company plus extras for the occasional passengers.)

Life rings or horseshoes (If possible they should be equipped with a mercury-switched light that comes on when in an upright position. Two are sufficient, mounted in easy reach somewhere aft on each side of the ship.)

Fog horn

Bell

Life lines and stanchions

(So much for safety equipment above deck. The life preservers can be stowed below but should be near a hatch and not buried under gear or groceries. Everyone should know their locations.)

Spare rope, cable, chain, marlin and sail twine

Spare set of sails

Stove fuel

Flags (Courtesy, pratique [quarantine], club burgee, and national emblem [determined by registry])

Dock lines

Boat hook

Fenders and fender planks

Anchors

Anchor chain or line and shackles

Spare anchor line (minimum of 350 feet)

Fire extinguishers (Below, they should be located in the galley and each cabin.)

Boarding ladder

Rope-working tools

Canvas-sewing kit

Sail canvas

Paint and varnish

Brushes, turpentine, linseed oil, thinners

Paint remover

Caulking cotton

Seam compound

Caulking iron

Spare slides, turnbuckles, jibsnaps, swivels, blocks, and fittings

Gasket material

Sheet metal

Lumber, assorted

Insect screening

Sea anchor (or means of improvising one)

Ax, hatchet, maul

Faucet washers

Wood cover for glass areas

Spare keys (for flush plugs, cabins, ignition, strongbox, etc.)

Diving gear (masks, snorkels, regulators, and tanks—if possible suits, fins, boots, and hoods)

Mop and pail

Plastic buckets

Brass polish

Measuring sticks

Trouble light with extension cord

Harness and safety lines (web with cable or line fitted with snap—one for each crew member)

Storm clothing for all hands

Winch handles

Lead-and-line
Clear plastic bags
Silicone, spray and grease
Emery and sandpaper
Gasket cement
Electrician's tape
Rust solvent
Grease, lube oil, graphite
Cotton waste
Rags and cloths
Glue, plastic wood, putty
Small pouring funnels
Fuel transfer pump
Spare parts for heads, stove, plumbing, all machinery
Bilge sweetener
Tools (standard tool chest, carpenter, electrician, and machinist tools)
Assortment of nuts, bolts, screws, nails, tacks, brads
Ignition coils (if any gasoline engines aboard) and breaker points or spare distributor head, spark plugs, condenser
Fuses
Spare copper tubing and rubber hose
Oil-filter cartridges
Strainers for fuel
Cranks
Wheel puller
Spare parts for all power plants (auxiliary engine, generator, pumps, blowers, electric and outboard motors)
Spare light bulbs
Hydrometer
Electric wiring lengths
Plugs, male and female
Spare parts and fuses for electronic gear, radio, etc.

Leakproof dry cells (for flashlights and torches, transistor radios and record players, walkie-talkies, etc.)

Schedule 2—Housekeeping and steward's lists

Candles
Drano
Sewing kit (not sail)
Clothespins
Scissors
Fly swatters
Sharpening stone
Paper plates, cups, towels
Wax paper, Saran, foil
Masking tape
Twine
Toilet tissue, bowl brush, cleaner
Cleansing tissues
Plastic or waxed garbage bags
Linens, bedding, pillows
Berth spreads
Disinfectants
Spray gun
Ash trays
Window cleaner
Broom and dustpan
Scrub brush
Chamois and cloths
Cleaning compounds, powders
Detergent
Bottle stoppers
China and silver service (the "china" ideally plastic)
Bottle openers
Can opener
Pots, pans

Cutlery, spatula, wooden spoons
Corkscrew
Ice pick and tongs
Plastic food bags
Unbreakable glassware
Ammonia, bleach
Salt-water soap
Steel wool or copper wool
Matches
Stove parts
Bar supplies
Insecticides, repellents, and rodent poisons
Bond seals for liquor and weapons

Schedule 3—Food

There are companies that offer excellent canned foods specially put up with marine menus in mind, including canned butter, canned bread, and canned milk requiring no refrigeration. The cook should be in on the planning for this list and must consider balance of diet and individual tastes of company members. The calculated number of meals required should be inflated for margin.

Food stowage must consider easy access. The cook should be acquainted from the outset with stowage locations, and should supervise the loading of food.

Liquor
Wine
Beer
Tobacco (supplementing individual supplies.)
Gum, mints, candy
Beverages (juices, soft drinks)
Extra fresh water. (The ship's fresh water supply should be in three stocks: ship's tanks, where most of it is stored; emergency supplies—lifeboat and rafts; and an

extra supply in jerry cans or plastic jugs, against possibility of leakage or spoilage.)

Schedule 4—Medical supplies

2 rolls adhesive tape 10 yds. x 3 in.
3 rolls adhesive tape 10 yds. x 2 in.
3 boxes eye pads
2 Ace bandages
2 Cepacol antibiotic
2 razor blade dispensers, filled
6 bottles (100 each) salt tablets
2 tubes blister ointment
2 bottles eye lotion
12 tubes (one oz. each) Polysporin
4 tubes (4 oz. each) zinc oxide
3 bottles (9½ oz. each) medicated powder
1 triangle bandage
2 packages gauze sponges (100 each)
1 large bottle aspirin
1 bottle Excedrin
4 tubes first-aid cream
100 gauze pads
1 box adhesive bandage strips (assorted)
2 pints alcohol
1 box medium butterfly closures
1 box small butterfly closures
2 bottles (1½ pints each) milk of magnesia
500 cotton balls
1 clinical thermometer
5 dental poultices
1 bandage scissors
1 clamp
2 tweezers
12 plaster of Paris bandages

1 bottle procaine (30 c.c.)
Dulcolax suppositories
1 Steritube
24 ⅜ circle reverse cutting sutures with silk thread
12 Demerol (2 c.c.) ampoules
12 disposable syringes
10 ampoules (1 c.c.) adrenalin chloride
100 tablets cascara
3 bottles paregoric
1 bottle Kwell lotion
1 vial powdered opium
1 vial benzedrine
1 vial seconal
1 vial codeine
1 vial (24) Bonine
1 bottle (11 tablets) Aralen 250 mg.
1 vial Aralen 250 mg.
Instructions for use of hypodermic syringes (unless a doctor is aboard)
Globaline tablets

Schedule 5—Clothing and personal gear

Although each individual will draw up his own list, voyaging conditions and space limitations make the suggested list valuable as a starting point.
Passport
Birth certificate
Identification
Health certificate
Credit cards
Licenses (driver's and other)
Traveler's checks
Addresses and phone numbers
Stationery

Reading matter
Pocket knife
Spare eyeglasses and sunglasses
Camera and film
Transistor radio
Toilet articles
Plastic clothing bag
4 pair sox (nylon)
2 drip-dry shirts
Swim suit
Sweatshirt
Topsides shoes
Boat jacket
Light sweater
Underwear (easily washable)
Sport shirts
Jeans
One four-in-hand tie
Belt
Sport jacket or blazer
Shorts and slacks (cotton)
One light raincoat (shore use)
One laundry bag
Tobacco needs and lighter
Travel alarm
Underwear (heavy)
Extra lighter fluid (cook takes a dim view of using up ship's matches)
Foul-weather gear (for use on board)

Schedule 6—Strongbox and lock

Ships papers
Passports
Personal valuables

Insurance papers
Canal permits and papers for transit
Cash and traveler's checks
Letters of introduction
Letters of credit
Ammunition
Crew lists

Schedule 7—Navigation Supplies

Plotting tools (pencils with erasers, sharpeners, dividers, parallel rules, single straightedge, protractor, small-area plotting sheets, graph paper, blank paper)

Work forms (Napier diagram for compass deviation, H.O. 211 and H.O. 214 forms)

Charts for route (Ocean pilot, area, harbor, detail)

(It is recommended that in addition to these charts one have aboard charts of coastal areas near points to be visited, in the event of being driven on or having to put into these places for one reason or another.)

Hand bearing-compass
Pelorus
Patent log
Binoculars (at least 2 pair)
Chronometer
Stop watch
Barometer
Flashlights (waterproof)
Beam torches
Sextant
Depth finder (useful but not essential)
Radio direction finder (useful but not essential)

Schedule 8—Books, lists, and handbooks

Tide tables

Tide current tables

Light lists and supplements

Radio beacon lists

Chapman: *Piloting, Seamanship, and Small Boat Handling*

Mixter: *A Primer of Navigation*

Bowditch: *American Practical Navigator*

Log books (ship, radiophone, wheel to be kept in plastic bag in cockpit with flashlight and pencils)

Stores and stowage lists

Manufacturers' handbooks and parts lists (auxiliary engine, generator, bilge pumps, stove, radiophone, any other machinery)

American Red Cross First Aid Handbook

Merck's Manual (medical)

Natural History Field Book of Classification

Coast pilot with latest supplement

Sailing directions

Ocean passages for the world

Nautical Almanac (current)

Air Almanac

Sight Reduction Tables

H.O. 211 (one copy stowed in lifeboat cache)

H.O. 214 (volumes for all latitudes planned)

Catalog of U.S. Coast and Geodetic Survey

World Port Index

International Code of Signals H.O. 103

Miscellaneous books for recreational reading

Schedule 9—Recreation

Decks of cards

Chips

Dice

Fishing equipment

Chess set
Record player (transistorized, battery-driven—with records)
Scuba gear (*Schedule 1*)
Games

☆ Appendix III
Preparation Countdowns

~~~~~~

THE FOLLOWING is a series of countdowns that I used from the early stages of preparation right up to D-day. I confess that it looks positively Prussian, it's so methodical. But some sort of progressive reminder like this is essential for the many things that must be accomplished in order.

Minus 2 years

Study ships and prices.
Rough out costs of provisioning, surveying, outfitting.

Minus 18 months

If starting from scratch, this is the latest date at which one should start studying *and practicing* navigation.

Even if someone else is going to navigate, it will not be quite your voyage unless you too have the capability. There are navigation schools in metropolitan centers with complete eight-week courses, but it is possible to learn navigation from books (*see Appendix II, Schedule 8*) provided you can get out on the water enough to make certain you can apply the book knowledge.

If you intend to operate long-range radio voice transmission, eighteen months is a minimum time to equip yourself with the training and licensing necessary. This is by no means essential to voyaging however (*see notes on radio, Appendix IV*).

Minus 12 months

Marine survey of ship. (This is not too early. If the ship passes a thorough scrutiny, it is not going to rot in a year and a record of damage and repair will be checked at shakedown and at final hauling and inspection.)

Minus 6 months

Solidify your roster of shipmates. By this time, you should know whom you want, who is serious about going and can make it, and have in mind a couple of emergency alternates.

Check and apply for ship's radio licensing.

Minus 5 months

Complete list of charts (*Appendix II, Schedule 7*) and assemble them. Radio beacon and light lists, tide and tide-current tables, yachtsman guides, sailing directions (U.S. Hydrographic Office), safety literature and equipment, almanacs, and navigation tables.

Meet with cook for menu planning and draw lists, decide on sources, and plan stowage areas.

Minus 4 months

Draw medical list (*Appendix II, Schedule 4*) with advice of physician, who can order prescription items.

Minus 3 months

Order canned provisions and galley needs, including extra fresh-water containers. (Thick-walled, clear plastic, five-gallon collapsible jugs recommended.) If storage space is available near point of departure, this is a good time to assemble all needs. In case of items in short supply, starting this early will permit tracking them down from other sources.

Start checking chronometer for accuracy.

Special permits for canals, ports, or waterways. Check on procedures for visas, tourist cards, inoculations, vaccinations, bonds to be posted, if any, and firearms laws for ports contemplated. This is good time to gather general information on the places you'll be visiting. (Tourist bureaus are happy to provide this material.)

Minus 8 weeks

Passports in order with extra pictures.

Minus 7 weeks

Navigation brush-up and cram.

Minus 6 weeks

All supplies (provisions, gear, tools, utensils, etc.) assembled in location to load.

Minus 4 weeks

Physical and dental checks for all.

Shakedown cruise: If this can be arranged for a minimum of twenty-four hours offshore overnight, it will acquaint the crew with the ship and each other. Snags brought to light now can be corrected the following week during hauling and inspection. Instruct the company in: boat drill, fire fighting, use and location of life preservers and rings, safety harness, first aid and medical supplies, the stove, and the ship's plumbing, rigging, electrical systems, and pumps. Brief exposure to the ship's behavior and handling in dark and daylight, the watch schedule, bunk assignment, distribution of foul-weather gear and life harness by fit, and some last minute pilotage and navigation practice can be accomplished in this time.

Minus 3 weeks

Haul and inspect. Check through-hull fittings, clean the bottom (it can make a big difference in speed); check for corrosion and electrolysis; check shaft, propeller, bearings, zinc collars, rudder fittings, etc.

Shots for everyone. Health certificates in passports.

Minus 3 days

Load provisions and supplies, except fresh foods. Keep stowage records and recheck all lists and schedules.

Minus 2 days

If there is a going-away party, this is the day for it. Casting off at departure time with a shipload of hangovers has its disadvantages.

Minus 1 day

Post watch schedule.
Load personal gear.
Stow fresh foods.

Fuel and fresh water.
Radio check; weather check.

Departure day

Load ice. Load all hands and follow regular departure check list, below.

☆ *Appendix IV*
Standard Procedures Check List

~~~~~~~~~~~~~~~~~~~~~~~~~~~~~~~~~~~~~~~

THE FOLLOWING are useful check lists for approach, arrival, and departure.

Approach

Ready lists—food and other needs.
Ready mail and laundry.
Fly quarantine flag, ensign, and burgee.
Ready courtesy flag.
Ready papers and customs clearance.
Seal liquor.
Ready anchor.
Set shore watch.
Update wheel, radio, and ships logs.

Arrival

Arrange for: fuel—diesel, gasoline, alcohol; fresh water, ice, chandlery, laundry, mail.
Check bilge level, pumps.
Deck and line check.

Clear and stow quarantine flag.
Run up courtesy flag.

Departure

Check all loaded provisions properly stowed.
Extinguish fires during gasoline transfer.
Treat water if necessary.
Latch freezer.
Lock fresh water.
Check pumps and bilge level.
Secure stowage.
Vents and filler plugs OK.
Colors correct.
All hands accounted for.
Visitors and stowaways ashore.
Course orders to helm.
Weather advisory.
Radio time check.

☆ *Appendix V*
Miscellaneous Notes

~~~~~~

1. *Watches*

A watch schedule depends on the number of people aboard. Here is the one I used on the voyage. It worked well for us.

Four hours in the daytime and three at night seem to be good lengths of time for watch periods. The three night hours often seem longer than the four daylight ones. Pete Jackson suggested this, and I found he was right. We used these periods: 6:00 A.M. to 10:00 A.M.; 10 to 2 P.M. and 2 to 6 P.M. in the daytime. The night watches were 6 to 9, then 9 to 12, 12 to 3, and 3 to 6 A.M. We got a natural change of periods from day to day because there was an uneven number of watch periods. For example, if you worked the 6 A.M. to 10 A.M. trick, being on one and off two, the next two watches you'd be free—10 to 2 and 2 to 6. Your next watch then would be 6 to 9 P.M. Then you'd be off 9 to 12 and 12 to 3. You'd be on 3 to 6 A.M. the following day. Each day you worked one watch period earlier than the day before until after three days you came back to the same schedule. Nobody got stuck with unpopular hours this way. Further, to offset the formation of cliques aboard, I rotated the watch partners so that every three days a team of two was broken up and reformed. At the end of fifteen days, you would have stood watches with every one of the other members. This system works well with six standing watches. Connie, as cook, had no deck duty, although she frequently spelled us at the wheel.

Once per week another person did the cooking for Connie. This let her off Sundays. A cook should not be required to work seven days a week.

A day was midnight to midnight. Occasionally a team would get a five-hour watch when a new time zone was entered. Forrest Nelson told me that in the old days freighters used the dateline as an excuse to rob hands of whole days off and reduce payment until the seamen formed unions and did some navigating on their own.

2. *Navigation*

While on occasion I used the Sight Reduction Tables and the Air Almanac, I found I did my best work with the Nautical Almanac and H.O. 214 tables for the latitudes sailed (0° to 30°). I used plotting sheets, transferring the fixes in light pencil to a chart when I was nearing land. I did the work in a vertical form I had devised based on the Mixter 214 forms and kept the figures, dated and with the fixes added in latitude and longitude. I could set a day's work with the sun in three columns—morning, noon, and afternoon sights, using running sun lines with the dead reckoning. Star sights were not too important when far from land, I found, but they were useful for practice and to corroborate sun sights. They also gave us something of a check on D.R. (D.R.— dead reckoning—comes from the original "ded. reckoning," meaning deduced reckoning.) I made star and planet sights and used the moon when the horizon permitted. Several moon-and-sun fixes were possible.

With the radio time ticks and a Rolex GMT wrist watch, I found I did not need the ship's chronometer at all. The Plath is a micrometer sextant free of error and with filters having the magic property of giving the limb of the sun a sharp edge through cloudiness. I had little difficulty getting reasonable accuracy of height and used the system of taking five or six shots spaced a minute to two minutes apart. Plotted on graph paper, these sights made a straight line and afforded the opportunity for working a sight at a time and altitude not actually observed.

I made some sights with the refurbished antique vernier sextant, which performed quite satisfactorily.

Noon sights near the equator, where declination and latitude matched, were of course impossible with a horizon sextant, but we didn't seem to miss them. Morning and afternoon sun lines gave enough information. If it were clear enough to get these, it would generally be clear enough to see any land far enough away that the lack of accuracy was not critical. (This was not the case in the Tuamotus, where the islands are so low they are not visible for more than eight or ten miles.)

Horizons were not difficult in rough seas, I found, if I used patience in getting a sight when the ship was on top of a wave. This probably affected the dip correction, but in taking it into account, I chose to err on the under side, as the height of waves is easily exaggerated from the deck of a small ship.

3. Radio Equipment

The oceans are crossed often, even today, in sailboats with no radios. Many that have radios aboard have receivers for time ticks and weathercasts but no transmitters. Transmitting and receiving equipment capable of reaching anywhere on a voice basis used to require, before the advent of solid-state electronics, a large volume of space and would have worked a hardship on a small yacht. It is possible today, but few yachts have it.

I had it aboard partly as a safety precaution—if we were to lose the ship en route it would have been possible to radio a position, thereby narrowing a lifeboat's search—but mostly I was catering to a habit of communicating by broadcast.

Until I met Virgil Bowers, I had not dreamed it would be possible from far out to sea to speak directly, two ways, with my wife at home. Virgil introduced me to the possibilities of single side-band transmission on a mobile basis, and explained what he had done with it in many locations on this planet. I later found that his explanation of his activities was modest. He is one of the top ham operators in the world.

There are many aspects of ham radio. Each ham finds that particular angle that interests him most. Some like to build equipment, others like to experiment. Many like to chew the rag with another ham a couple of blocks or ten thousand miles away, or perhaps sit in on a round-table conversation among New York, California, South America and Europe.

Virgil Bowers' particular interest is handling what are called phone patches, telephone conversations patched into ham stations and bringing callers together over immense distances without long lines. Within this field of activity, Virgil's specialty is working ships with military personnel aboard whom he connects with their homes. His satisfaction in carrying this off on an almost daily basis is equalled only by the pleasure it gives those he connects.

Thane had a Ray-Jeff ship-to-shore phone aboard (good for islands on certain limited frequencies and at distances up to 150 miles). She also had a transistorized portable RCA radio-direction finder, a model similar to one I'd used in New England waters and around the Florida Keys. I did not use it on this voyage because I wanted all navigation done by pilotage and celestial—I suppose for esthetic reasons. My approach was not stringently purist, as I got the correct time and weather reports through the radio, but then, when you make your own rules . . .

Virgil brought with him an incredible array of electronic gear. He had a Collins KWM2 "transceiver"; power supplies for 110 volts AC, and a 12-volt DC supply for use with the ship's batteries; a Collins 30 L-1 linear amplifier; an extra receiver for time checks and also to cover the high seas marine frequencies.

He also installed a Simpson ship-to-shore radio with a large number of crystals; put aboard a Wollensak tape recorder, a pair of five-watt walkie-talkie units, and an airline solid-state emergency transmitter about the size of a large loaf of bread.

Virgil's antenna arrangement was very special, and was the result of a series of tests. It was a balun-fed inverted "inverted-V," trapped for fifteen and twenty meters. He arrived at this arrangement after much effort of trying to brace up some kind of a beam, then he realized that no beam could stand the shipping around it would receive at the top of a sixty-five-foot mast. The problem was to get an antenna above the steel cable of the standing rigging to allow signals to get out without being absorbed, and pick up received signals.

He started with a "Telrex" fifteen- and twenty-meter inverted-V kit. Instead of putting both legs of the dipole toward ground with the balun at the high point, he put one of the legs of the dipole on a plastic pole, which he fastened to the top of the main mast. This put one leg straight up above the mast (to about eighty feet above the water) with the balun fastened to the main truck (the top of the sixty-five-foot main mast.) The other leg of the dipole was stretched aft to the mizzen mast. This arrangement put the whole antenna above and clear of the rigging.

The mizzen had a short antenna mounted atop it for the ship-to-shore radiophone. After storm damage to the main antenna, we were forced to use this, and woefully inadequate as it was, together with the damage to both the transceiver and linear amplifier. We still managed to be heard thanks to the vigilance and large antennas of some stateside hams who kept frequencies clear for our schedules.